The Balance of Pow

WITHDRAWN

This text examines one of the guiding principles behind international politics. For over three hundred years the balance of power has been central to both the study and practice of international relations. In his book, Michael Sheehan analyses the eighteenth- and nineteenth-century workings of the classical balance of power system and traces its evolution through the twentieth century. He discusses the new 'deterrence' variant that was introduced into international power politics by the superpowers' acquisition of nuclear weapons and the new European balance of power that will arise out of the end of the cold war.

The Balance of Power looks at the different meanings the concept has held through history and the key thinkers and statesmen who have influenced its development. It addresses arguments about morality and the value of the principle as a foreign policy guide. The book supplies the reader with a highly comprehensive account of the balance of power, showing how the principle and the structures it produced changed alongside political thought and international society.

Michael Sheehan has written widely on the subject of defence and arms control. He is the co-author of two recent books on international defence and the author of *Arms Control: Theory and Practice* and *The Arms Race*.

The Balance of Power
History and Theory

Michael Sheehan

London and New York

First published 1996
by Routledge
11 New Fetter Lane, London EC4P 4EE

Simultaneously published in the USA and Canada
by Routledge
29 West 35th Street, New York, NY 10001

Typeset in Times by Florencetype Ltd, Stoodleigh, Devon
Printed and bound in Great Britain by
Mackays of Chatham plc, Chatham, Kent

British Library Cataloguing in Publication Data
A catalogue record for this book is available from the
British Library

Library of Congress Cataloguing in Publication Data
A catalogue record for this book has been requested

ISBN 0-415-11930-8 (hbk)

ISBN 0-415-11931-6 (pbk)

For my mother, Norah Sheehan

Contents

Preface

The balance of power principle has been central to both the study and practice of international politics for three centuries. It has guided governments in the conduct of foreign policy and provided a structure for explanations of some of the recurring patterns of international relations. For many analysts it comes closer than any other idea to being the guiding principle behind international politics. It has always been controversial, both in terms of its power to explain the workings of the international system and in terms of its wisdom and moral virtue as a foreign policy strategy. It is a concept riddled with ambiguity and the fact that it has demonstrated such longevity and resilience shows that it has served an important purpose in thinking about international relations. That purpose emerged in Europe in the seventeenth century, and though subsequently modified, its power as an 'image' explains its survival as a centre-piece of the post-Renaissance international system.

This book attempts to give an explanation of the complexity of the balance principle and practice in history and seeks also to give the reader an introduction to the vast literature on the subject. It attempts to explain the mystery of the enduring fascination of the balance of power image and to introduce the reader to the controversies that have surrounded it. For a subject that has been analysed or discussed so often in the past three centuries, the balance of power idea is surprisingly nebulous. It is an idea which has been given many different meanings and this creates difficulties when it comes to trying to reduce the concept to its essence, to provide a clear explanation of what the phrase 'the balance of power' does and does not mean.

However, in an important sense, this effort is not necessary, indeed, it would be counter-productive. Although it is possible, and worthwhile, to isolate various meanings of the concept and explain them, one of the most important features of the idea's history is that it has had so many meanings. In particular, as this book will argue, it has been conceptualised in two distinct senses over the three hundred years since it first emerged in Western Europe. The development of these two interpretations are traced through the book.

Because of its myriad meanings and long history, it is easy to lose perspective when dealing with the balance of power idea and become swallowed up by its complex manifestations. The focus in this book is upon the development of the concept and the varying ways in which it has been understood and used. It has always been used for a purpose. Conceptualising international relations in terms of balances of power predisposes the analyst to identify some features and not others. Advocating it as a way of understanding the world, therefore, always serves a particular political purpose. However, as the central chapters of the study argue, the particular variant of balance thinking that is crucially important to twentieth-century 'realist' explanations of international politics is in fact only one of the key manifestations of the concept and therefore represents the privileging of one particular world-view.

This book examines the various meanings given to the balance of power over the centuries and traces the historical evolution of the theory and practice through steadily more complex forms. It describes the balance principle in practice, both as a guiding light of national foreign policies and as a structural explanation of how the international system operates. The central portion of the book examines the workings of the classical balance of power systems of the eighteenth and nineteenth centuries before going on to trace its evolution in the twentieth century, particularly in the novel 'deterrence' variant produced by the invention of nuclear weapons by the great powers. In addition, Chapter 7 looks at some of the historical alternatives to the balance of power approach and explains both the similarities and differences they show compared to the balance of power.

I am deeply indebted to Dr Moorhead Wright of the University College of Wales, Aberystwyth, for first introducing me to the subject of the balance of power and for his helpful advice over many years. I would also like to thank Pamela Strang for her cheerfulness while typing successive drafts of the book.

M.S.

1 The meaning of the balance of power

> Students of international politics do not need to be told of the unsatisfactory state of balance of power theory. The problems are well known: the ambiguous nature of the concept and the numerous ways it has been defined, the various distinct and partly contradictory meanings given to it in practice and the divergent purposes it serves (description, analysis, prescription and propaganda); and the apparent failure of attempts clearly to define balance of power as a system and specify its operating rules.
>
> Schroeder, 1989: 135

INTRODUCTION

If the idea of the balance of power is so laden with contradictions, why then should we study it at all? The answer to that question is that, for all its faults, the balance of power has been one of the most important ideas in history. It is a concept which for centuries students of international relations believed held the key to understanding the recurrent patterns of behaviour of states living in a condition of 'international anarchy'. At the same time, it was a guide for many statesmen, who saw in it a method for securing the continuing independence of their states. This is the critical importance of the balance of power concept, that whatever its limitations as a tool for analysis or a guide to policy, it has historically been a reality; a reality that deserves to be analysed and understood.

However, when it comes to seeking the essence of the idea of the balance of power, the difficulty is not that its meaning cannot be discovered, but rather, as Inis Claude (1962: 13) has pointed out, that it has too many meanings. At its heart the balance of power seems a simple concept, readily understandable by statesmen and ordinary citizens. Confusion exists, however, because throughout history its advocates and critics alike have used the term too freely, so that an analysis of the countless references to it in the literature throws up a host of examples which confuse rather than enlighten. Ernst Haas uncovered eight different meanings of the phrase 'balance of power' (1953: 447–57) while Wight (1966: 151) went one better with nine. George Liska (1977: 5) has argued that it is counter-productive to attempt to pin down the balance of power concept too exactly and that there is 'a misplaced desire for precision in a concept that is at once the dominant myth and the fundamental law of interstate relations, and as such with some reason, highly elastic'. Nevertheless, this elasticity has contributed to the confusion surrounding the concept.

DEFINITIONS

Before plunging into the trackless swamp of the alternative inter-pretations, it is worth noting at the outset that at the heart of the balance of power idea is a straightforward concept as, following the approach used by Zinnes (1967: 270–85), a select number of definitions will suffice to make clear.

1   'An equal distribution of Power among the Princes of Europe as makes it impractical for the one to disturb the repose of the other'.

Anonymous, *Europe's Catechism*, 1741

2   'action by a state to keep its neighbours from becoming too strong ... because the aggrandisement of one nation beyond a certain limit changes the general system of all the other neighbours ... attention to the maintenance of a kind of equality and equilibrium between neighbouring states'.

Fenelon, 1835

3   'The balance of power, however it be defined, that is, whatever the powers were between which it was necessary to maintain such equilibrium, that the weaker should not be crushed by the union of the stronger, is the principle which gives unity to the political plot of modern European history'.

Stubbs, 1886

4   'History shows that the danger threatening the independence of this or that nation has generally arisen, at least in part, out of the momentary predominance of a neighbouring state at

once militarily powerful, economically efficient, and ambitious to extend its frontiers or spread its influence, the danger being directly proportional to the degree of its power and efficiency, and to the spontaneity and "inevitableness" of its ambitions. The only check on the abuse of political predominance derived from such a position has always consisted in the opposition of an equally formidable rival, or of a combination of several countries forming leagues of defence. The equilibrium established by such a grouping of forces is technically known as the balance of power'.

Crowe, 1928

5 'an arrangement of affairs so that no state shall be in a position to have absolute mastery and dominate the others'.

Vattel, 1916

6 'the balance of power assumes that through shifting alliances and countervailing pressures no one power or combination of powers will be allowed to grow so strong as to threaten the security of the rest'.

Palmer and Perkins, 1954

7 The balance of power 'operates in a general way to keep the average calibre of states low in terms of every criterion for the measurement of political power ... a state which threatens to increase its calibre above the prevailing average becomes subject, almost automatically to pressure from all the other states that are members of the same political constellation'.

Toynbee, 1934

8 The balance of power 'refers to an actual state of affairs in which power is distributed among several nations with approximate equality'.

Morgenthau, 1978

9 'when any state or bloc becomes, or threatens to become, inordinately powerful, other states should recognise this as a threat to their security and respond by taking equivalent measures, individually and jointly, to enhance their power'.

Claude, 1962

10 'The balance's underlying principle ... was that all the nth disengaged powers would tend to intervene on the side that seemed in danger of losing any ongoing war, to ensure that

such a loser was not eliminated from the system and absorbed into an emerging colossus'.

Quester, 1977

As Dina Zinnes notes, a listing of definitions in this way shows almost complete agreement on the key feature of a balance of power system. A balance of power involves 'a particular distribution of power among the states of that system such that no single state and no existing alliance has an "overwhelming" or "preponderant" amount of power' (Zinnes, 1967: 272).

When the essence of the concept is distilled in this way, it is easy to agree with Hume that the balance of power is founded upon 'common sense and obvious reasoning'. Although it must be said that Hume's argument is based upon a crucial assumption, which is that the independence of states is a more important goal to pursue than a process of political unification under a hegemonic power. This may indeed be a desirable goal, but it is a goal identifiable with a particular post-Renaissance European manner of looking at international relations.

There are a variety of methods by which this basic objective might be sought, generating alternative policies and different balance of power systems. For example, in the unusual case of a two-power system, only an equality of power can prevent preponderance, in the manner called for by the balance of power approach. As the number of states in the system increases beyond this, however, a wide variety of distributions of power becomes acceptable. 'In effect, any distribution is permissible as long as the power of each unit – state or alliance of states – in the system is less than the combined power of all the remaining units' (Zinnes, 1967: 272).

BALANCE OF POWER AND 'REALISM'

Balance of power thinking is usually conceived of as belonging within a particular tradition of thinking about international relations, that of 'power politics' or 'realism'. Dougherty and Pfaltzgraff (1990: 81) have listed what they see as being the four basic tenets of this perspective.

1   Nation-states are the key actors in an international system composed of independent sovereign states.
2   Domestic and foreign policy are clearly separated areas of national policy.

3   International politics is a struggle for power in an anarchic international environment.
4   States have different capabilities to achieve goals and defend
interests.

These four assumptions draw upon a particular interpretation of
older traditions. It could be argued that Thucydides, Machiavelli,
Hobbes and Rousseau fall within the power politics world-view.
A classic statement of this perspective was Hans Morgenthau's *Politics Among Nations* (1978). Morgenthau asserted that the world is
the result of forces inherent in human nature and that:

> moral principles can never be fully realised, but must at best be
> approximated through the ever temporary balancing of interests
> and the ever precarious settlement of conflicts. This school, then,
> sees in a system of checks and balances a universal principle for
> all pluralist societies. It appeals to historic precedent rather than
> to abstract principles, and aims at the realisation of the lesser evil
> rather than that of the absolute good.
>
> (Morgenthau, 1978: 1–2)

Morganthau laid out six principles which he felt distinguished the
concept of political realism.

1   Politics, like human nature, is seen as being governed by objective laws that have their roots in human nature. Once
identified, these 'laws' will be of enduring value – 'the fact
that a theory of politics was developed hundreds or even thousands of years ago – as was the theory of the balance of power
– does not create a presumption that it must be outmoded and
obsolete' (1978: 4). Statesmen will make decisions on the basis
of rational choices between alternative options.
2   The key concept which enables the realist to make sense of
the complexities of international politics is the concept of
interest defined in terms of power (1978: 5). Morgenthau admits
that realism emphasises a rational foreign policy which is never
quite attainable in practice, but he argues that this does not
detract from its utility.

> Far from being invalidated by the fact that, for instance, a
> perfect balance of power policy will scarcely be found in
> reality, it assumes that reality, being deficient in this respect,
> must be understood and evaluated as an approximation to
> an ideal system of balance of power.
>
> (Morgenthau, 1978: 8)

3   The kind of interest determining political action in a particular period of history depends upon the political and cultural context within which foreign policy is formed. The same applies to the concept of power. Therefore, Morgenthau accepts that power and the use of power can change during periods of time, but argues that this will be more likely to result from a general shift in the balance of power within the international system. Power here is defined as 'anything that establishes and maintains the control of man over man' (1978: 9). The contemporary connection between interest and the nation-state is seen as the product of a particular period of history. Alternatives to the nation-state could evolve in the future and, by implication, could have been key actors in the past.

4   Realism does not accept the validity of universal moral principles in an abstract sense, but argues that they must be 'filtered through the concrete circumstances of time and place' (1978: 173). Above all, Morgenthau argues that the state has no right to allow moral principles to get in the way of, or detract from, its duty to pursue the objective national interest.

5   However, Morgenthau qualifies this by arguing that, in fact, states' policies are influenced by their moral judgements in a way that tends to encourage moderation, and that this encourages a live-and-let-live approach where states recognise that just as they are pursuing their own national power aspirations, so too are other states. Individual states should therefore respect each other.

6   Morgenthau goes on to argue that realists and politicians should subordinate non-political criteria such as morality to the requirements of political reality.

The realist image of international relations is one of inevitable clashes between nation-states as they seek to maintain their autonomy and increase their wealth and power. 'The fundamental nature of international relations is seen as being unchanged over the millennia. International relations continues to be a recurring struggle for wealth and power among independent actors in a state of anarchy' (Gilpin, 1981: 7). This latter point is a feature of most balance of power thinking. There is a tendency to argue that balance of power politics is an inevitable feature of any international system, because it reflects the nature of mankind and human nature is seen as being essentially unchanging. This view was expressed in the eighteenth century by David Hume when he argued that the ancient Greeks, who understood human nature so well, must therefore have been familiar exponents of balance of power politics.

There is a major problem involved here. Classical realist thought looks at the world in a particular way. Realists have identified this approach as being a natural or inevitable way for human beings to look at the world of interstate relations. Perhaps inevitably, they have projected this particular image of international relations back into history, finding evidence from past eras which support their world-view and citing earlier thinkers such as Thucydides, Machiavelli and Rousseau, as well as statesmen in many eras, as supporting their perspective.

However, as later sections of this study will demonstrate, the balance of power approach, which is central to realist theorising, is far from being an instinctive human approach to international politics. On the contrary, it appears to be the product of a peculiar combination of factors in seventeenth-century Europe, and the particular model of the balance of power which realists promote is significantly different from the concept as it originally emerged and as it periodically reasserted itself. Moreover, for the majority of recorded human history, the balance of power approach has been conspicuously absent from the record of interstate relations.

THE CENTRALITY OF POWER

The concept and measurement of power, together with the ability of states to translate this power into defined national goals, is one of the most fundamental characteristics of realist perspectives. Most realists assume that it is in the interests of the state to acquire as much power as possible and, having acquired it, to exercise and maintain that power.

One intellectual problem immediately thrown up by this assumption is that power is a concept, or term, interpreted differently by different people. For some it means the use of force, usually military force, but also political or economic force. For others, power is not a specific thing or activity, but is an ability to influence the behaviour of other states. Gilpin (1981) defines power as an actor's ability to impose his or her will despite resistance, and defines prestige or authority as being different from power. Prestige and authority constitute only the 'probability' that a command will be obeyed. However, Gilpin still acknowledges that any prestige or authority eventually relies upon traditional measures of power, whether military or economic.

Closely related to the notion of power is the concept of national interests, and the objectives of using power. Realist assumptions regarding concepts such as sovereignty and anarchy lead the realists to argue that because international politics is anarchic, that is, there is no superior governing authority, then the independent sovereign states basically have to struggle to secure their own interests. Nicholas Spykman argued that the basic objective of a state's foreign policy must be to preserve territorial integrity and political independence.

Thus, the processes and activities of states in the realist image of international relations become naturally limited to achieving the short-term or immediate goals of security and survival, since no single state can reasonably plan for its long-term future and security.

This condition of realist international politics has been described by some writers as the security politics paradigm or more generally as the security dilemma. It sees states perpetually competing, conflicting and fighting over issues of national security. The implication of this is that states must do whatever is necessary to survive in this highly dangerous environment. If most states are ruthlessly behaving in this way, then those that do not will become victims in the struggle for security. The nature of the system in which all the states exist then becomes a determining factor in their behaviour, forcing them to play the balance of power game if they are to survive. This characterisation is central to the explanation of the balance of power advanced by 'structural' or 'neo'-realists such as Kenneth Waltz (1979: 118).

The balance of power theory sees international society as unequal; power versus weakness. But this basic inequality among states can be balanced, that is, all states can be kept in check regarding each other's position, and this can therefore prevent hegemony, allowing states to preserve their identity, integrity and independence, and perhaps deterring aggression or war.

Balance of power theory is thus closely in line with the traditional, realist image of international relations. The task of statesmen is to identify and prioritise the national interests according to any changes that occur. Because the international anarchy militates against any long-term security or stability, nation-states may well encourage balance of power systems, so that in absolute terms their security, stability, power and influence can be more readily enhanced. Morgenthau (1978) therefore argued that the balance of power and foreign policies which were designed to achieve or maintain it were not only inevitable, but were crucial mechanisms for stabilising international society.

Realism and balance of power thinking are linked because their assumptions are so similar. However, Morganthau himself believed that balance of power theory offered only a partial solution to the problem of anarchy and change in the international system. This, in his view, was because states involved in the international anarchy must in practice seek, not 'a balance or equality of power, but a superiority of power on their own behalf' (Morgenthau, 1978: 227). This argument seems to run counter to the whole essence of balance thinking. Superiority is clearly not the same thing as equality. It is one of the problems of examining the balance of power idea that even its proponents can use the term in ways which are clearly contradictory. The many alternative uses of the term are looked at later in this chapter, but it is worth noting here that the pursuit of superiority rather than balance need not necessarily indicate imperialistic intentions. Balancing power is difficult because power defies exact measurement and states will tend to insure themselves against underestimating their opponents' power or overestimating their own by acquiring a margin of safety, a capacity to match a greater-than-anticipated threat. In a flexible multipolar system such an effort is unlikely to threaten predominance. In a simple bipolar system, however, this would not be the case and any success-fully acquired 'margin of safety' would in practice represent superiority.

Trevor Taylor (1978) argues that what is significant about the power-politics approach is not so much the obvious point that a state's influence in the international arena depends upon the power it has, but rather the suggestion that 'if a state is to succeed, it has little choice but to make the acquisition of power its central, immediate aim' (Taylor, 1978: 122). In other words, the struc-tural realist assumption. Although critical of the assumptions of the realist approach, Taylor notes that it is virtually impossible to prove or disprove, because the arguments about whether it is correct or not are based upon a subjective judgement, so that the approach is likely to remain in vogue indefinitely. If this is the case, then so will the balance of power idea, which shares most of the same assumptions.

The raw material for the power-politics approach is history. Schwarzenberger (1964: 14) describes power politics as being 'an abstraction reached inductively by the study of International Relations of the past and present'. Taylor (1978: 125) gives an example from Morgenthau, and the same approach can be seen in Butterfield, Wight, Aron, Spykman and other members of the realist school. Much of this writing can be criticised as being selective in its choice of historical examples. Thus, Rosecrance (1973: 25) declared that 'history is a laboratory in which our generalisations about international politics can be tested'. Yet earlier power-politics writers, rather than using history in this way, tended to selectively pick out particular historical cases to illustrate their points and thereby support them. Indeed, one historian, Schroeder (1991), has called into question the whole edifice of twentieth-century balance of power theorising by challenging the historical interpretations on which it is based.

Writers of the power-politics school also drew inspiration from political philosophy and, because they shared an essentially pessimistic view of human nature, chose to highlight the insights of thinkers such as Hobbes and Machiavelli, 'whose works emphasised the dark side of human behaviour' (Taylor, 1978: 126). However, as Little (1989: 92) has pointed out, in doing so, such writers established the dominance of a *particular* image or interpretation of the balance of power, and indeed, of power itself. At the same time, they effectively eclipsed an alternative, associative image of the balance of power, without which it is difficult to explain certain periods of the operation of balance of power policies in history. In particular, this specific interpretation of the concept is a poor basis for understanding the important balance of power system of the early nineteenth century in Europe and, most crucially, it is an inadequate basis from which to comprehend the seventeenth-century origins of balance of power thinking itself.

A key departure point of realism is the idea of state personality – that like an individual, a state has a sense of purpose and is capable of rational action. E. H. Carr describes this assumption as 'a necessary fiction or hypothesis' (1946: 148–9) without which it would be impossible to conceptualise international relations – a point made also by Purnell (1978: 27–8) with regard to the ancient Greek state system. This assumption is by no means universally accepted by international relations theorists, but it is central to realist thought. Once it is accepted that a state has personality, it can be assumed that there is indeed a 'national interest' conceived of in terms of the well-being of the entire people rather than just a particular group within the state. This national interest is generally identified with security on the grounds that 'unless a state is secure it cannot be sure that it will survive and, if it does not survive, it will not be able to fulfil any other goals favouring its citizens' welfare' (Taylor, 1978: 127).

As noted earlier, the power-politics perspective is underpinned by a particular view of human nature. This emphasises its worst aspects and therefore argues that in order to be successful people and states must protect themselves against the evil of others. Political leaders are seen as being obsessed with the desire to increase and employ power for its own sake. Humans are viewed as dangerous and untrustworthy. Conflicting, rather than complementary interests are emphasised. For the realist, conflict is inevitable and natural. To a large extent, functioning balance of power systems are a reflection of these attitudes. By its very nature, the balance of power mentality breeds an obsession with the relative power of states within the system and a pervasive spirit of rivalry. The competitive elements of the system are not even really mitigated by the use of alliances, since the balancing process is present both within and between alliances. Even current allies must be constrained and at all times there is the awareness that the ally of today may become the enemy of tomorrow.

THE PURSUIT OF POWER

For a balance of power to come into being there must exist an international system, that is, a community of states in regular contact with each other. These states will have certain policy objectives, some of which will conflict with the policies of other states. Each state's most important objective will be the continuing existence and independence of the state itself. In order to maintain their independence, states will rely on diplomacy supported by military power – primarily their own, but supplemented by that of allies if necessary. As each state moves to match the efforts of its rivals a balance of power will emerge which sustains a basically stable system. Power must be countered by matching power.

This is very much the conventional wisdom. However, it should be noted that system is not the same thing as society. An important school of thought within international relations theorists has consistently argued that international relations is not simply a state of warlike anarchy whose social elements are minimal. They have argued instead that there is such a thing as 'international society', that states and governments are bound by rules and therefore form a community with one another, a society. This way of conceptualising international relations can be traced at least as far as the seventeenth-century Dutch jurist Hugo Grotius. In the thinking of Hedley Bull in the late twentieth century it was important to this study, because Bull explicitly linked the idea of the balance of power with the notion of international society. He did so by asserting that theories of the state system, in so far as they present the balance of power as a product of deliberate state policy and argue that states are obliged to seek to produce such a balance, 'must be taken also to embody the idea of international society and of rules binding upon its members' (Bull, 1966: 39).

Quincy Wright distinguished between a 'static' balance of power and a 'dynamic' one. This can be identified with the distinction between balance as a system and balance of power as a policy. Wright described a static balance as 'the condition which accounts for the continued coexistence of independent governments in contact with one another', while a dynamic balance 'characterises the policies adopted by governments to maintain that condition' (Wright, 1942: 445).

An obvious feature of all traditional balance of power reasoning is the obsession with power. Hans Morgenthau, a leading proponent of balance of power politics declared that 'the aspiration for power on the part of several nations, each trying to maintain or overthrow the status-quo, leads of necessity to a configuration that is called the balance of power' (Morgenthau, 1978: 173). States are seen as being engaged in a struggle for power, indeed, the accumulation of 'power' is their sole foreign policy objective; all other objectives being viewed as simply means to that end.

This simple approach is clearly flawed. States do not by any means devote their entire resources permanently to the accumulation of power. Governments have a variety of demands upon their available resources, and varying domestic political and cultural traditions mean that by no means all states pursue a policy of power accumulation.

Robert Gilpin modified this simple image to some extent by describing international relations as being 'a recurring struggle for wealth and power among independent actors in a state of anarchy' (Gilpin, 1981: 7). Power is seen as a means to an end – protecting and advancing the well-being of the state's citizens, but is *also* an end in itself.

For Morgenthau, the balance of power created a 'precarious stability' in interstate relations, one that needs constantly to be re-established. The phrase 'balance of power' implies a certain permanence – a 'balance' is a finished product. The reality of international relations, however, is that movement and change, not stasis, are its characteristic features. Even a balance of power, therefore, cannot hope to produce permanent stability. Power is never permanently balanced, rather the states must be permanently engaged in the act of balancing power, of adjusting and refining it in response to the perpetual ebb and flow of power within the system. In this sense the balancing process is designed not to be an obstacle to peaceful change, but rather to influence its form so as to avert destabilising developments.

Power can be seen as the capacity of an individual or an organisation to achieve its objectives. But power does not exist in the abstract. It is a function of the relationship between the power-holder and the state which it is trying to influence. Until such a relationship exists, power remains implicit and a state's power varies according to the context in which it is trying to use it. In their search for security, states are seen as seeking to acquire, retain and increase their national power, since this is the principal means by which they can achieve security. International relations is seen as a jungle, a Hobbesian State of Nature, where the search for power has to be unending if survival is to be assured. Classical realist scholars such as Morgenthau, Schwarzenberger and Schuman all argue essentially that hostility between states is a natural and inevitable feature of international relations which leads almost instinctively to the emergence of balance of power politics and a balance of power system.

In addition, though the nature of power itself is hardly if ever defined by balance of power theorists, it is implicit in their writings that by power they mean *military* power. According to Hedley Bull, 'the idea of the balance of power rests on the abstraction of the military factor'. E. H. Carr (1946: 109) argues that the military instrument is crucial because 'the *ultima ratio* of power in International Relations is war. Every act of the state in its power aspect, is directed to war, not as a desirable weapon, but as a weapon which it may require in the last resort to use'.

C. Wright Mills (1959: 27) argued that the leaders of the nuclear superpowers during the cold war assumed that 'military violence and the whole supporting ethos of an overdeveloped society geared for war are hard-headed, practical, inevitable and realistic conceptions'. This demonstrates the importance of ideas (such as the balance of power concept) in international relations, for in this sense ideas are facts, which shape both perceptions and actions and are therefore crucial in creating the 'reality' with which statesmen believe themselves to be dealing.

Clearly, military power is an important element in the foreign policy of many states, and it is therefore logical that the nature of such power and its comparative distribution among states will be an important element affecting outcomes in international politics. Its importance is summed up by a comment by Liska that 'the key structural guarantee of minimum order in a pure multistate system is the distribution of antagonistic power in a reciprocally countervailing pattern' (Taylor, 1978: 132).

A balance of power is never a static phenomenon and can never be taken for granted. It is always tending to move towards an imbalance. It therefore has to be constantly adjusted, either towards the restoration of an earlier equilibrium, or – more usually – the creation of a new one. Lasswell (1965) spoke of the balancing of power, rather than of a balance, since the attempt toward equilibrium can never be a wholly successful one.

Lord Bolingbroke, an eighteenth-century British Foreign Minister recognised this, but cautioned that the implication for states was that they needed to maintain a constant vigilance.

> The scales of the balance of power will never be exactly poised, nor is the precise point of equality either discernible or necessary to be discerned. It is sufficient in this, as in other human affairs, that the deviation be not too great. Some there will always be. A constant attention to these deviations is therefore necessary.
>
> (Maurseth, 1964: 125)

Although states might in theory desire a preponderance rather than a balance, rational leaders are aware that beyond a certain point in the drive for preponderance the law of diminishing marginal returns comes into operation. A balance emerges because the states comprising the system reach at least an adequate, if not an absolute, degree of security and realise that efforts to enhance their security still further would either strain the demands upon their national resources to the point where cut-backs and set-backs would be seen in other areas of national power or they would trigger a more than offsetting loss in relative military power because of political realignments against them (Liska, 1957: 35). Moreover, a continuous aggressive drive for hegemony pursued simultaneously by all the states within a system would undermine the fabric of the international *society* of which states form a part. International society is crucially composed of cooperative as well as conflictual elements and, at a minimum, must provide the 'rules of the game' within which competition takes place.

To the extent therefore that statesmen are conversant with balance of power thinking and used to viewing foreign policy in terms of interaction within a state system, they will be alive both to the need to recognise and act against threats to the equilibrium posed by other states, and to the fact that their own ambitions will be similarly monitored by the other states in the system.

ALTERNATIVE MEANINGS OF THE BALANCE OF POWER

The British historian A.F. Pollard once turned to the Oxford English Dictionary to find 'balance' defined in twenty different ways, 'of' given sixty-three meanings and 'power' eighteen. The various permutations of meaning could therefore turn into the thousands, so that it was hardly surprising that the phrase had been used in so many different ways throughout history. According to Pollard

> The balance of power may mean almost anything; and it is used not only in different senses by different people, or in different senses by the same people at different times, but in different senses by the same person at the same time.
>
> (Pollard, 1923: 58)

A number of analysts have investigated the various alternative ways in which the phrase has been used throughout its long history. Hans Morgenthau believed that the term was used in four distinct senses –

> as a policy aimed at bringing about a certain power distribution; as a description of an actual state of affairs in international politics; as an approximately equal distribution of power internationally; and as a term describing any distribution of political power in international relations.
>
> (Morgenthau, 1978: 173)

Martin Wight (Butterfield and Wight, 1966: 151) identified nine distinct meanings, or at least nine different ways in which the concept has been used. Not all can be held to have equal validity, though all have been commonly used. An incorrect usage remains that even if it is used frequently. Some of the meanings given to the phrase in the list which follows, clearly diverge sharply from the core meaning identified at the outset of this chapter.

1 An even distribution of power.
2 The principle that power ought to be evenly distributed.
3 The existing distribution of power. Hence, any possible distribution of power.
4 The principle of equal aggrandisement of the great powers at the expense of the weak.
5 The principle that our side ought to have a margin of strength in order to avert the danger of power becoming unevenly distributed.
6 (When governed by the verb 'to hold':) A special role in maintaining an even distribution of power.
7 (Ditto:) A special advantage in the existing distribution of power.
8 Predominance.
9 An inherent tendency of international politics to produce an even distribution of power.

The first meaning noted by Wight is the core meaning identified earlier in this chapter; an even distribution of power in the international system which precludes any one state or alliance from achieving a preponderance. This includes the simple or 'bipolar' balance and the multiple balance forms. This is the closest thing there is to a generally accepted definition of the balance of power. But, as Wight's eight other meanings make clear, it is very far from being the only sense in which the phrase is commonly used.

The second use of the phrase sees it changing from a purely descriptive to a normative use; the idea that equilibrium is beneficial and that power *ought* to be evenly distributed. This usage found clear expression in the Treaty of Utrecht of 1713, which brought the War of the Spanish Succession to an end. The treaty preamble justified its terms on the grounds that it would produce 'a just Balance of Power (which is the best and most solid foundation of mutual friendship and a lasting general concord)'. When used in this sense the phrase 'balance of power' is being given a positive moral connotation. Advocates in extolling the balance of power promote the features that are deemed to accompany it, such as moderation in foreign policy means and ends, the preservation of sovereign independence, and for some, the deterrence of war. This type of usage is worth noting because balance of power politics are often contrasted with idealist foreign policy, whereas in certain historical periods the balance of power idea itself has been invested with overtones of idealism. However, criticisms of balance of power policies have also been made on ethical grounds, notably by the American President Woodrow Wilson.

However, as already noted, power defies exact measurement and states will constantly be seeking to insure themselves with a margin of error. Even if a stable equilibrium does come into existence, it is likely to favour some states more than others and will be seen as imperfect by revisionist states who feel it discriminates against them. Thus, Hitler told Italy in 1936 that 'Any future modifications of the Mediterranean balance of power must be in Italy's favour' (Wight, 1966: 151). Here the phrase is being used in its third sense, to simply refer to the existing distribution of power, as a synonym for the prevailing political situation. It is in this sense that statesmen will refer to the balance of power moving or leaning, for example an Israeli leader might have suggested that the balance of power was swinging towards the Arab states, or favoured Israel's enemies. Martin Wight argues that this use of the phrase can be extended to mean *any* possible distribution of power and quotes Winston Churchill in 1942, 'no man can see how the balance of power will lie or where the winning armies will stand at the end of the war' (1966: 15). Here all sense of a genuine balance or equilibrium has been lost and the phrase has become simply a synonym for the distribution of power at a particular time. Historically, this can be seen in the way that the balance of power was identified with a particular political settlement at the end of a major war. This was true of the arrangements created in Europe by the Utrecht treaty of 1713 and the Vienna treaty of 1815. In the seventeenth and eighteenth centuries such a particular order was often called a 'system', as for example 'the system of Westphalia'. What this meant in reality was the *status quo* produced by the war.

The fourth use of the phrase, the principle of equal aggrandisement of the Great Powers at the expense of the weak, is based upon the record of certain states historically pursuing foreign policies justified in the name of the balance of power, particularly the partition of Poland in the eighteenth century and the division of Africa and China in the nineteenth.

The policy of partition has always been a controversial one for both advocates and opponents of balance of power policies. Wight himself declares vigorously that 'nothing in European history has done more to discredit the idea of the balance of power than the belief that it led naturally to such a crime as the Partition of Poland' (1966: 157) and quotes the outraged terms of Friedrich von Gentz

who bitterly declared that those who divided Poland in the name of
the balance of power, 'whilst they inflicted the most fatal wounds
upon the spirit and very existence of this system, borrowed its
external forms, and even its technical language' (von Gentz, 1806:
77). Whether partition was indeed a perversion of the balance of
power concept depends upon one's interpretation of the overall
purpose of a balance of power system, that is, whether it is
designed to preserve the sovereignty of *all* the states in the system,
or merely that of the great powers, the 'essential national actors'
identified by Morton Kaplan (see Chapter 4). As a technique
it simply represents one possible way of interpreting the balance of
power principle.

More controversial still is the fifth possible meaning, the principle
that 'my side ought to have a margin of strength in order to avert
the danger of power becoming unevenly distributed'. Here the
distinction is between an objective and a subjective balance of power.
Thus, for example, Reinhold Neibuhr, a 'realist' advocate of balance
of power policies was able to argue during the cold war that 'the
idealists must learn that nothing but a preponderance of power in
the non-Communist world can preserve the peace' (Davis and Good,
1960: 302). Indeed, Walter Lippmann, in the same era argued that
a balance of power, far from providing security, had the opposite
effect during the Allies–Axis confrontation and that 'when the
alliance is inadequate because there is an opposing alliance of
approximately equal strength, the stage is set for a world war. For
then the balance of power is so nearly even that no state is secure'
(Lippmann, 1943: 106). Although proponents of this view have justified it in terms of the balance of power, it is essentially a perversion
of the balance of power ideal. True balance of power policies are
pursued without regard to ideological divisions and the aim is a true
equilibrium, not a preponderance for one side. A preponderance
remains exactly that, whichever side possesses it. It was in this sense
that Pollard (1923: 59) argued that supporters of the balance of power
thought of 'balance' in the sense of a bank balance, that is, a surplus
rather than equality.

The sixth meaning is that of 'possessing a special role in maintaining an even distribution of power', and is seen most clearly in
the form of the 'balancer' state described in Chapter 3. Here, a state
derives political advantage, but has special responsibilities, because
its diplomacy is responsible for maintaining the system in balance
by committing its strength periodically in support of the weaker
element(s) of the simple balance. This was a policy attributed to

Britain in the eighteenth and nineteenth centuries and one attempted on occasion by Sweden, Savoy and Venice with varying degrees of success.

The fact that a balancer's power is normally uncommitted, giving it a manoeuvrability denied to the powers of the central balance produces yet another usage of the phrase 'balance of power', one implying 'the possession of a special advantage in the existing distribution of power'. British statesmen of the eighteenth and nineteenth centuries frequently used the expression in this way.

So flexible has been the term 'balance of power' that it has even been used to convey the exact opposite of its traditional meaning and employed to describe the possession of *predominance*. It was this that Chester Bowles meant when he wrote in 1956 that 'the two-thirds of the world who live in the undeveloped continents . . . will ultimately constitute the world balance of power' (Wight: 1966: 165). Ernst Haas cites an example of this tendency from the historical literature. The Count of Hauterive argued that the balance of power demanded that France break the Treaty of Campo Formio in order to raise a confederation of continental states to oppose the dominant position of Britain 'and, incidentally, establish the hegemony of France' (Haas, 1953a: 449).

Here, according to Haas, the balance of power is 'a special case, either in its equilibrium or its hegemony connotation – in the general pattern of power politics'. As Inis Claude has remarked, 'while such tolerance of diversity is admirable, it is a strange theory that cannot choose between polar opposites' (Claude, 1989: 80).

Finally, Wight identifies a ninth meaning of the phrase, which is 'an inherent tendency of international politics to produce an even distribution of power', the idea of systemic equilibrium maintained by the processes of the system. This is the sense in which non-realist theorists use the term. The system is seen as operating irrespective of whether or not any particular state or states wish it to operate. Thus, according to A. J. P. Taylor, between 1848 and 1914 the balance of power appeared to be self-operating in the manner of the laws of economics. 'If every man followed his own interest, all would be prosperous; and if every state followed its own interest, all would be peaceful and secure' (Wight, 1966: 166). Even this final usage is itself plastic, tending to become a synonym for the 'endless shifting and regrouping of power, the scales perpetually oscillating without coming to rest' (ibid.).

Ernst Haas enumerated different meanings of the balance of power in much the same way as did Martin Wight. But though some of the meanings he identified were the same as those of Wight, a number of his categories were significantly different, and are worth noting.

1   Balance meaning 'stability' and 'peace'. Haas argued that many analysts effectively argue, not so much that the balance of power is an effective mechanism for producing peace and stability, but rather that 'peace and stability are identical with the balance of power' (1953a: 450), giving as an example F. G. Leckie's 1817 book, *An Historical Research into the Nature of the Balance of Power*. However, Fénelon was rather more explicit in claiming that the balance of power was a producer of peace, declaring that 'this care to maintain a kind of equality and balance among neighbouring nations is that which secures the common repose' (Wright, 1975: 41).

2   In sharp contrast, Haas also identifies a group for whom the balance of power means 'instability' and 'war'. This is clearly seen in the writings of such bitter opponents of the balance of power concept as Richard Cobden (1867) and commentators such as the Abbé de Pradt, who argued that 'the balance of power meant war, while peace is identical with the settling of all issues on their moral, economic and ethnographic merits' (Haas, 1953a: 451). Both the latter two ideas seem based upon an exaggerated image. A key mechanism for maintaining the balance of power was war, which was used to defend and redress the balance. In this sense, Cobden was right, although as the period 1815–1914 showed the balance might work to produce periods in which major wars were very infrequent. By the same token, however, Leckie clearly overstressed the pacifying effects of the balance of power system.

3   Haas also sees as a specific meaning of the phrase the 'notion of balance' as implying a universal law of history. This is an outlook clearly associated with Hans Morgenthau, for years the *doyen* of the 'realist' school of international relations theory. Haas himself quotes as an example John B. Moore, who declared that

> what is called the balance of power is merely a manifestation of the primitive instinct of 'self-defence', which tends to produce combinations in all human affairs, national as well as international, and which so often manifests itself in aggression.
>
> (Haas, 1953a: 452)

As always, the assumption here is of the natural and inevitable struggle of states for superiority and the equally inevitable resistance to such attempts.

Donnadieu described it in determinist terms, 'Destiny takes along him who consents and draws along him who refuses', said Rabelais. 'The balance of power is one of these necessary forces; in other words, it is the expression of a law in the life of nations' (Haas, 1953a: 453). Burke said of the balance of power that it 'had been ever assumed as the known common law of Europe, at all times, and by all powers'.

4 Ernst Haas also draws attention to the way in which 'the balance of power' has been employed as a vehicle for propaganda. The concept has, at certain periods in European history, been an extremely popular one. The reasons for this are explored in Chapter 2. Its emergence in an intellectual context generally favourable to the notion of balance or equilibrium in all fields made it an appropriate metaphor for political use. This very availability, and the advantage which politicians took of it, was one of the reasons its meaning subsequently became subject to dispute. The mechanism which politicians used to derive political advantage from association with the positive connotations of the balance of power was simply to identify it with whatever particular state of affairs the politician in question wished to commend. Thus, in calling together a coalition to take arms against the infant French democracy in 1792, Prussia appealed for intervention in terms of the balance of power.

The perfection of the balance of power was offered as a justification for German expansionism in the First World War and French expansionist policies during the eighteenth century, policies which were not in fact about balance at all, which indeed ran quite counter to it. As Haas notes what makes the use of balance terminology in this context significant is 'the fact that the users of the term felt so convinced of its popularity as to make its conversion into a symbol of proper policy propagandistically profitable' (Haas, 1953a: 463).

Haas, in an insightful analysis of this aspect of the use made of the balance of power, describes it as serving an 'ideological' function in its heyday. Ideology is here used to mean the belief in a set of symbols. These symbols may not be objectively true, but they serve an important purpose as the myths which produce the spiritual cohesion of the ruling class. The balance of power concept may have been used in this sense to explain policies 'in terms of natural laws, in terms of moral rightness, or in terms of historical necessity if the symbol chosen to "put it over" was a sufficiently widely accepted one' (Haas, 1953a: 463). Indeed, Justi, in his *Di Chimare des Gleichgewichts von Europa*, published in 1758, argued just this, calling it a 'camouflage'. 'States, like private persons, are guided by nothing but their private interests, real or imaginary, and they are far from being guided by a chimerical balance of power' (Haas, 1953a: 464). For Haas, however, balance of power thinking is genuinely ideological if statesmen believe that the need for balancing power is actually in the general interest. In this sense, Peter Gellman has argued that the phrase 'balance of power' is also 'an invitation to consider the moral dimensions of international politics' (1989: 157) in the sense that proponents have deemed it a force for good and a producer of peace and independence, while critics have denounced it as a source of instability and war and a mechanism for denying national self-determination. As will be seen in Chapter 2, the European background in which the balance of power idea emerged during the second half of the seventeenth century very clearly demonstrates the way in which the balance of power concept came to serve a crucial ideological function in the sense used by Haas.

With the concept given so many meanings, Schroeder (1989: 140–1) has argued that the phrase 'balance of power' should never be used without an accompanying phrase identifying the way in which it is being used. Noting that other concepts such as socialism and democracy acquired highly charged and divergent meanings which required clarification in this way, as with 'liberal democracy', 'authoritarian democracy', 'peoples' democracy', and so on, Schroeder calls for a similar qualification for the phrase 'balance of power'. Certainly, this would make it easier to realise which particular meaning of the phrase was being used at any particular time.

Schroeder also makes the interesting suggestion that because the phrase appears to have meant different things at different periods in history, then the concept itself is a dependent variable. 'Instead of the balance of power explaining what happened in European politics, what happened in European politics largely explains what happened to the idea of the balance of power' (1989: 141). This is an extremely insightful observation, for the concept has indeed experienced an evolutionary history of this kind.

The wide variety of ways in which the term 'balance of power' has been used has contributed to its popularity and longevity, but at the expense of clear comprehension. The most obvious problem, as Inis Claude noted, is that proponents frequently fail to distinguish between balance of power as a situation of equilibrium and as a system of states engaged in competitive manipulation of power relationships among themselves (1989: 77). Chapters 3 and 4 therefore examine these two distinctive ways of thinking about the balance of power as a phenomenon. Before doing so however, Chapter 2 looks at the historical origins of the theory and practice of the balance of power.

2 Intellectual origins and early development

It is a question whether the *idea* of the balance of power be owing entirely to modern policy, or whether the *phrase* only has been invented in the later ages.

David Hume, in Wright 1975: 59

Ideas are like rivers, arising in a swamp or moor region rather than in a mountain spring, and often they see the light of day only after they have run for miles through subterranean caverns.

Alfred Vagts, 1948–9: 87

THE GREEK CITY-STATES

Although it was not until the beginning of the Renaissance in Europe that there is clear evidence of the emergence of both balance of power policies and a balance of power system in operation, it is possible to go further back in time and find evidence of unsystematic balance of power thinking. Certainly, on occasion states and alliances attempted to match the power of their opponents or combined against a powerful third party. States also on occasion attempted to remain aloof from the struggles of two closely matched rivals, so as to gain the advantages of balancing, without such behaviour being described as balance of power. According to Evan Luard 'a true balance of power policy occurs only when a state allies itself with the *weaker* of two possible partners, because it recognises that the other may finally prove the greater menace' (Luard 1992: 1; emphasis in original). The Scottish philosopher and historian David Hume argued that interstate politics in the classical age of ancient Greece was governed by balance of power thinking. To Hume the policy of preserving a balance was such an obvious one that 'it is impossible it could altogether have escaped antiquity, where we find, in other particulars, so many marks of deep penetration and discernment' (Wright, 1975: 63).

However, Hume was writing in the mid-eighteenth century at a time when Britain's policy of maintaining a European balance of power was domestically controversial and Hume was seeking the support of antiquity for the policy he himself favoured. More recently, it has been argued that an ancient Greek complex balance of power existed and that it was the transformation of this system into a bipolar system dominated by Athens and Sparta that drew the whole of Greece into the catastrophic Peloponnesian War (Fleiss, 1966: *passim*). Morton Kaplan (1968: 399) also suggests that the Greek city-states went through a balance of power phase and that the classical Greek period conforms to a significant extent to the balance of power model.

However, the evidence on which these authors' views are based is slender and certainly the study of that period of history did not confer the idea of the balance of power upon later generations for a further 2,000 years. As Robert Purnell argues (1978: 19), 'we must start by admitting frankly that at no period of their history do Greek and Roman thinkers appear to have developed anything approaching a comprehensive and consistent theory of international relations', a surprising fact given the complex relations between the political entities in the Graeco-Roman world. Watson has argued that the common cultural norms which governed the Greek world justify the description of ancient Greece as an 'international society', but he notes also that Greek thinkers themselves did not conceive of relations between the city-states in this way. While writers such as Aristotle wrote at length about the nature of government within the city, there was no equivalent speculation about relations among the Greek states or between them and the wider world. There was no ancient Greek metapolitical theory (Watson, 1992: 50). What can be said is that in Thucydides' *History of the Peloponnesian War*, written 300 years before the birth of Christ, there is evidence of balance of power *thinking*. Thucydides believed that the basic cause of the war was the growth of Athenian power and the fear this raised in Sparta.

Greece at this time had developed a comparatively sophisticated state system composed of around 1,500 city-states, most of which were little more than towns. The most important of these were Sparta, Athens, Corinth and Thebes. The cultural homogeneity of the Greek world had produced a network of relationships involving trading and warfare and this had stimulated the development of an early form of diplomacy involving the occasional dispatch of heralds and embassies.

The Peloponnesian War was fought by two great coalitions, the Peloponnesian League, led by Sparta and the Delian League led by Athens. Sparta had steadily expanded during the sixth century BC until it dominated the Peloponnese and was the centre of a network of allied states who were bound by treaty 'to have the same friends and enemies' and to follow the Spartan leadership 'on land and sea' (Kagan, 1969: 11). Sparta and Athens were allies during the Greek wars with Persia and relations were cool, but correct, afterwards. Sparta had always been a 'great power' in Greek terms while Athens only became so after the Persian War when the Greek states bordering the Aegean Sea turned to her for leadership in the continuing struggle with Persia, because Sparta had withdrawn her forces from the Aegean once the direct threat of a Persian invasion had been averted. The Aegean states formed the Delian League to continue the struggle against Persia, and Athens dominated the League so effectively that in its later years it is referred to by historians as the Athenian Empire. Over time, the rivalry between the two states led to the majority of Greek states being encouraged or coerced into joining one of the two alliances.

The crisis came in 433 BC. Corcyra (modern Corfu), engaged in a struggle against Corinth, appealed to Athens for help. Corinth was an ally of Sparta and the Athenians were well aware that aiding Corcyra would risk a war with Sparta and her alliance. Yet the appeals by Corcyra were hard to resist. Sparta was a land-power as were all her allies except one – Corinth which had the third-largest navy in Greece. Athens was overwhelmingly a naval power. Her trade, her wealth, her ability to dominate the Delian League and the Aegean Sea, her basic security – all depended upon her position as the dominant naval power in the region. Corcyra had the second-largest fleet in Greece and the Corcyran envoys to Athens argued persuasively that war between Athens and Sparta was inevitable and that Athens dare not allow the Corcyran fleet to fall into the hands of an ally of Sparta.

> There are three considerable naval powers in Hellas – Athens, Corcyra and Corinth. If Corinth gets control of us first and you allow our navy to be united with hers, you will have to fight against the combined fleets of Corcyra and the Peloponnese. But if you receive us into your alliance, you will enter upon the war with our ships as well as your own.
>
> (Thucydides, 1954: 54)

This is evidence of a degree of balance of power reasoning, but at its simplest level, little more than the notion of gaining a numerical advantage over one's enemies. Only in a single speech by Demosthenes, the oration for the Megalopolitans, does the ancient world provide us with evidence of thinking about a balance of power *system*, with Greece seen in terms of many states, all concerned with the relative power of all the others. Thus, while one can detect behaviour in the ancient Greek system which is analogous to balance of power behaviour, it was not self-consciously done for that purpose, nor did it reflect a theory of international relations in which balance policies could play a logical role. Wight argues that the ancient Greek world lacked the prerequisites for the emergence of a balance of power system. These were

> Sovereign States that could effectively and continuously organise their human and territorial resources; a diplomatic system that provided them with a regular flow of information; and a sufficient sense of common interest among them. Ancient Greece had had the first, but not the second or third.

(Wight, 1973: 86)

It has been suggested that the reason that the Greeks never developed a theory of international relations was because they lacked what Manning called the 'meta-diplomatics' involved in attributing individuality and personality to states (Taylor, 1978: 27). The Greeks spoke not of 'Persia' or 'Thebes' as taking actions, but rather 'the Persians' and 'the Thebans', and this therefore constrained the Greeks in terms of theorising about relations between states as such. This was important, because, as was seen in the previous chapter, the balance of power concept is embedded in a certain outlook on the nature of man, of power and relations between states within a system of international relations. Unless these are present, it is difficult to conceptualise and theorise about balance politics and this may well explain why the concept did not properly emerge until the nation-state itself began to, and became fully-fledged only when Europe began to constitute a true international system. A rare example of the kind of thinking characteristic of a balance of power outlook was in the early Roman era when Polybius commended Hiero, the ruler of Syracuse, for supporting Carthage rather than Rome, because a Carthaginian defeat would have allowed Rome to dominate the Mediterranean region, as indeed it eventually did.

The balance of power idea is absent from the ancient Greek world. Modern reflections, such as that of Waltz (1979: 127), which identify balance of power policies in ancient Greece in order to establish a historical continuum of balance practice, are imposing a framework on a pattern of events whose explanation should instead be sought in the Greek world-view of the era.

Yet the absence of theorising about international relations and about balances of power in ancient Greece is striking. The Greek culture of this time demonstrated many of the elements which combined to produce balance of power theory in Europe 2,000 years later. That these factors did not combine to produce a similar effect in ancient Greece is important.

Greece was composed of a very large number of independent states, including a core group of 'great powers' of approximately equal strength. The Greeks were passionately committed to the idea of independence and the autonomy of the individual city-states. The idea of unifying Greece into a single state 'did not often occur to them, and when it did, it was usually greeted with genuine abhorrence' (Watson, 1992: 49). Opposition to hegemony was therefore as great, if not greater, than it was in the later European system. In these ways the Greek system mirrored the later European one. In addition, Greece demonstrated a similarity in the crucial philosophical elements of theory production. The Greeks of Asia Minor had produced the first theoretical philosophers a century before the outbreak of the Peloponnesian War. Thinkers such as Thales and Anaximander argued that nature was not a plaything of the Gods. Rather, it was governed by principles of order, by general physical laws which the human mind was capable of comprehending. These ideas were revolutionary and can be seen as the beginning of scientific thought. The early Greek cosmologists speculated upon critical areas for scientific advance (Perry, 1993: 123) including 'natural explanations for physical occurrences (the Ionians), the mathematical order of nature (Pythagoras), logical proof (Parmenides) and the mechanical structure of the universe (Democritus)'.

The striking similarities between the conditions present in ancient Greece and seventeenth-century Europe, in the sense of political pattern and a scientific revolution embodying a mechanical concept of the universe, make the failure of Greece to produce an international theory suggest two things. Firstly, that these factors were not enough in themselves to generate balance of power thinking, a point of great importance when the seventeenth century is examined. Secondly, that the argument of structural realists is not borne out by the historical record. Similar conditions do not produce identical outcomes. Reductionist theories are inadequate because social constructions are the product of a complex variety of factors.

As Butterfield points out, not only is the balance of power largely absent from the ancient world, but the scholars and writers of that period are silent about its absence. Thus, it is reasonable to conclude

> that the idea of the balance of power not only did not exist in the ancient world, but did not take its rise even from the modern study of ancient history. More than most of our basic political formulas, this one seems to come from the modern world's reflections on its own experience.
>
> (Butterfield, 1966: 133)

THE RENAISSANCE

The long era of the Roman Empire and the so-called 'Dark Ages' which followed were not conducive to the development of balance of power thinking. Rome was able to dominate the Mediterranean world for centuries, a fact which shows that there is nothing inevitable in the operation of the balance of power. Indeed, a striking feature of the historical record is the *absence* of the theory and practice of the balance of power approach from most of recorded history. Far from being an inevitable feature of international relations, it is very much a modern development, a child of the Renaissance. The feudal Middle Ages were not characterised by a state system, but by one whose sovereignties looked to the authority represented by pope and emperor. Nevertheless, this period did give evidence of thinking which presaged the development of true balance of power thought. Thus, for example, Commynes, a diplomat in the service of Burgundy and France in the late fifteenth century, described Europe as being a pattern where the power of states was balanced by that of their neighbours or nearby rivals. Thus, Scotland balanced England; England, France; Portugal, Spain; Venice, Florence; and so on. But this simply described the tendency of bordering states to be particularly concerned about the power and policies of their immediate neighbours; it was not a description of balance of power policy as such. It was only as the Middle Ages gave way to the era of the Renaissance and the state in its more modern manifestation began to emerge that new ways of thinking about international politics began to surface. It appeared not on the European plane, but in the microcosm of the late-fifteenth-century Italian city-state system, which Kaplan argues at first glance appears 'to constitute as close a historical approximation of the model as we are likely to find under the constraints of the real world' (1968: 399).

To a certain extent the practice preceded the development of the theory. Many historians have characterised late-fifteenth-century Italy in terms of a balance of power system, in which the five most powerful city-states attempted to prevent Italy being dominated by any one power. Butterfield, for example, argues that the geographically and politically distinct Italian sub-system produced a state system in miniature and that 'within such an arena, states will want to support the power of which they are less afraid against the power of which they are more afraid' (1966: 133). The main threat was identified as being Venice, and the leading proponent of balancing policies Florence under Lorenzo de Medici. A classic statement of this thesis is that of Nelson. Nelson argues (1943: 125) that modern international relations can be dated from around 1450 in Italy, if the criteria are taken to be the existence of a state system, and balance of power policies regulating competition between centralised territorial states. Nelson asserts that the competition between the five major Italian states 'gave rise to balance of power politics in the fullest sense' (1943: 125). The five great powers were Venice, Milan, Florence, Naples and the Papal States. Venice was the most powerful and the most aggressive of these states and for much of the period 1450–99 her power was 'balanced' by a fluctuating constellation of alliances of which the most frequent was the triple alliance of Florence, Milan and Naples. The irruption of French power into the Italian peninsula in 1494 destroyed the Italian system, 'but for the preceding fifty years, the Italian peninsula had been secured in a relatively peaceful condition through the operation of balance of power politics' (Nelson, 1943: 126). Certainly, in the early part of the sixteenth century many Italians looked back on the 1480s as a golden age in which Italy was, in Machiavelli's words, '*in un certo modo bilanciata*'. Machiavelli played an important though indirect part in the development of the balance of power concept. He never wrote about balance policies as such, but he did help establish the foundations of international relations theory, within which balance of power theory is rooted. In particular, Machiavelli established the idea that the state was a moral force, with a claim upon the loyalty of its citizens and a political entity with 'rights' which could be defined and defended (Savigear, 1978: 35). The full acceptance of this concept had to await the secularisation of politics and was not fully consummated until the Peace of Westphalia in 1648.

The second great contribution made by Machiavelli was the idea that the state was defined not just by its internal workings, but by its relationships with other states, that there existed an international order which related states to each other, an order with a particular structure (Savigear, 1978: 37). Machiavelli did not reflect upon the rationale of the alliances constructed by the Florentine leaders to contain the expansionist states in Italy, nor does the underlying structure of international relations which he detected emerge as one governed by the principle of balancing power.

The Florentine scholars Rucellai and Guicciardini similarly described Italy in the 1480s as being balanced between expansionist Venice and the alliance of Florence, Naples and Milan. According to Guicciardini, the foreign policy of Florence under Lorenzo de Medici was designed to ensure 'that the Italian situation should be maintained in a state of balance, not leaning more toward one side than the other' (Wright, 1975: 9). Guicciardini here goes further than Machiavelli, who never showed any understanding of what a balance of power system was or how it might be maintained, arguing, for example, that a state should help the *stronger* side in a war in order to share in prestige – an idea totally at variance with balance of power thinking and medieval rather than modern in outlook.

As Butterfield (1966: 134) points out, Machiavelli's failure to think in terms of the balance of power is all the more surprising because he was deeply interested in the question of how a state should behave when its neighbours were at war. In later centuries this issue would invariably be considered through the prism of balance of power thinking, yet Machiavelli shows no evidence of having thought in these terms. Although Guicciardini also had a limited grasp of the balance of power concept, he did make a significant contribution to the development of the theory by describing Italy in terms of a system of forces which had been brought to a certain equilibrium (Butterfield, 1966: 137). Guicciardini attributed the operation of the Italian balance of power to the genius of Lorenzo de Medici of Florence, supported by Ferdinand of Naples. Nelson quotes Guicciardini's description of the Italian system as one where the alliance against Venice was designed 'to keep down the power of the Venetians, who were without question superior to any of the confederates separately, but not able to cope with them when united' (Nelson, 1943: 130–1). Guicciardini felt that the system operated effectively to maintain an overall balance in which *all* the states watched each other carefully, and thereby prevented any of the states from dominating the peninsula.

This idea that states operate as part of a 'system' was a major step forward. Certainly, the way in which Guiccardini described Italy in his history influenced subsequent generations of historians into accepting that there had been a balance of power system in operation in Italy in the late fifteenth century. This balanced system may have been largely a myth as some modern scholarship has suggested (for example, Pillinini, 1970), but it was certainly an extremely powerful myth which did much to legitimise the idea of a balance of power among subsequent generations of thinkers outside Italy. In particular, Guicciardini raised the reputation of Lorenzo de Medici under whom Florence was alleged to have become 'the tongue of the balance' in the Italian city-state system. Lorenzo's letters reveal a clear concern with the relative strengths of the various powers in Italy, but do not demonstrate any understanding or sympathy with the balance of power in the sense that subsequent generations came to understand it.

In this period the balance of power idea was clearly developing significantly. It was a long way from reaching a fully developed form, however. There were still important elements of the theory missing, a holistic conception of the international system for example or a non-ideological approach to foreign policy. These developments had to await the evolution of the interstate system reflected in the Peace of Westphalia and the final triumph of secularism. It is dangerous to read too much into the sixteenth- and early-seventeenth-century writings on the idea of balance. The concept was still very much *sui generis*.

Guicciardini's eulogising of Lorenzo de Medici was repeated by Alberico Gentili, a Protestant Italian jurist who stressed the necessity for secular values in international relations and thereby paved the way for the emergence of the kind of balance of power thinking which he favoured. Gentili argued that war should be seen as a political rather than a moral concern. In his *De Jure Belli Libri Tres* (1598), Gentili used a scientific metaphor to promote balance of power policies, arguing that,

> the maintenance of union among the atoms is dependent upon their equal distribution; and on the fact that one molecule is not surpassed in any respect by another. ... This it is which was the constant care of Lorenzo de Medici, that wise man, friend of peace and father of peace, namely that the balance of power should be maintained among the princes of Italy. This he believed would give peace to Italy as indeed it did so long as he lived and preserved that condition of affairs.
>
> (Gentili quoted in Wright, 1975: 13)

It is noticeable that in this period proponents of balancing strategies argued that it would produce peace. Giovanni Botero in *Reason of State* (1956), written in 1589, advocated balances as a means to produce peace and claimed that Lorenzo de Medici had kept Italy at peace for many years by balancing the powers.

Although the use of the terminology of equilibrium antedated the practice of balance of power policies in Italy by some 50 years it is significant that it did emerge in Italy at this time. Alfred Vagts, in a seminal essay written in the late 1940s, drew attention to the way in which political language tends to be borrowed from other fields such as the arts, religion, philosophy and the sciences, and that the more commonly used a term is, even when it is being used in many different ways, the greater its political usefulness (Vagts, 1948–9: 88–9). This was certainly the case with the concept of 'balance' or 'equilibrium' in Renaissance Italy. Thus, music was governed by the principles of 'counterpoint' and 'harmony', the health of the body was determined by the balance of good and evil 'humours'. A critical factor in the dissemination of these ideas and images was the invention of printing, a development whose importance is difficult to overstress. Printing was first perfected in Europe in Mainz round about 1450. Within 50 years European presses had produced some six million books, 'more books, probably than had been produced in western Europe since the fall of Rome' (Rice and Grafton, 1994: 7).

The rapid spread of printing throughout Europe accelerated both the diffusion of images and the spread of ideas. It meant that the particular interpretation of Italian history put forward by Guicciardini, Rucellai and Gentili could rapidly be received and absorbed by literate Italians and that this conception of the Italian state system would spread through Europe as their works were translated, to offer a model for later ages when circumstances propitious for its general adoption emerged in northern Europe.

However, while the use of metaphors drawn from mathematics and geometry was instrumental in bringing about the adoption of the balance of power concept as the basic description of international relations, it did not make clear the degree to which the balance was to be seen as a description of the nature of international relations, or as a prescription and guide for statesmen, providing rules and producing policies which would stabilise relations between states (Savigear, 1978: 41).

Despite this overwhelmingly favourable intellectual environment, balance terminology was slow to enter the vocabulary of international politics, and when it did so it encouraged a conceptualisation that was highly simplistic. Because the terminology of the balance was derived from that of the physical sciences there was always a tendency (which would become particularly marked in the eighteenth century) to discuss alliances almost as if they were chemical formulae. In addition, for a number of reasons, the earliest model of a balance of power system to become popularised was the simple bipolar model.

This development was partly a result of the dramatic dualities that characterised Europe in the sixteenth century, the struggles between France and the Habsburgs, between Christianity and the Turks, between Catholics and Protestants. But it was also encouraged by the balance metaphor itself. The popularisers of the balance of power concept used the well-known astrological symbol of *Libra* or the scales to convey their meaning as simply as possible. This bipolar balance model was to be a powerful influence upon European balance of power thinking until well into the eighteenth century. Certainly, a bipolar balance made it easier to assess the relative strengths of the parties in the system and more likely that the balance image would become part of the popular consciousness.

Nevertheless, despite the simplicity of the form in which it entered the European political culture, the balance of power concept performed a vital function. Because it promised a degree of stability and predictable behaviour between states it appeared to 'establish a link between two apparently incompatible but essential aspects – completely free states and some kind of social order among nations – of European civilisation' (Greene, 1964: 219). It was this feature which would become central to the widespread acceptance of the balance of power principle in the final decades of the seventeenth century.

It is difficult to trace the process of transmission between the Italian city-state system and the wider European balance in the sixteenth century. Indeed, it has been argued that the European balance would have emerged without the Italian example, because of the struggle between France and the Habsburgs (Wight, 1973: 91). It is doubtful if this would in fact have been the case, for the classical Greek example demonstrates that there is nothing *inevitable* about the development of balance of power thinking, even when circumstances seem favourable. Moreover, as will be argued later, there were critical features largely unique to the seventeenth century which help to explain why the principle achieved its general acceptance during that period. However much truth there might be in this statement, the Italian example certainly prepared the ground for the emergence of balance of power thinking in northern Europe. Venice, the object of balancing policies in the 1480s, became a proponent of the balance of power in the next century as her power declined. It is worth noting that although Venice was more often the object of balance of power diplomacy in the fifteenth century, Anderson (1993: 151) argues that the earliest clear reference to an Italian balance of power was made in 1439 by the Venetian Francesco Barbero. Barbero insisted that Venice was interested in the maintenance of such a balance. Venetian doctrinal support for the theory was significant because Venice maintained an elaborate diplomatic network and through this she spread support for the balance of power throughout Europe.

Indeed, by 1605 the Italian prelate Giovanni Botero, in discussing the balance of power concept in his *Relatione della Republica Venetiana* (Venice, 1605) was able to declare that the balance of power idea was based upon 'natural order and the light of reason' (Botero quoted in Wright, 1975: 22). Like Guicciardini, Botero praised what he saw as the subtle policy of Lorenzo de Medici who he felt had managed to keep 'Italy at peace for a long time by balancing the powers' (Botero, 1956: 125). It is noteworthy that at this stage of the concept's development, it was seen by many of its proponents as a way of maintaining peace. This objective was far less prominent in later centuries. The balance of power idea was clearly spreading in the first half of the sixteenth century. As early as 1535 Mary of Hungary, the Habsburg regent in the Netherlands, was referring to the balancing techniques of the Italian princes and in mid-century noted that in Italy the small states had sought to balance the power of the great powers intervening in Italy (Anderson, 1993: 151–2).

The translation of the historical works of Italian writers such as Machiavelli and Guicciardini into other European languages also had an impact. In 1579 the first translation of Guicciardini's *History* introduced Italian balance of power thinking to a wider English audience. Significantly, the translators of the work dedicated it to Queen Elizabeth I and flatteringly assured her that, 'God has put into your hand the balance of power and justice, to poise and counterpoise at your will the actions and counsels of all the Christian kings of your time' (Vagts, 1948–9: 97). This was a clear advocacy of the balancing policy, and the timing of the appeal was appropriate, for in the following decade England under Elizabeth began to oppose the hegemonic drive of Spain.

It was in fact in the struggle against Philip II of Spain that the mechanism of the grand alliance, which Martin Wight has called 'the master-institution of the balance of power' (1973: 93) made its first tentative appearance. In 1584, as Spain moved to crush the Dutch revolt, Sir Francis Walsingham presented a memorandum to the English Privy Council proposing aid to the Dutch and, should this be approved, discussion of 'whether it be not fit that the French King should be moved to concur in the action' (Read, 1925: 73–4).

The implications of growing Spanish power were forcing English policy-makers to begin framing foreign policy in a wider European context. The struggle against Spain encouraged English balance of power thinking just as the later struggle against Louis XIV of France spread such attitudes throughout Europe. Policy was forced almost unconsciously to follow balance of power lines, while analysis of the necessities of a balancing strategy was encouraged. Thus, for example, anticipating the need to ignore religious or ideological sympathies in seeking alliance partners, Lord Burghley declared in 1589 that England would ally with any state opposed to the threatening power of Spain (Wight, 1973: 105).

THE SEVENTEENTH CENTURY

By the time the Anglo-Spanish struggle ended, English thinking about the balance of power had advanced considerably. In 1609 Sir Thomas Overbury (1903: 154) described Christendom as a double balance : Spain, France and England in the West, and Russia, Poland, Sweden and Denmark in the East, with Germany a self-contained equilibrium in the middle. Overbury was anticipating the concept of sub-balances contained within the general European equilibrium, an issue which was to be of profound importance to Europe in the period between 1700 and 1730.

Three years after Overbury published his *Observations*, Sir Francis Bacon in his essay 'Of Empire' was outlining specific policy guidelines for maintaining a balance of power. Bacon urged that 'princes do keep due sentinel, that none of their neighbours do overgrow so (by increase of territory, by embracing of trade, by approaches or the like), as they become more able to annoy them than they were'. Bacon argued that Henry VIII, Francis I of France and the Emperor Charles V had followed such a policy with respect to each other with the result that 'none of the three could win a palm of ground, but the other two would straightways balance it, either by confederation, or if need were, by a war; and would not in any wise take up peace at interest' (Bacon quoted in Maurseth, 1964: 121). Bacon went on to argue that danger to the balance of power justified preventative war.

Although Spain and France were the central actors in the struggle for supremacy in seventeenth-century Europe, both states produced thinkers who encouraged their rulers to frame their foreign policy in balance of power terms. An example of such advocacy can be found in the anonymous adviser to Archduke Albert, ruler of the Spanish Netherlands at the turn of the century. England and Spain had long been engaged in a bitter struggle which had culminated in the Spanish invasion attempt of 1588. The Duke's adviser, however, recommended making peace with England in order to allow England to emerge as a counterweight to the rising power of France, arguing that an alliance between England and Spain would

> 'be a salutary counterweight to the might and power of France, which nation, by virtue of the peace and order which her King maintains, will soon present a threat to daunt the princes of all Christandome' and the rising threat of France meant that in future 'the same case which joined France and England in alliance in these latest wars – which is to say the power of the King of Spain – must now unite Spain, England and this country'.
>
> (Wright, 1975: 25)

Indeed, by 1612 the idea of lesser states combining to prevent a great power from achieving 'universal monarchy' had become so well-established that the Italian writer Boccalini could describe it as a generally received opinion (Anderson, 1993: 153).

Peace between England and Spain was finally concluded in 1604. Although Britain was to become the advocate of balance of power policies during the eighteenth century, she contributed little to the development of either the theory or the practice during the first three-quarters of the seventeenth century. She was too caught up in the domestic struggle between King and Parliament to play a major role in European affairs. The Treaty of Westphalia, which brought the Thirty Years War to an end in 1648 can be seen as a crucial watershed in the long process by which the balance of power became the central guiding principle of European international relations in the eighteenth and nineteenth centuries. In order to work effectively, a complex balance of power requires the existence of a functioning international system in which the sovereign independence of states is the central goal of national policy and in which there is comparative moderation in foreign policy objectives and an absence of ideologically based interstate bitterness. The Peace of Westphalia can be said to have formalised these conditions in Europe and thereby provided the foundation for the acceptance of balance of power logic as a determinant of foreign policy behaviour. It brought an end to the century-long Christian wars of religion in Europe, it formally recognised the concept of state sovereignty and it refuted the aspirations of the Papacy and the Holy Roman Empire to recreate a single Christian imperium.

France was rising to the position of great power, though she herself had but lately recovered from the turmoil of the Wars of Religion and experienced the rebellions of the Fronde between 1648 and 1652. The first half of the seventeenth century did however see a number of French contributions to the development of balance of power theory. The long struggle between France and the Habsburgs rein-forced the image of a bipolar balance envisaged in terms of a pair of scales, seen for example in Duke Henri de Rohan's description of France and Spain as 'the two Poles'. Rohan's contribution to the development of the theory lay in his emphasis on the idea of national interest. He argued that as Spain had attempted to dominate Europe, it was natural for another great power to arise (in this case France) to act as a counterbalance. But this general systemic effect having occurred, 'the other Princes join the one or the other, according to their interest' (Wright, 1975: 35).

This was an advance on the thinking of earlier French writers such as Philip de Commynes who had noted the tendency of balanced pairs of enemies to appear, such as England–France, Spain–Portugal, Bavaria–Austria, but had seen their rivalry purely in terms of geographical proximity, without showing any awareness of differing national interests within a broader state system. Rohan, however, does not argue that equilibrist sentiment *as such* should govern the choice of state interest. In this regard his contemporary, Philippe de Bethune was more profound. Bethune argued that neutral states should clearly support the weaker of the two dominant powers and by producing an equality of power bring both sides to foreign policy moderation, for the safety of states consists 'in an equal counter-poise of power on both sides, and the greatness of a Prince drawing after it the ruin of his Neighbours; it is wisdom to prevent this' (Wright, 1975: 34). Bethune also noted that power is relative. The threat posed by any particular state reflected both the size and resources of a particular state, and the ability of the state to project that power abroad. Domestic ingredients of power potential such as economic wealth, size of armed forces, quality of weaponry and so on Bethune termed a state's 'absolute power'. Other, less tangible factors he called 'conditional power'. An example of the latter was distance, for 'a Neighbour Prince of mean forces, may more easily or sooner hurt or succour us, than a great Prince which lies far off' (ibid.).

It was difficult for French writers to move beyond a simple bipolar image of the balance. Since France clearly was one of the two 'poles', she could seek support to balance Spain or Austria, but was unconvincing when she aspired to any more subtle balance role. Notwithstanding this, some efforts were made during the premiership of Cardinals Richelieu and Mazarin to acquire the image of 'balancer' state even while acting as the basic counterweight to Spain. Cardinal Richelieu in 1616 claimed the title 'arbitre de la Chrestiante' for the King of France, while Mazarin's despatches in the 1640s made several references to the balance of power. Mazarin, for example, identified the Venetian Republic with a balance of power policy (Butterfield, 1966: 139). By the middle of the seventeenth century the ideologically positive connotations of 'the balance of power' were already becoming accepted. In the treaty between France and Denmark signed in 1645 the two states refer to the need to maintain the longstanding balance of power (*ancien et salutaire équilibre*) 'which has until now served as the foundation of peace and public tranquillity' (Anderson, 1993: 155).

Even before the restoration of Charles II in 1660 Britain had begun to take a more active role in European diplomacy once more. In 1657 Cromwell signed an alliance with France which led to English participation in the war with Spain. Although Cromwell's action increased England's prestige and won her army laurels at the Battle of the Dunes in 1658, it was criticised subsequently. A pamphlet by Slingsby Bethel, published in London in 1668 strongly criticised Cromwell because he went to war with Spain instead of with France 'bringing the first thereby under and making the latter too great for Christendome and by that means broke the balance between the two Crowns of Spain and France' (Bethel, 1668: 368).

Bethel's analysis of Cromwell's policy is interesting for a number of reasons. His basic argument was that Cromwell had followed the form of traditional English foreign policy without appreciating its spirit. England under Cromwell had continued to make war on Spain, as it had done for over a century, without realising that the reason England had opposed Spain in the past, that is, that she was the most powerful European state and committed to extending her continental dominions, now applied to France, not to decaying Spain.

Bethel was arguing for a mobile foreign policy in which old antagonisms are not allowed to stand in the way of the requirements of the day. It is interesting also that Bethel believed that this policy of opposing the strongest power in Europe had always been English policy, a view that bears only cursory examination. Bethel was writing during the reign of Charles II and his observations, while superficially criticising the policies of Cromwell, also criticised those of Charles II, since in this regard their policies were the same. As a republican writing under a restored monarchy he was forced into this oblique method. It was Charles II's pro-French policy that was the true object of his attack. For, in fairness to Cromwell it may be said that the relative decline in Spain's position *vis-à-vis* France was not as obvious in Cromwell's day as it was after the Treaty of the Pyrenees in 1659. Though Spain was undoubtedly weak, it appeared that France was in no better position. The years which preceded Cromwell's French alliance had seen France prostrated by the upheavals of the Fronde rebellions, so that her latent strength was disguised.

Although highly critical of England's supine attitude towards France during the reign of Charles II, Bethel was astute enough to realise that the England of Charles II did not possess the strength to determine the outcome of a European conflict itself, given the continuing decline of Spain and the weakness of the Austrian Habsburgs. The alternative, as Bethel saw, was for England to add to her own strength by alliance with other nations and thereby produce a third force, capable of exercising the role of balancer with credibility. Bethel was therefore enthusiastic in his praise for the Triple Alliance between England, Sweden and the Dutch Republic in 1668, an alliance formed for the purpose of mediating a 'reasonable' peace between France and Spain and for guaranteeing the peace once it was concluded. Although this surprise grouping of the northern powers did not fundamentally weaken France, it did come as a major diplomatic upset, not only because England was traditionally wary of peacetime alliances, but also because England and the Dutch Republic had barely emerged from the second Anglo-Dutch War. The 'mediation' of the northern powers was therefore a significant factor in the ending of the War of Devolution between France and Spain which had begun in 1667. Though Bethel compared the wisdom of Charles II's balancing policy with that of Queen Elizabeth I (1671) the King very quickly reverted to a pro-French and anti-Dutch policy. Nevertheless, Bethel clearly identified the possibilities open to England for playing the role of balancer and recommended the best method for maintaining it, the alliance. Nor was Bethel alone in thinking along these lines. Baron de Lisola, the imperial minister in Brussels published a pamphlet in 1667 in which he accused France of seeking to achieve a 'universal monarchy' and, rather ironically, recommended that the states of Europe follow the advice of the Frenchman de Rohan and realise that they needed to 'hold the balance' between the powers of France and Spain if they were to secure their independence and maintain peace in Europe.

The architect of the dramatic 1668 Triple Alliance is generally agreed to have been Sir William Temple, one of Charles II's most able and trusted diplomats, who served as envoy both in Brussels and the Hague. He was an opponent of the King's pro-French policy and an advocate of alliance with the Dutch. Temple's constantly reiterated warnings to Charles II about the dangers to Europe from a preponderant French power were often couched in balance of power terminology, and he is especially interesting on the mechanisms for maintaining equilibrium.

The French aggression in the War of Devolution alarmed both London and the Hague. Charles II's objective in concluding the Triple Alliance was the same as that which motivated the Dutch. Both saw the French advances in the Spanish Netherlands (modern Belgium) as a threat to their own security, and yet both had their own reasons for not wanting to offend Louis XIV too much. The Dutch were still technically allied to France, while Charles II was still intent on pursuing a basically pro-French foreign policy. For these reasons the Anglo-Dutch alliance of 1668 was disguised as a mere offer to mediate between France and Spain. In fact, England, the Dutch Republic and Sweden secretly agreed that, if necessary, they would use military force to compel France to reach a compromise peace with Spain. This was a highly significant development, anticipating the balancing role England would play in the next century.

The possibility of needing force to dictate a settlement compelled Britain to think about the mechanisms of balance politics. In order to be decisive, Britain needed an enhanced military capability and the King asked Parliament for money to strengthen the Navy. Temple explained this in a letter to the Grand Pensionary of Holland, de Witt, in March 1668, 'since we only draw a war upon ourselves by desiring a peace, to endeavour on the contrary to draw on the peace by making all the appearances of desiring a war'.

Unlike earlier writers on the subject, Temple clearly saw national balance of power policies as operating within a wider European state system. He was perceptive enough to see that other states might legitimately use balance of power thinking to constrain England when necessary. For example, he saw the interests of the Dutch Republic as being to 'preserve themselves by an alliance with England against France, and by that of France against England as they did formerly by both against Spain' (Sheehan, 1988: 28).

Both Temple and Slingsby Bethel demonstrated an awareness of the significance of subsidiary balances of power, Temple advising the Dutch 'to balance in some measure the two lesser crowns of Sweden and Denmark, as well as the greater of France and Spain'. Bethel similarly praised the Long Parliament for allying 'with Holland in the preserving of Denmark as necessary for the Balancing of Sweden' (ibid.: 29). Bethel recognised that a balance of power in the Baltic was necessary if important naval supplies, especially timber, were to continue to reach Britain, which depended on naval power for her security.

The contributions of Temple and Bethel to the development of balance of power thinking in England were significant because they were made at a time when the idea held no favour with the nation's leadership, nor had it done so for generations. Much the same could be said of George Savile, Marquess of Halifax, who through the reign of the Francophile Charles II was well known for his concern at the growth of French power on the continent.

Unlike many of his fellow countrymen, his antipathy to France sprang not from religious bigotry or xenophobia, but from a clear perception of what he saw as the French threat to the liberties of Europe. In his writings he emphasised that France was the inheritor of an 'overbalancing power', and that to oppose French aggrandisement was the correct response, just as it had been right to oppose the power of Spain in the previous century. Whereas it had sometimes been argued that the Spanish expansionism in Europe in the sixteenth century was the result of their 'popery', or the peculiar wickedness of the Spanish as a nation, Halifax argued that the replacement of the Spanish menace by the French showed that it was the prevailing power situation that accounted for such aggrandisement and that therefore the ally of today could become the feared aggressor of tomorrow. Halifax laid emphasis on the fact that a balance of power policy cannot be guided by traditional friendships or animosities, but only by the requirements of the present. The movement to oppose a preponderant power must be automatic, no matter what the source of the threat.

In *The Character of a Trimmer* (1969), published in 1685, Halifax declared that he had no bias either for or against France and accepted that when Spain had been at the height of its power it had used the same methods which the French had subsequently adopted. It was not partiality that moved him, but rather the fears of an overgrowing power. He even went so far as to approve of the French action in opposing England during the Anglo-Dutch Wars. This was correct, he argued, because when England gained the upper hand 'then the King of France, like a wise prince, was resolved to support the beaten side, and would no more let the power of the sea, than we ought to suffer the monarchy of Europe, to fall into one hand' (Halifax, 1969: 89). Halifax resembled Bethel in as much as he projected England's balance of power policies centuries into the past, calling sixteenth-century England the 'perpetual umpire' between France and Spain and also in criticising Cromwell for his war with Spain as being injurious to the prevailing balance of power (ibid.).

The expansionist policies of France under Louis XIV produced a rapid acceleration in the development of balance of power theory. As Martin Wight noted, 'if the struggle against Philip II had brought a balance of power into systematic operation, it was the struggle against Louis XIV that raised it to the level of theory' (Wight, 1973: 97). By this point the idea of the balance of power had quite clearly entered into the mainstream of European thinking about international relations. Butterfield has drawn attention to the fact that references to the balance of power can be discovered from the sixteenth century, but they are fairly few in number, while from 1600 onwards not only are such references more numerous, their meaning is also clearer. From the middle of the century onwards 'references begin to come in an amazing flood. And, so far as I can see, it is only at this point in the story that the doctrine has its remarkable development' (Butterfield, 1966: 139).

It was no accident that the concept of the balance of power in international relations blossomed during Newton's era at the end of the seventeenth century, an era dominated by an intellectual fascination with the mechanics of the universe, for as Wight (1979: 168) noted, 'the balance of power is the principle of what might be called the mechanics of power politics; and the mechanistic metaphor is useful for describing international relations'. The laws of planetary motion were published by Kepler in 1619 and by 1687 Newton had developed the laws of gravity. The material for analogy was thus increasing steadily.

EUROPEAN EQUILIBRIUM AND THE GENERAL CRISIS

In explaining the triumph of balance of power thinking in the final decades of the seventeenth century in Europe a number of features stand out and are obviously important. They include the emergence of the sovereign state in Western Europe and the centralisation of political and military power that went with it. The example of the earlier Italian state system and, perhaps more importantly, the reflections upon it by a later generation of Italian historians, was critical. Printing spread their interpretations throughout Europe. The confessional division of Europe produced by the Reformation and the acceptance of the principle of *cuius regio, eius religio* ended the unity of Christendom and helped produce a state system composed of a large number of states of comparable strength. The scientific revolution produced a wealth of metaphors and a fascination for mechanics and balance. All these factors help to explain why the balance of power idea emerged so strongly, but they are not in themselves sufficient. Indeed, previous studies of the origins of balance of power politics have identified many such important contributing factors. What they do not fully explain is why these factors were so instrumental after 1650. Many of them were present in the sixteenth century without producing a similar effect, and some similar factors had existed in the ancient Greek world without triggering the same outcome. The answer to this anomaly lies in the phenomenon often referred to as the 'general crisis' of the seventeenth century, which was itself the result of forces set in motion in the previous century. In his excellent study of the subject, Theodore Rabb argues that the crisis in question concerned the location of authority, 'in a world where everything had been thrown into doubt, where uncertainty and instability reigned, could one attain assurance, control, and a common acceptance of *some* structure where none seemed within reach?' (Rabb, 1975: 33).

The crisis of authority had been triggered by the Renaissance and the Reformation. These two phenomena brought about a total reshaping of the view of the world held by Europeans, and of the place of mankind in the universe. Medieval Europeans had shared a world-view in which the universe was seen as a hierarchy with God at the apex. Humankind was sinful and lowly. The social order was a rigid hierarchy whose highest temporal and spiritual leaders ruled in accordance with God's teaching. As the highest of God's creations, humankind lived on a world which was the centre of the universe.

Philosophy and the arts revolved around theological issues and representations.

With the Renaissance and the Reformation, the orderly structure and perspective of the medieval European world steadily disintegrated. Renaissance humanist thought broke with the rigid divisions of medieval society and initiated trends towards individualism and secularism. The dominance of the Church was broken, a process accelerated by the onset of the Reformation which shattered the unity of Christendom. New states emerged, engaged in a steady process of centralising power.

In addition, Renaissance thinkers subverted the comforting belief that the Earth was the centre of the universe and humankind a uniquely important species. Copernicus and Galileo demonstrated that the Earth was a planet, undermining the complicated theology of the Medieval Church. The certainties of the medieval era were replaced by doubt and a profound sense of insecurity. As the French scientist Blaise Pascal put it, 'engulfed in the infinite immensity of spaces of which I am ignorant, and which know me not, I am frightened' (Perry, 1993: 71). The Reformation exacerbated this intellectual anguish by removing a common framework for exploring these issues and triggering ideological warfare between Christians. Many Protestant sects threatened traditional authority still more by challenging monarchical authority.

The Renaissance gave Europeans a fundamentally new perspective. In the case of art this was quite literally true. In the fifteenth century Italian artists developed the technique of linear perspective, allowing the representation of reality as seen from a particular point of view. This technique 'allowed the artist a sharper, more penetrating presentation of reality; but at the same time it showed very clearly the limitations and ambiguities of human perception' (Koenigsberger, 1987: 22). In a broader sense, the discovery of the 'New World' by Columbus in 1492 and the arrival of European explorers in the Indian Ocean, changed the image of the world held by Europeans.

Nearly two centuries passed between the emergence of a primitive balance of power system in Italy in the final decades of the fifteenth century and the triumph of balance of power thinking in Western Europe at the end of the seventeenth century. The hesitant spread to acceptance of the concept puzzled historians of international relations like Herbert Butterfield, but what is significant is not the slow transmission of the original idea, but rather the reasons for its eventual acceptance.

As Rabb has convincingly argued, the period from the sixteenth to the early seventeenth century was a time of turmoil, change, excitement and anguish in Europe. This long period was characterised by painful attempts to come to terms with a vast array of new ideas in every field, ideas which had swept aside the old medieval certainties.

> As expectations lost their cogency, an atmosphere of groping and unease descended. Europe's leaders, philosophers and artists grappled with a world that seemed to be crumbling about them. . . . The sense that all solid landmarks had disappeared pervades the writing of the age – either because men were toppling the landmarks or because they were seeking them in vain.
>
> (Rabb, 1975: 37)

This intellectual uncertainty could not continue indefinitely and, perhaps ironically, it was science, which had helped to generate doubt by undermining the Aristotelian model of the Cosmos, which in the end found a reconciling solution to the intellectual *travails* of the era with the emergence of a new unifying conception of the universe expounded by Newton.

It was this reconciling and harmonising function that was critical and which explains the success of the 'mechanical' metàphor in popularising balance of power theory in this period, as noted by Haas. The preceding hundred years had been characterised by religious discord, political turmoil and war. In virtually all areas of European thought in the seventeenth century this produced a search for harmony, a characteristic feature of the Baroque era.

Given the turmoil brutally exemplified by the Thirty Years War (1618–48), it was hardly surprising that the quest for harmony and order was particularly marked in international relations, producing a succession of proposals for perpetual peace (for example Sully, Penn, and Bellers) and the formalisation of principles of international law by Grotius. In *On the Law of War and Peace* (1625), Grotius argued that international law was based on natural laws common to all mankind. He accepted the ultimate sovereignty of states and proposed rational efforts to limit the horrors of war, though he did not think that war could be abolished.

Subsequent generations would relate these ideas to the balance of power conception popularised by the Newtonian revolution in science. As late as the early twentieth century Oppenheim could argue that, 'an equilibrium between the members of the Family of Nations is an indispensable condition of the very existence of

International Law (1905, I: 73–4). The logic of Oppenheim's argument, which was the view held at the turn of the eighteenth century, was that, in a system without an overall authority, respect for international law is sustained by a balance of power which ensures an approximate equality of strength between the great powers such that none can flout the conventions of international society with impunity.

As Rabb has argued, Newton's model of the universe was rapidly adopted as the new consensus because it offered an end to a long period of intellectual uncertainty for Europeans. 'What the age wanted to hear was that the world was harmonious and sensible; that human beings were marvellously capable, endowed with an orderly Reason that could solve all problems' (Rabb, 1975: 114). Newton and Locke were embraced because their ideas fulfilled a compelling need for an epistemology that would end, at least for the next two centuries, the anguished doubts about the sources of order and authority that had characterised the previous 200 years. A new world-view coalesced around the structure of all-embracing frameworks, an outlook into which the earlier Italian model of a balance of power between the major powers could be smoothly integrated.

A feature which is noteworthy here is that the balance of power as a concept emerged with two characteristic, but not entirely harmonious features. The first saw the balance as part of a method for maintaining the independence of the states within the system by establishing a mechanism for triggering alliances against states with hegemonial aspirations. This perception, predominant in Britain, became the definitive interpretation of the balance concept among English-speaking realist scholars in the twentieth century.

The second perspective saw the balance of power in a 'Grotian' sense providing the harmonising framework sustaining the international society which had emerged from the Westphalia settlement of 1648. Although counter-hegemonic alliances feature here also, this second conceptualisation owes more to the effects of the scientific revolution on European thinking and emphasised the idea of Europe as a *system* of states, comprising a society co-determinous with vanished Christendom. It was this conception which proved amenable to the German-speaking world and the states of the Holy Roman Empire in particular. It was also the theme which dominated during the phase of 'concert' diplomacy in the first half of the nineteenth century.

By the end of the seventeenth century, the balance of power concept was gaining general acceptance as the organising principle of European diplomacy. Yet, as Anderson (1993: 159–63) has pointed out, this was not an inevitable development and the concept was strongly criticised in a still highly religious age for its secular and amoral aspects. Indeed, the competing image of a unified Christendom able to confront the Muslim world as a single entity continued to be put forward, particularly in Catholic states. For religious idealists, the balance concept, which advocated flexible alliances and action against co-religionists was deeply shocking.

Just as the principle of the balance of power had to compete for acceptance with more traditional alternative outlooks, so too the practice of balance policies was far from winning wholehearted acceptance. The last three decades of the century witnessed alignments that can justly be described as balance of power coalitions, but at the same time many states saw fit to ally with the threatening power, either through fear or the hope of making territorial gains, a phenomenon which a later century would call 'bandwagoning' and which is the antithesis of a balancing policy.

THE WAR OF THE LEAGUE OF AUGSBURG AND THE RISE OF BRITAIN

Between 1683 and 1689 a fundamental readjustment occurred in the European power situation. The previous 20 years had witnessed an imbalance in favour of France. The Habsburg monarchies were prostrate between 1660 and 1683. Spain continued its remorseless decline, while Austria had been weakened by the dreadful Thirty Years War (1618–48), which at the Peace of Westphalia had ended in a reduction in her prestige and influence in Germany. Austria was also under pressure from the Ottoman Empire and was thus in no condition to provide an effective counterweight to French power. By 14 July 1683 Austrian fortunes had reached their nadir. The Turkish army was laying siege to Vienna and the Emperor had fled north to Passau.

From this point on, however, Austria began its vital recovery. On 12 September 1683 the Turkish Army was routed at the battle of Kahlenberg by imperial forces under John Sobieski, King of Poland. An Austrian counter-offensive followed, in which the imperial forces drove the Turks from Austria and recaptured much of Hungary, where the Habsburgs were proclaimed as hereditary monarchs. Transylvania, Croatia and Slavonia soon followed as Austrian accessions. Though the war continued until 1699 these Austrian gains meant that the Habsburgs were secure against the Turks. The Turkish threat to Christian Europe was finally on the ebb. The Austrian victories vastly enhanced the prestige of the Emperor and revitalised Austrian morale. In addition, they gave the Habsburgs a markedly increased territorial base, greatly outweighing the losses of 1648, so that by the 1690s the Habsburg Emperor was in a position to perform the role of counterbalance to the power of the King of France.

In the same period equally significant developments were taking place on the western margins of Europe. The 'Glorious Revolution' of 1688 which placed William of Orange on the throne of England was decisive in bringing Britain into the European balance. The 'revolution' was precipitated by the combined follies of James II and Louis XIV. While James II was busily engaged in losing popularity in England, Louis XIV made three major blunders, two of them mistakenly influenced by his policy of divide and rule in the minor balance, the third an ill-timed return to the religious intolerance of a previous generation.

The latter, the revocation of the Edict of Nantes in 1685, had many important effects on the European equilibrium. France lost the skills of her Protestant population and the exodus strengthened those states to which the Huguenots fled, especially England, Prussia and the Dutch Republic. Moreover, as well as thoroughly alarming the English Protestants, the arrival of large numbers of Huguenots greatly stimulated the development of an informed opinion on European matters in England.

Even more injurious to the cause of France were the actions of Louis XIV in 1688. By invading the Palatinate that year, France enabled William of Orange to sail for England secure in the knowledge that the French armies were fully occupied far from the Dutch borders. Moreover, France could have used its fleet to contest William's passage to England, but chose not to do so in the mistaken belief that William's landing would produce a long civil war in England, embroiling the Dutch leader and leaving France free to pursue her European ambitions. In the event, William of Orange's accession to the English throne was to all intents uncontested, and was to be decisive in the re-establishment of a European equilibrium and the acceptance of balance of power ideas in England.

William III's accession brought to the English throne a king whose knowledge and experience of continental politics was greater than that enjoyed by any English king for centuries. Whereas the later Stuart kings had pursued dynastic foreign policies in which the interests of the nation were subservient to the interests of the Royal House, the very presence of William of Orange in England in 1688 was due to the fact that he wanted England to assume her

European responsibilities. William crossed the North Sea in order to bring England into the balance against France rather than to educate her in the finer points of balance theory but, thanks to him, Britain rapidly developed into a state capable of self-consciously pursuing a balance of power foreign policy throughout the following century. Like Bethel and Halifax, William III asserted that his opposition to France was inevitable only because France was the preponderant power. Had a similar threat been posed to Europe by Austria, he insisted, he would have opposed the Habsburgs equally energetically. He had said as much to Sir William Temple in 1675, remarking that in the event of Habsburg aggrandisement he would be 'as much a Frenchman as he was now a Spaniard' (Gibbs, 1969: 6).

As the Imperial Army advanced on Belgrade in the summer of 1688, Louis XIV could not fail to see that the conditions for a bipolar balance of power in Europe were beginning to reassert themselves. He therefore gambled on a swift offensive that would enable France to make major gains in Western Europe, before the Habsburg Emperor could bring the full weight of his growing power to bear in the West. At the same time, a French offensive would bring some relief to their Turkish allies. The French armies enjoyed initial success, the Imperial Armies being preoccupied with the Turkish war and William of Orange being distracted by the need to fight a campaign against James II in Ireland. In 1689, however, the first of the great coalitions had been constructed to 'contain' French power.

The 'Grand Alliance' was composed of the Dutch Republic, Spain, Saxony, Bavaria, Swabia, Savoy, Britain and the Austrian Habsburg Empire. The coalition was not constructed without difficulty. Based upon the League of Augsburg, many of its members were uneasy allies. Only the tenacity and diplomatic genius of William of Orange held the alliance together.

Despite the tensions within it, the coalition possessed considerable strengths. It had powerful armies, naval superiority and above all, sound financial resources. By 1693, with the French armies making little, if any, progress in Flanders or the Rhineland and the allied blockade beginning to bite, cautious peace talks were opened, which continued through the winter of 1693–4. The talks did not remain secret and prompted wide debate within the allied nations. One English pamphlet writer opposed the terms offered by the French because they would not produce a Franco-Austrian equilibrium, which Britain must support in order that she might play the role of balancer, a position Britain could exploit 'to maintain the Empire of the Sea, which we have regained the possession of in so glorious a manner, but even to enable us to decide the success of Wars and the Conditions for the future' (Anon, 1694).

There is a clear recognition in this pamphlet (which may have been written by Daniel Defoe) that Britain was not in a position to play a significant role in determining the outcome of European politics except in conditions of equilibrium and that it was therefore of paramount importance that she should strive always to maintain a balance of power on the continent. It is worth noting that the writer saw the continental balance as being needed to allow Britain to maintain her position of naval superiority. The idea of a balance of naval power, though it was being discussed in Britain at this time, for example, in Molesworth's *Account of Denmark*, published in London in 1694, never became a popular conception, for obvious reasons. Britain strongly espoused the cause of a balance of power on land, but as the dominant naval power, had no incentive to support a concept that might threaten her naval advantage. On land, however, the situation was different. England was militarily weak and lacked the resources to balance a power bidding for continental hegemony, except in alliance with other powers.

In 1697 the peace negotiations were concluded with the treaties of Ryswick and Turin. These represented a severe check on French ambitions. The Dutch gained a barrier of fortresses in Flanders and France made considerable concessions on the Rhine–Moselle frontier. The two treaties indicated that a new system had arisen in Europe in which balance considerations would play a major role. Almost immediately, however, the European equilibrium was threatened by the question of the Spanish succession. The Spanish succession issue had a decisive influence on the development of both the theory and practice of the balance of power in Europe.

In 1698 the last Habsburg King of Spain was old, terminally ill and childless. It was Louis XIV who took the initiative and suggested to William III that they jointly devise a partition of the Spanish inheritance which would avert a war. The first attempt came to nothing when the intended beneficiary of the scheme, the electoral Prince of Bavaria, suddenly died. A year later in 1699 a second partition treaty was devised. By this the French Dauphin would receive Lorraine, Naples and Sicily, while Spain and the remainder of its global empire would go to Archduke Charles of Austria.

Although France would have made significant gains under the terms of the second partition treaty, the main acquisitions went to the Austrian Habsburgs and the purpose of William III had been to strengthen Austria as a counterweight to French power. In the event, however, the Austrian Emperor rejected the Partition Treaty as not giving him enough. When the childless Charles II of Spain died in 1700 he was found to have left a will giving Spain and all her possessions to Philip of Anjou, grandson of Louis XIV. The French king was placed in a tremendous dilemma, and seeing little hope of the other major powers actively supporting the terms of the second Partition Treaty, he decided to accept the terms of Charles II's will. When England formally declared war on France as a result of this action, in May 1702, the British document declared that the purpose of the alliance against France was to 'preserve the liberty and the balance of Europe and to curtail the exorbitant power of France'.

CONCLUSION

Although balancing strategies can occasionally be identified in the historical record, it was only at the end of the Renaissance period in Europe that true balance of power thinking began to emerge. The crucial feature of such thinking being the willingness to ally with the weaker states in the system in order to defeat an actual or potential hegemonic aspirant. The sophistication of balance of power thinking developed significantly between the mid-fifteenth and mid-seventeenth centuries, but only flowered into the modern concept of the balance of power at the end of the seventeenth century. Before this development could take place it was necessary for Europe to undergo the ordeal of the religious wars, which produced a recognisable state system and ended the era of foreign policy driven by religious ideology. In addition, a crucial factor was the scientific revolution and the concomitant resolution of the intellectual crisis of authority which had plagued the European mind for two centuries. With the emergence of new powers and a greater flexibility in alliance formation, the stage was set for the classic era of balance of power politics, the eighteenth century.

3 Balance of power policies

INTRODUCTION

In discussions of the balance of power one can distinguish between a prescriptive and a descriptive element: the balance of power as a policy and the balance of power as a system. As policy it endorses the creation and preservation of equilibrium, the confrontation of power with countervailing power to prevent a single power laying down the law to all others. As system it implies interdependence: 'a collection of states, autonomous units of power and policy, involved in such intimacy of interrelationship as to make reciprocal impact feasible' (Claude, 1962: 42). The first meaning may be seen as the logic of a balance of power response to a 'Hobbesian' international relations, while the latter reflects the 'Grotian' version of the concept. This chapter looks at the balance in the first sense, as policy, while Chapter 4 will examine the question of the balance of power as a system.

Students of the balance of power have long noted its attractiveness as a guide for foreign policy-makers. Ernst Haas felt that historically it had been seen as an extremely useful principle which explained the nature of the state system and the rules that states should follow to ensure their survival.

> Its merits lay in its objectivity, its detachment from ideology, its universality, and its independence from short-term considerations. It stressed the essentials, timeless and inescapable, in international affairs: power and power relationships.
>
> (Haas, 1953a: 370)

States are not normally intrinsic supporters of balance *per se*; that is to say that a state's government does not pursue policies with the object of seeing its own room for manoeuvre constrained. On the contrary, for statesmen the balance is like good advice, something valuable for others, but not for oneself! The best balance is one which leaves one's own state free while constraining all the others. This, however, is extremely difficult to achieve, and is closest approached in the role of the 'balancer' state. The complexity of balance of power policies from the point of view of individual governments is that states are pursuing incompatible goals – seeking to engage actively to prevent imbalance emerging, yet at the same time attempting to minimise the scale of their own commitment and burdens; seeking to support a system that constrains all, while hoping to maximise their own freedom of action. Not surprisingly, policies composed of such elements will not function smoothly or predictably.

Organski identified six methods by which states might attempt to maintain the balance of power, these being to arm, to seize territory, establish buffer zones, form alliances, intervene in the internal affairs of other nations, or divide and conquer (1968: 267). None of these techniques is peculiar to balance of power politics, they are simply foreign policy techniques and can just as easily be used by a major state to attempt to create an empire, or by a small state simply to increase its own power. However, they are all techniques that have been used historically in an attempt to maintain a perceived balance of power.

The various techniques can be divided into two basic categories: those that attempt to build up one's own power and those that attempt to weaken or diminish the adversary. The more commonly used techniques are looked at below.

ALLIANCES

As Gulick (1955: 58–60) noted, the most logical way to promote a balance of power among states would be to ensure that all of them had the same power. A preference for such an arrangement has underlain a number of proposed balance of power schemes, such as those of Sully in the early seventeenth century and Bellers in the early eighteenth. For Martin Wight, such a preference reflected a Grotian approach and has normative connotations (1991: 165). In reality, such a scheme faces overwhelming obstacles. Even to ensure that the *major* states in the system are approximately equal in power is extremely difficult and the most thoroughgoing attempt at doing this, the Vienna Congress of 1814–15 fell far short of the ideal, leaving Russia and Austria far larger than Prussia, even when the latter had gained enormous territories in an attempt to create a check on both Russia and France.

Since equality of states cannot be attained, the next best option is to use fluid alliances to create an effective equality of power between the states making up the system. The territorial and military inequality of states can be corrected through a system of alliances.

Alliances provide states acting within a balance of power system with a capacity for flexibility and rapid reaction to threats which they cannot find simply by looking to their own resources. States can increase their power by internal reform, but it is difficult to produce major increases of power at very short notice by this method. The fastest way to achieve this end is by adding to one's own strengths the strength of allies or relatively, by decreasing the strengths of an adversary by luring away its allies (Organski and Kugler 1980: 16).

It has been argued in this regard that what distinguishes the late twentieth-century from the eighteenth- and nineteenth-century international systems is not the pursuit of deterrence through balanced power, but rather the means chosen for achieving this end. In the eighteenth and nineteenth centuries the preferred method was not matching a rival's power by increasing one's own military capability, but rather by matching power through forming a coalition of all the states that saw themselves as being threatened by an aggressor's growing power. The historical systems were not characterised by an increase in the power of a single state or even the system as a whole. Instead, power was rearranged to counter aggression (Ziegler, 1977: 172). In the bipolar 'balance of terror', by contrast, strategic nuclear power was directly balanced with reference to a single nuclear adversary.

States join alliances to protect themselves from states or coalitions whose superior resources could pose a threat. To ally *with* the dominant power means placing one's trust in its continued benevolence. The safer strategy is to join with those who cannot readily dominate their allies in order to avoid being dominated by those who can. Thus, Henry Kissinger advocated *rapprochement* with China rather than the Soviet Union because he believed that, in a triangular relationship, it was better to align with the weaker side (Kissinger, 1979: 178).

States do not simply ally against power *per se*. There has to be an accompanying perception of threat. For the states of Western Europe, American power was not seen as threatening after 1945, whereas Soviet power was. In addition, states will understandably react more rapidly and energetically to threats from nearby states.

As Walt (1985: 10) points out, 'because the ability to project power declines with distance, states that are nearby pose a greater threat than those that are far away'. In short, the more aggressive or expansionist a state appears, the more likely it is to trigger an opposing coalition.

In a balance of power system alliances should be flexible and temporary. States should be prepared to desert old allies and seek new ones whenever such a realignment would serve to benefit the balance of power. Midlarsky (1983: 762–84) has described this behaviour as 'the absence of alliance memory', making all other states potential allies or enemies, regardless of past friendships or hostility, and allowing for random changes in alliance partners. Because of this need to avoid permanent commitments, *ad hoc* alliances best suit a balance of power system. The more states there are in the system, the easier it will be to make the adjustments necessary to maintain the balance, because the number of potential allies will be greater. Thus, Organski (1968) argues that the large number of major powers that formed the eighteenth-century state system allowed a very high number of possible alliance combinations and this was one of the key reasons why the balance of power system worked so effectively during that period.

Not all potential allies would have much to offer in terms of diplomatic, economic or military strength. Nations seek allies who can counterbalance the power of rival states and their allies, and they therefore try to find allies that can supplement their own capabilities. The principle involved is simply the balancing of power with power; a state seeks allies to cope with a danger that it cannot overcome unaided.

Thus, in a balance of power system alliances will tend to form as states seek to augment their own power with the power of allied states, in reaction to a perceived threat. A number of writers have argued that the size of the alliances thus produced is predictable. William Riker, for example, has argued that states will create alliances 'just as large as they believe will ensure winning and no larger' (1962: 32). This assertion clearly contradicts the historical record, but Riker explains this by pointing to what he calls 'the information effect' (ibid.: 77). The uncertainty of the real world and the absence of perfect information about the capabilities and intentions of one's likely opponents mean that alliance building tends to aim at 'a subjectively estimated minimum coalition rather than at an actual minimum' (ibid.). This latter formulation accords more closely with the opinion of other writers on the subject who have argued that larger than minimum winning alliances will occur, for example, Russett (1968: 291).

Thus, in a balance of power system one would expect alliances to occur, and these alliances to be fairly large. Friedman in fact argues that *status-quo* alliances (and an alliance devoted to the maintenance of the existing balance of power must be deemed a *status-quo* alliance) will be larger than the minimum winning alliance. This is because the 'gain', that is, the maintenance of the *status quo*, satisfies all the members of the alliance (Friedman, Bladen and Rosen, 1970: 261). In this respect it is worth noting Strausz-Hupé's comment that alliances which are meant to deter will only be successful if they can assemble overwhelming force (Strausz-Hupé and Possony, 1950: 231-2). However, a number of balance theorists, such as Jervis (1976: 110), have argued that the larger an alliance becomes, the more difficult it becomes for it to perform its function effectively, because the states involved have to devote more time to managing the controversies within the alliance and therefore have correspondingly less time and energy to devote to addressing the external threats for which the alliance was created in the first place.

In periods marked by ideological rigidity but strategic stability, states may follow their ideological preference when it comes to joining alliances. When faced by great danger, however, ideological compatibility is far less important; one takes whatever allies one can get, as the alliance between the Western democracies and the Soviet Union during the Second World War demonstrates. Balance of power alliances are by their very nature temporary arrangements. Once their objective has been achieved the cement that held them together – fear of the imperialistic power – dissolves and the alliance fragments. Thus, the alliance or coalition does not itself go on to become a threat to the other states in the system. This pattern of behaviour can be seen following the end of the great coalition wars in 1715, 1815, 1918 and 1945.

Balance of power doctrine puts a tremendous emphasis on diplomatic manoeuvrability. Niou *et al.* (1989: 96) make the important point that it is not always formally existing alliances that help to maintain the balance of power. Sometimes the threat of potential alliance has the same effect. For example, the real balancing dynamic in Europe from the early 1870s onward was between the potential threat of a Russo-French alliance (which did not actually materialise until 1892–4) and the potential counterthreat of an Austro-Italo-German alliance (which was not actually consummated until 1892).

Even the 'balancer' concept involves a direct consideration of alliances. The most commonly cited example of the balancer is Britain, yet during the eighteenth century Britain did not see herself as acting alone in this role, but rather as the core of a group of states sufficiently powerful to tip the balance. British policy was therefore not to intervene alone as the 'balancer state' but rather to act as the core of a balancer alliance of medium powers, adding this alliance to the weaker of the two central powers to form what they invariably called a 'Grand Alliance' for the maintenance of the balance of power.

Britain seems always to have tried to assemble the largest alliance her diplomatic skill and financial resources could produce. There was no attempt to limit the alliance to 'minimum winning' size, even allowing for overestimation of what that might require. It has been said that multilateral alliances somehow seem less aggressive than bilateral alliances, and there may have been an element of this kind of thinking in the British approach. The frantic alliance-building to which Britain was prone was denounced by William Pitt in 1755 as 'a wild comprehensive system'.

This preference for large alliances may have been partly inspired by the British view of the European system as being fundamentally bipolar. As well as being seen as the dominant 'poles' of the European system, France and Austria were seen as being approximately equal in power. However, despite this condition of near equilibrium, Britain felt that her own power was insufficient to tip the balance one way or the other. Hoadly declared in 1727 that the alliance between Britain and the Dutch Republic constituted 'the Turn of the Balance of Europe, whenever they join themselves to any other great Power of Europe; and Both of them together, but barely sufficient for this Purpose' (1727: 78). Without the aid of the Dutch, it was believed, Britain should never take the risk of entering a continental war. In a bipolar system, it has been suggested, alliance leaders will try to gain as many allies as possible, even if many of them can contribute little to the military strength of the alliance. In practice, Britain was attempting to create a coalition rather than a simple alliance.

The difference between an alliance and a coalition is essentially one of size. Gulick, for example, defines an alliance as 'a bilateral or trilateral agreement for offensive or defensive purposes', and a coalition as 'a similar agreement signed by four or more powers or a conjunction of several alliances directed toward the same thing' (1955: 78).

The other major difference between alliances and coalitions, which arises from the consideration of size, is a qualitative difference in membership. Alliances are based around states with a certain number of common interests. Coalitions tend to be based on a single common interest, but one of sufficient importance to override their differences on other issues. An alliance is a grouping of two or three powers, whereas a coalition involves four or more. Coalitions may in practice be formed by the coming together of several alliances whose traditional suspicion of one another is overcome by the overriding threat to the system. For this reason coalitions have appeared 'only in the great war crises of the balance of power, at times when the very existence of the state system seemed shaken and in danger' (Gulick, 1955: 77). The formation of a coalition therefore involved the breaking of traditional alignments and could only be expected in exceptional circumstances. Gulick restricts his definition of coalition to the alignments against Charles V, Louis XIV, Napoleon I, the Central Powers in 1914–18, and the Axis Powers in 1939–45.

Liska (1977: 5) argues that the regulatory function of alliances within a balance of power system is crucial, because balance of power is an approach which is full of anomalies, many of which can be overcome through the workings of the alliance system. In particular, alliances act as the critical link, in both the theory and the practice of the balance, between the actions and policies of individual states and the overall results for the system.

Alliances are deemed to foster parity in so far as they help to adjust the gains made by states within the system and help modulate constraints, which limits the rise or decline of the power of participating states.

THE RESORT TO WAR

With regard to the relationship between the balance of power and war there is a division in the literature, but in this case there exists a clear majority in one school of thought. According to Blainey,

> its clearest theorists and practitioners, the Metternichs and Castlereaghs – 'all thought of war as an instrument to preserve or restore a balance of power'. In essence a balance of power was simply a formula designed to prevent the rise of a nation to world dominance. It merely masqueraded as a formula for peace.
>
> (Blainey, 1973: 111–12)

In a general sense, Blainey's criticism is unfair, since proponents of the balance of power have not as a rule made the preservation of peace its primary objective. There are those who have argued that balance of power systems can produce peace, such as Organski and Kugler (1980: 14), who suggest that 'when power is more or less equally distributed among great powers or members of major alliances peace will ensue', though even they assert that power distributions do not generally determine the likelihood of war (ibid.: 49). However, from earliest times, observers of international relations have argued that there is in fact a very strong link between power *distribution* and the outbreak of war. Thucydides, writing in the fifth century BC argued that 'what made war inevitable was the growth of Athenian power and the fear which this caused in Sparta' (1954: 49).

The detailed study of the late nineteenth-century balance of power system by Rosecrance *et al.* (1974) was inconclusive in this regard. They pointed out that it ought to be possible to determine whether a balance of power made war more or less likely. However, their investigation revealed no clear relationship in this regard.

The 'power alignment' column indicates the relative power of each element within the balance of power system (state or group of states). The c/c column indicates the degree of conflict (less than 50) or cooperation (more than 50) present in the system in any one year. However, no clear pattern emerges. In the five years in which there was a marked four-against-one imbalance, the degree of cooperation varies tremendously.

The consecutive years 1873 and 1874 highlight the lack of pattern. 1873 was marked by a significant power imbalance, yet conflict levels were low while cooperation levels were high. The following year was also characterised by a dramatic power imbalance, yet in 1874 levels of cooperation were very low.

The lack of identifiable pattern in this case study is important because structural realist theory argues that there is a direct link between systemic stability (defined as the absence of system-wide wars) and the number of states in the system. Yet there does not appear to be a direct correlation between balance and conflict, though Waltz has argued that a bipolar balance is the most stable of all.

The threat of force and its actual use are the two major instruments of balance of power diplomacy. In the periods leading up to the great coalition wars of 1914–18 and 1939–45, balancing policies were pursued through threats of force rather than with force itself.

Table 1 Balance of power patterns and level of cooperation/conflict in the major power sub-system

Year	International alignment	Power alignment	c/c major power sub-system
1870	Germany/France Austria Britain/ Russia	3/10/2	48.406
1871	AFGRB	15	56.805
1872	AFGRB	15	57.118
1873	F/GARB	4/11	57.858
1874	FARB/G	12/3	48.795
1875	FARB/G	12/3	55.186
1876	AFGRB	15	51.654
1877	FAR/B/G	8/4/3	54.334
1878	AGBF/R	13/2	53.814
1979	AGBF/R	13/2	52.464
1880	AFGRB	15	57.381
1881	B/AGR/F	4/8/3	55.394

Source: Rosecrance *et al.* (1974: 22)

War was an instrument to be used sparingly, but statesmen could not escape the fact that the balance of power would not simply look after itself. They knew that in the final analysis they had to be willing to take their countries into war against the state expanding in pursuit of a hegemony.

War was a necessary corollary of balance of power policy. In the classical period of the balance of power, war was of a limited rather than a total nature and moderation in the objectives in pursuing a war was crucial. For the balance of power system to work effectively it needed to be composed of a number of comparable powers, so that diplomatic flexibility in alliance formation was possible. It was essential, therefore, that defeated states should not be eliminated, but should be permitted to take part in the revived balance as quickly as possible, as was France after 1815, for example. The final third of the eighteenth century, which saw plans to defeat and dismember Prussia, and the actual partition of Poland, was an aberration in this respect.

Proponents of the balance of power have not generally included prevention of war as being an objective of balance of power policy. The object was rather to prevent the domination of the system by one state or alliance, using war to achieve that end if necessary. War was not glorified, it was simply the bitter price that often had to be paid for maintenance of the independence of the states within the system.

But for those for whom war represented a pathological condition, a disaster to be avoided whenever possible, the balance of power system produced far too many occasions when the bitter price was necessary. Critics of balance policy, such as the conservative Edmund Burke in the eighteenth century, argued that the system not only allowed wars, but generated 'innumerable and fruitless wars. That political torture by which powers are to be enlarged or abridged, according to a standard ... ever has been ... a cause of infinite contention and bloodshed' (Luard, 1992: 16).

Liska argues, controversially, that the maintenance of the balance of power justifies preventative war (1957: 34). Such warfare is seen as being legitimate if it is associated with the limited objective of 'containing' an expansionist adversary. According to Liska, intervention is justified if the adversary is attempting to increase its power through external expansion, but is not legitimate if its power is growing as a result of internal reforms. But this comes very close to recognising a general right of the community to intervene in the internal affairs of other states. Moreover, it begs the question of why peaceful internal reforms should not also trigger such intervention, if they create a latent capability to bid for hegemony.

Some authors, such as Spanier (1972: 10), have argued that the balance of power has had as one of its purposes the deterrence of war. Similarly, Van Dyke (1966: 221) and Organski (1968: 280) argued that one of the benefits to be derived from a balance of power system was the preservation of peace. However, the majority of authors of whom Gulick (1955: 89), Liska (1957: 38) and Wight (1979: 184) are representative, have argued that its function was not to preserve peace, but to preserve the system and, within it, the autonomy of the major states. Thus, for example, Wight argues that

> It is easy to point to occasions on which the final move in recti-
> fication of the balance has been war. It is not remembered how
> often the balance of power has averted war. For the balance of
> power is not the 'cause' of war; the cause of war, however one
> chooses to identify it, lies in the political conditions which the
> balance of power in some degree reduces to order.
>
> (Wight, 1979: 184)

Not all observers would share Wight's sanguine view. In the after-math of the Holocaust of the First World War, many blamed the rigidity of the alliance systems and the European balance of power for the outbreak of war in 1914. This interpretation has received some support from more recent writers on the balance of power. For example Midlarsky (1989: 6–7) argues that when a bipolar balance between two large coalitions dominates the balance for an extended period of time, as was the case with the confrontation between the Triple Alliance and Triple *Entente* before 1914, then the balance of power is equivalent to exact polarisation. All the major powers are actively linked to one or other alliance. Thus, while international relations scholars would be unlikely to subscribe to the view that the balance of power 'of itself' is a progenitor of systemic war, a 'tight' bipolar condition runs a high risk of breaking into all-out conflict and, as in the decade before 1914, the two conditions may on occasion be effectively identical.

THE SEPARATE PEACE AS A TACTIC

One of the features of Britain's 'balancer' foreign policy in the eighteenth century was her habit of reneging on treaty obligations. The most interesting aspect of this behaviour, however, was her habit of concluding a separate peace at the end of a war. The British participation in the War of the Spanish Succession, the War of the Austrian Succession, and the Seven Years War, all ended with Britain abandoning her major ally. This raises the question: to what extent can this habit be considered a natural balance of power tactic?

Antipathy to permanent alliances is a clear balance of power tenet. *Ad hoc* alliances should be preferred, and strong powers opposed in turn. Nicholas Spykman wrote of Britain that once a war has been successfully fought and the enemy defeated, 'Britain is apt to shift her diplomatic and economic support. The former ally is deserted because he is now on the strong side; the former enemy supported because he is now weak' (Spykman, 1942a: 25). During the eighteenth century, however, Britain generally moved to abandon her allies even before the war had ended.

This tendency can be explained in other ways than as a balancing tactic. George Liska, for example, has suggested with regard to the eighteenth century that different though complementary conflicts may result in the formation of rival alliances and account for their composition, without clearly identifying either alliance as offensive or defensive in nature. Liska gives as his example the conflicts between 1740 and 1763 over the German and overseas balances. Liska's argument is basically that such a situation means that any one ally is unlikely 'to support any other ally to the point of achieving total victory in the contest that concerns him in particular' (1977: 7). This is because to do so would probably terminate the alliance, since one ally would have achieved its aims.

Thus, just as Riker argued that a minimum winning alliance is probable, so Liska declares that a 'minimal victory' alliance will be produced. A minimal victory alliance is described as a winning alliance 'just sufficient to satisfy the irreducible objectives of members' (Liska, 1977: 7) and to deny even those to some allies if the final settlement has been precipitated by a separate peace.

As has already been noted, the British alliance-building technique does not fit the 'minimum winning' model. However, the British practice of concluding a separate peace does fit the 'minimal victory' model. Although Britain did tend to make peace early, without achieving all her allies' aims, she did so only when the threat to the balance of power seemed to have been averted. The preservation of the balance of power thereby satisfied the *minimum* aims of all the allies. Since in 1711 and 1748 Britain made peace when the threat had been eliminated, and indeed in 1711 partly because Austria herself was beginning to pose a threat to the balance, the British were pulling out of the war with the main war aim of the allies satisfied. This had the incidental effect of satisfying the third rule in Morton Kaplan's framework, that is, 'to stop fighting rather than eliminate an essential national actor' (1957: 23).

In the War of the Austrian Succession, Britain deserted her Austrian ally early in 1748. The preliminaries of peace were signed by Britain, the Dutch Republic and France in April of that year. Abandoned by her allies, Austria was eventually forced to agree to the Anglo-French peace terms, even though they included none of her major objectives. In 1762 Britain withdrew from the Seven Years War by signing a separate peace with France, leaving Prussia to struggle on alone.

The clear strains within the wartime alliance of 1941–5 between Britain, the United States and the Soviet Union were in large part caused by Stalin's fears that his Western allies might be tempted to conclude a separate peace with Germany. It was these fears that prompted his constant appeals for the Anglo-Americans to open the 'second front' in the West, and the insistence upon 'unconditional surrender' by Germany, leaving no scope for a bargained war termination with the Western allies. Intra-alliance strains towards the end of a successful war are by no means rare in history. Even before a war is over, the shape of the post-war world comes to dominate diplomatic manoeuvring, rather than simply the successful conclusion of the war.

The tendency of allies to withdraw from coalitions or wars once the minimal anti-hegemonic aim has been achieved certainly has the effect, whether consciously sought or not, of reducing the danger that one or more of the victorious wartime allies will themselves rapidly emerge as a threat to the balance.

THE BALANCER

The question of the importance of the 'balancer' in balance of power systems has generated strong opinions from both critics and proponents. According to Organski (1968: 288), 'There is no such thing as a "balancer" and there never has been'. Padelford and Lincoln (1967: 300), by contrast, argue that, 'in theory and practice any balance of power system, whether limited or global, requires "balancers"'.

The balancer policy is one to which any state can aspire, though few can fulfil its requirements. It is curious that the balancer role has not received more attention, for it exercises a strong attraction for statesmen, indeed, in many ways it is the most desirable role for a great power to play. The reasons why this is so will be looked at in more detail below, but at this point it is worth noting that the balancer acts outside of the central balance, and because its power is not effectively balanced anywhere else in the system, it possesses a margin of disposable power.

The basic function of the balancer is to prevent the occurrence of a permanent disequilibrium in the international system, that is, the existence of a situation in which one state or alliance is able to exercise a hegemony over the others, or even to establish an *imperium*. All variations of the balance of power system have this basic function, that is, the preservation of a system based upon numerous sovereign states. In many ways the balancer role is the clearest example of a state pursuing a conscious balance of power policy. Whereas methods such as alliance formation involve groups of states acting together and overlap to some extent with the idea of balance of power as a *system*, with all the states involved in some way in the balancing process, the balancer role is simply one state perceiving that its own individual policy is crucial to the maintenance of a balance.

The operation of a balancer assumes the existence of an international system structured in such a way that the alignment of the balancer with one state or alliance in the system will be sufficient to redress any developing imbalance of power. The balancer maintains the balance through its diplomatic flexibility, shifting its support from one side to another, supporting the weaker against the stronger, if necessary even up to the use of military force. It is implicit in this function that the balancer acts within a system often characterised in terms of 'a pair of scales', that is, one dominated by two approximately equal states or alliances. In a genuinely multipolar system there is no need for a specific balancer, since the kaleidoscopic readjustments of the many actors in a system of equal and genuinely unaligned states would obviate the need for a balancer. For a balancer to play a determining role, either the system must be bipolar or it should be multipolar, but with a tendency towards bipolarity in times of crisis. Thus, for example, in the 1730s the European system was multipolar, but as the crises of 1739–40 and 1756 unfolded, the states took sides in such a way that two blocs emerged which dominated events. The Duke of Newcastle in 1733 declared that 'there are two great contending powers in Europe', to which the Earl of Stafford added that he hoped that there would always be such a rivalry, for it could only end 'by one of them being swallowed up by the other', which would be an 'unlucky' thing for Britain and Europe (Cobbett, Vol. 8: 1240). A similar bipolarisation is evident in the decade before the First World War. If the two major blocs are fairly evenly matched, then the previously uncommitted power of the balancer is likely to prove decisive in determining the outcome of any conflict.

If the function of the balancer is straightforward enough, the question of its importance to balance of power systems is not. There is a clear division in the literature between a number of writers who believe that a balance of power system cannot operate efficiently without the existence of a balancer, and a number who argue that a balancer is not only unnecessary, but also that its very existence would subvert a genuine balance of power system.

For the first group of writers, the balancer is the key to the successful operation of the system, indeed, they argue that without the balancer the whole idea of a balance of power is rendered unrealistic. This is because it is only the existence of the balancer, a state devoted to the maintenance of the general equilibrium, that can ensure an actual or potential preponderance to the side prepared to maintain the *status quo*. In Lerche's words, a balance can be sustained 'only when a major state or bloc of states makes the preservation of the balance the major component of its policy' (1956: 129).

Critics of the balancer role are equally emphatic. Henry Craik declared that a balance of power 'ceases to be true as soon as its adjustment is entrusted to anyone. It must either be maintained by its own equilibrium, or it becomes a pretence, sustained only by the application of arbitrary force' (Pollard, 1923: 59). This view is supported by Kenneth Waltz, who argues that the balancer concept derives from a distortion of balance of power theory, the distortion being the idea that 'if a balance is to be formed somebody must want it and must work for it' (Waltz, 1959b: 38). Both Craik and Waltz advocate a conception of the balance of power in which the system operates mechanistically, somewhat in the way an economy is supposed to be operated by market forces under *laissez-faire* economics. The distinguishing element in this 'automatic' conception of the balance of power is, according to Inis Claude, the assumption that 'equilibrium may be produced or preserved without actually being willed by any state' (1962: 46). Kenneth Waltz goes further and criticises those writers who advocate policies designed to preserve the balance, on the grounds that it has proved to be 'an unfortunately short step from the belief that a high regard for preserving a balance is at the heart of wise statesmanship to the assumption that states must pursue balancing policies if a balance of power is to be maintained' (Waltz, 1959b: 38).

Clearly the 'automatic' balance conception leaves no place for a balancer. However, Claude (1962) offers two other conceptions. A 'manually operated' balance is one willed by the leading statesmen, who conduct their states' foreign policies with this end in view. In this version the balance is not produced by the automatic processes of the system or by the efforts of the balancer alone, but by skilled multilateral diplomacy. The other alternative is the 'semi-automatic' system, in which the balance of power is assumed to be largely self-sustaining, but should a major danger threaten the balance, the additional power of the balancer is available to retrieve the situation.

The balancer is a state whose power is not normally committed to any of the alliances of approximately equal strength which constitute the central balance. However, in a situation where two alliances are balanced and one state is non-aligned, one is looking not at a balanced system but at an unbalanced one, since nowhere within the system is the power of the balancer balanced itself. Thus, if power balanced is power neutralised, then the non-aligned state is in an exceedingly powerful position. The advantage of the balancer is that its power is applicable in a way that the power of the states enmeshed in the central balance is not. Because its intervention produces a preponderance, albeit one 'devoted to the protection of legitimate rights', then in Organski's words, the 'intervention by the balancer brings about the very thing that it is said to be designed to prevent' (Organski, 1968: 287).

Organski is supported by Sterling, who argues that to become the balancer is to come 'as close to achieving actual domination as a diverse, multipolar system permits'. The balancer role is particularly expedient since, in comparison to an outright bid for empire, 'it involves a minimum expenditure of resources, a minimum of opposition and hence a minimum of danger' (Sterling, 1972: 57). Yet, as Daniel Defoe noted, 'every power which overbalances the rest makes itself a nuisance to its neighbours'. Why should the balancer be different? For Organski this is a fatal flaw in balance of power theory. He does not accept that a preponderance in the balancer's hands represents a stabilising factor where in any other state's hands it would be a threat.

In terms of strict logic, Organski is clearly right. A preponderance is not a balance. Yet, equally clearly, at certain periods particular states have successfully played the balancer role, thereby imbuing the concept with a certain credibility. This needs to be explained.

In the case of the British claim to the role, there were a number of domestic factors which traditionally constrained Britain's influence on the European continent. Distrust of large standing armies, suspicion of continental involvement and a preference for naval power, unsuited to continental conquest, all acted to restrain Britain. To have a credible claim to the balancer role a state ought to possess an array of cultural and political values which have the effect of restraining her desire to gain political or territorial preponderances *in the area for which she aspires to perform the balancer role*. They need not be the same factors which restrained Britain, but they must have the same practical effect.

A second restraining factor is the nature of the balancer's power. The fundamental object of the balance of power, as von Gentz noted, was to ensure that no single European state 'must ever become so powerful as to be able to coerce all the rest put together' (von Gentz, 1806: 55). The important element here is the emphasis on singularity. The balancer does not of itself constitute a preponderance because its influence derives from its marginal disposable power *vis-à-vis* the states of the central balance, that is, its ability to add a winning margin to one side. Only if allied to another state or alliance within the system can it exert a decisive influence. Since it does constitute the winning margin it has tremendous bargaining power in obtaining concessions from the side which it supports. On the other hand, there are also obvious limits. It is always clear *which* side the balancer will defend, that is, the *status-quo* side or, if the situation is not a threat to the entire system, the weaker side. It is never going to be in the balancer's interest to support the strongest or revisionist side, since that would lead to the overthrow of the system and the loss of the balancer position. Moreover, in a situation where the balancer provides a margin to a larger alliance, the other allies are unlikely to accede to any balancer proposals which give a genuine political preponderance to the balancer, since to do so would be to simply exchange one danger for another. The balancer's power, therefore, while inflated by its diplomatic position, is still well short of hegemonial, and the balancer cannot add its weight to the revisionist forces without overthrowing the system.

It is generally accepted that the balancer must be a major power. Morton Kaplan is exceptional in this regard, arguing that 'any national actor' is qualified to fill the role (1969: 42). This is doubtful. It seems clear that a balancer must be a major power if its intervention is going to be decisive. Thus, commenting upon Italy's attempts to act as European balancer in the decade before the First World War, Hans Morgenthau noted that 'it had not enough weight to throw around to give it the key position in the balance of power' (Morgenthau, 1978: 202). Similar failures for the same reason attended the efforts of Venice to act as balancer in Italy after the battle of Pavia in 1525, and of Sweden in the Baltic region during the minority of King Charles XI between 1660 and 1672.

A further attribute required of the balancer is a certain degree of strategic security to go with its power, for, as Reynolds has noted, 'a policy involving shifting friendships is likely to earn one enemies' (1971: 200). Strategic security also enables the balancer to stay outside the central balance and to remain uncommitted until the moment when its intervention can be decisive. What is required are geographical security advantages, such as might arise from mountainous frontiers, a desert hinterland or sheer extent of territory. Morgenthau (1978) gives a further requirement – aloofness. In order to operate impartially the balancer should have its major interests outside the region covered by the central balance. Thus, France under Louis XIV could not be the European balancer because her primary foreign policy objective was acquiring territory in Europe. Britain was a better claimant since her primary interests were overseas and extra-European, in commerce and the colonies.

This argument is not universally accepted, however. Hartmann argues that the central balance itself is made more complex and flexible if the states involved have interests outside the central balance area which lead them to cooperate on occasion against the balancer (1952: 118). Newman, however, argues that if a balancer has interests of its own to protect outside the area of the central balance, those interests will exert a centrifugal force on the balancer, pulling it away from involvement with the central balance. According to Newman, these outside interests 'will either divert the holder from his concern with that balance, or will bring about conflicts that cut across the alignments within the balance, thus weakening it' (1968: 188).

The key variable is the attitude of the balancer towards the central balance. Although both Morgenthau and Newman used Britain as an example, Morgenthau was looking at Britain's record in the eighteenth and nineteenth centuries, Newman at Britain's actions in the 1919–39 inter-war period. The difference between Morgenthau and Newman was prompted by the fact that the key attitudes of the balancer were quite different during these two periods. This suggests a general rule about the impact of the balancer's foreign policy priorities. If the balancer has interests outside the balance, but none the less sees the maintenance of the central balance as a key objective, then the effects of the outside interests will be beneficial. Outside interests will make the balancer less susceptible to the temptation of aggrandisement in the area covered by the central balance. However, if the balancer becomes so obsessed by these outside interests that it begins to neglect the central balance then this is clearly disadvantageous. Overall, therefore, the balancer should be aloof, but not unduly so.

To an extent, the balancer's role will be made easier if the major balance actors themselves are seeking expansion elsewhere. Extra-European imperialism seems to have acted as a 'safety valve' for the European balance in the period from 1871 to 1914. This feature can only operate if the balance system is not already truly global, as it was after 1945.

Unlike general balance of power theory, which, it can be argued, 'is not a theory of state policy, but rather a theory about environmental constraints' (Waltz, 1959b: 41), writers on the balancer have always asserted that there are certain ways in which such a state *has* to behave if it is to perform its function. These may be summarised briefly.

The statesmen of the balancer should view the competition for advantage between the other states impartially, noting the shifts in the distribution of power among the states, but keeping the balancer itself unaligned. However, once the emergence of a state or alliance capable of posing a serious threat to the overall balance becomes clear, the balancer intervenes, allying itself with the weaker or non-revisionist elements in the system. The addition of the power of the balancer allows this latter grouping to overawe or, if necessary, to physically overcome, the states which threaten the system. Once this has been achieved, and the states comprising the system are brought into overall balance again, the balancer withdraws to take up its position of neutral but watchful guardian once more.

The balancer's intervention should be guided only by a desire to maintain or restore the international equilibrium. This objective should override all other considerations. The balancer can have neither permanent friends nor permanent enemies, only the permanence of its balancing strategy. There ought, therefore, to be no such considerations as 'old alliances', 'ancient enmities' or 'special relationships', nor, logically, ideological solidarity. The balancer cannot afford to become identified with the policies or aims of any of the states or alliances which constitute the central balance. Any state or alliance which aspires to hegemony must be opposed. Thus could Winston Churchill declare that, 'it is a law of public policy which we are following, and not a mere expedient dictated by accidental circumstances, or likes and dislikes, or any other sentiment' (Churchill, 1960: 193).

The balancer is immune to appeals based on concepts such as trust and loyalty. It should ignore past friendships and react only to present danger. Some writers have argued also that the commitment to preserve the balance overrides basic tenets of international law, such as the injunction not to interfere in the domestic affairs of other states. Taken to its extreme, this argument could be used to justify efforts by the balancer to deliberately accentuate the animosities and divisions among the states comprising the central balance. In the long run, however, acquiring a reputation for behaviour of this sort would make it extremely difficult for the balancer to gain the allies necessary for the effective performance of its role.

PARTITION AND COMPENSATION

It might at first appear paradoxical that partition should be included as one of the means by which states might seek to maintain the balance of power. It was, after all, noted at the outset of this book that the fundamental purpose of the balance of power system is to prevent the emergence of a dominant power and thereby to preserve the sovereignty and autonomy of the states which make up the international system. States are supposed to operate with an understanding that, if they wish to preserve their own independence then they must be prepared to support the independence of the other states in the system. Such a perception is implicit in the 'Grotian' image of the balance of power as the mechanism underpinning the international society of European states which emerged at the beginning of the eighteenth century.

However, there is a division in the balance of power literature on the question of whether, in acting to prevent the emergence of a preponderant state or alliance, states are expected to preserve the independence of *all* the constituent units in the system or merely of some of them.

According to Brougham (1872), the use of partitions and annexations to maintain the balance of power was a case of mistaking the means for the end, because 'the whole object of the system is to maintain unimpaired the independence of nations', an objective which applies as much to small and weak states as to the large and strong. Von Gentz (1806: 58) similarly believed that the balance of power was a guarantor of the independence of all states.

In practice, however, it is arguable if this was so. During the course of the eighteenth century, the idea of the balance of power was still evolving, and was increasingly coming to be seen as a device for stabilising the system through the interaction of the great powers, rather than of every single member of the state system. The balance was frequently maintained at the expense of the smaller states. Many of the major peace settlements saw small states disappear in large numbers. The Treaty of Vienna in 1815 cost many small states their independence, while large states such as Saxony were dismembered.

The attitude of the larger powers in these instances was that of seeing partition as an unpleasant necessity. The preference of France and Austria regarding the possible partition of the Ottoman Empire was that if at all possible partition should be prevented and the Empire preserved intact, but that if it could not be prevented then France and Austria must join in the partition. In Count Tolstoy's words 'if the cake could not be saved, it must be fairly divided' (Gulick, 1955: 72).

In Morton Kaplan's 'rules' for operating a balance system (discussed in the next chapter), two important ones are 'stop fighting rather than eliminate an essential national actor' and 'permit defeated or constrained essential national actors to re-enter the system'. It is the use of the word 'essential' that is the key to the paradox. In a balance of power system all states are equal, but in George Orwell's telling phase, 'some are more equal than others'. Small states or large weak states have historically been victimised by the balance of power, used as make-weights to appease the political or territorial designs of the more powerful actors in the system. In January 1805, for example, the British Prime Minister William Pitt argued that many of the small states of Europe could not have any solid existence in themselves and should therefore be disposed of to the benefit of the larger states because 'there is evidently no other mode of accomplishing the great and beneficent object of re-establishing ... the safety and repose of Europe on a solid and permanent basis' (Gulick 1955: 145).

The great powers were protected by the operations of the system because their existence and continuing effectiveness were essential to the successful working of the system. The weak states, by contrast, were not, and therefore were not protected to the same extent. Poland historically has suffered particularly from this feature, being partitioned between rapacious neighbours three times during the eighteenth century and once in the twentieth. Germany suffered the same fate in 1945. The division of regions into 'spheres of influence' for great powers is less dramatic, but also represents a significant restraint on the sovereignty of those states in the region. Examples of this latter behaviour include the Anglo-French *entente* of 1904, which divided North Africa into spheres of influence and the division of the Baltic states between Germany and the USSR's influence in 1939 (Handel, 1981: 177).

The balance of power system has traditionally been operated by the great powers, both because they have the greater capacity to influence outcomes and because they have the biggest stake in the established order. As great powers they have clearly benefited from the existing system and it is therefore most clearly in their interest to defend it.

The reality of the way in which the balance worked historically was that while each state had an interest in preserving a multi-state system, it did not follow that the membership of the state system had to remain constant, and thus the exact identity of the states making up the system might change over time. From a systemic perspective this was good, since it increased the system's flexibility and enabled it to accommodate the necessity for change. From the point of view of smaller or weaker states, it undermined the protection offered by the system, since they were the most likely to be partitioned to accommodate the need for flexibility and change.

While it can be argued that sacrificing weak states to maintain the balance of power serves the good of the system, it will clearly weaken the commitment of weak states to the balance of power as a system, since it does not serve their interests in the same way that it does those of the great powers. This has often led weak states to pursue what Annette Baker Fox (1957) has called 'anti-balance of power' behaviour, deserting the weaker side in the balance in order not to become the victim of the stronger in the event of war. Thus, Belgium moved away from cooperation with France to a position of neutrality as German strength and assertiveness increased during the 1930s. An essentially self-help system such as the balance of power has less to offer the weaker states, who would gain more from a more ordered international society than the anarchy reflected and protected by the balance of power.

MODERATION

The policy of reciprocal compensation runs counter to one of the other policies identified as an important component of a successful balance of power system, which is that of moderation, or the preservation of the states which are the system's components. Gulick argues that 'preserving the state components is a crucial corollary of the balance of power' (1955: 73). The eventual elimination of Poland at the end of the eighteenth century stands as a stark exception to this, but one can argue that in other cases of partition there is a clear difference between losing *some* territory and losing *all* territory and ceasing to exist.

Moderation, in this context, has a restricted meaning. The victorious states after a balance of power war should seek neither to humiliate or to destroy their recent enemy or enemies. The reason for such 'restraint' is that the recently vanquished will be important counterweights in the post-war balance of power system and their presence may be essential to restrain one or more of the recent victors who subsequently aspire to a dominant role themselves.

Such moderation is generally extended to large, rather than small powers, that is, to the major players within the system. Gulick argues that a spirit of moderation can be seen as a key element in a statesman's balance of power policy because 'only such an attitude can carry with it a willingness to think of the state system as a whole, and not exclusively of one state' (1955: 77). In the end, moderation is an effective factor because it is in each state's own interest to show such moderation. Each state has an interest in preserving any other important state because it would rather that state survived than that it be swallowed up by potential future enemies.

The historical record is patchy in this regard, however. While it is possible to identify such moderate foreign policies within balance of power systems – Bismarck's generous treatment of defeated Austria in 1866, for example – it is also possible to find states or alliances which appear to have completely ignored this precept. In 1740 an alliance went to war with Austria which, had it been successful would have entirely dismembered the Austrian Empire. Similarly, in 1756 the war aims of the allies united against Prussia effectively called for the elimination by partition of the Prussian state. Only defeat or stalemate in war prevented these aims from being realised.

CONCLUSION

The balance of power concept is an idea that has resonance at many levels. Historically it has been used to explain the actions of states in an essentially insecure environment. It has been used by statesmen to explain and justify their chosen foreign policies, and finally it has been recommended as a guide to wise statesmanship.

One of the curious aspects of the history of the balance of power concept is that for most its history none of its advocates went so far as to systematically work out the corollaries of the balance of power (Gulick, 1955: 52). No helpful handbook on 'how to implement a balance of power policy' ever appeared. Statesmen were left to work that out for themselves within the general moral and political framework of their day. Given the inherent ambiguities and inconsistencies of the balance of power idea, it is hardly surprising, therefore, that statesmen were inconsistent in the manner in which they attempted to apply balance of power policies.

This inconsistency of application is crucial if one assumes that a balance of power can only be produced through the self-conscious foreign policies of states directing their efforts towards that end. A complexity of the theory, however, is that proponents argue that states ought to pursue balance of power policies, but also that even if they fail to do so consistently, a balance of power *system* may, indeed probably will, still emerge.

4 Balance of power systems

INTRODUCTION

One of the many senses in which the phrase 'balance of power' has traditionally been employed is to describe or explain an historical state system. It is one of the ways in which the balance conception can be said to have played a critical part in the historical development of international relations. Historians have applied the 'balance of power' description to the European international systems of the eighteenth and nineteenth centuries. In the eighteenth century itself, statesmen referred to the balance of power system created by the treaties which ended the War of the Spanish Succession as 'the system of Utrecht'.

Balance of power thinking in fact represents one of the earliest example of holism, that is, thinking in terms of the natural tendency of groups of units to form themselves into wholes. It is the defining characteristic of a systems approach and its adoption predated by several hundred years the application of systems theory to other aspects of international relations. Kant, for example, said that the system of states reflected a 'predetermined design to make harmony spring from human discord' (Gulick, 1955: 21–2).

The systems approach assumes that, 'despite the complexity and confusion displayed by the amalgam of interactions, there are a set of structures which describe the international system, and explain the behaviour of the individual states' (Little, 1978: 189).

The key feature about the systemic approach to the balance of power is that it posits a direct relationship between the structure of the state system and the behaviour of states within the system.

Modern general systems theory originated outside the social sciences as a tool of engineering science. It was not until the 1950s that elements of systems thinking began percolating into the social sciences, and the study of international relations was one of the last to be so influenced. This is surprising, given that there have always been elements of systemic thinking present in international relations. The balance of power is the classic example of this. Many thinkers in the so-called 'Golden Age' of the balance of power, such as Rousseau and Kant, believed that Europe formed a political 'system' and that the balance of power operated in an essentially automatic manner.

Instead of leading the way in introducing the application of systems theory to social science, international relations as an academic discipline was one of the last to embrace it. While other social sciences were investigating its possibilities soon after the end of the Second World War, international relations was engaged in an academic debate over the rehabilitation of the balance of power concept.

After the end of the First World War there occurred a reaction against balance of power policies by both politicians and academics, who saw in the workings of the balance of power system one of the major causes of the outbreak of the war. Led by President Woodrow Wilson, who called the balance of power 'an unstable equilibrium of competitive interests determined by the sword', opponents rejected the balance of power as a way of organising international relations, and sought to promote collective security instead. However, following the Second World War there was a strong reaction to this approach, and writers like E.H. Carr and Morgenthau successfully undermined the idealist school of thought and replaced it with the realist state-centric view of the world. In particular, Morgenthau reasserted the importance of the balance of power idea which he elevated to a 'universal concept' determining the behaviour of any society of sovereign states. He also identified the balance of power as a 'self-regulating mechanism', in the manner of Rousseau.

Morgenthau placed enormous emphasis on the balance of power mechanism because he believed that it held the key to understanding the nature of interstate relations at the systemic level. As a 'realist', Morgenthau believed that all states were engaged in a continuous struggle to expand their own power. Yet, despite this, no state was able to emerge as a dominant political hegemon, and therefore the international system remained an 'anarchy', a system comprised of sovereign, independent states. According to Morgenthau (1978), this paradox could only be understood in terms of the effects of the balance of power system. Morgenthau therefore used the balance of power to explain why the fundamental structure of the interstate system has remained so stable over the past three and a half centuries.

As was noted in Chapter 1, Morgenthau, and the other members of the 'realist' school of international relations thought, saw the pursuit of power by states as the defining characteristic of the international system. The allegedly 'anarchic' nature of the system forced this behaviour upon states. Thus, the desire to maximise power should not be explained in terms of the individual preferences of states, but rather as a function of the nature of the system. Given the nature of the system, Morgenthau argues, what prevents continuous conflict and disorder is the self-regulating balance of power mechanism.

Kenneth Waltz, another member of the realist school, places so much emphasis on this particular aspect of state behaviour that his theory is described as 'structural realism'. Waltz argues that in an international anarchy, where a state can only rely upon itself for the maintenance of its security, the states are compelled to be functionally alike, to behave in the same way. If states fail to emulate the policies of their successful neighbours they will fall by the wayside. As others emulate them, power balancing takes place and the international order becomes governed by balance of power politics. According to Waltz, for a balance of power system to form only two requirements are necessary: 'that the order be anarchic and that it be populated by units wishing to survive' (Waltz, 1979: 121).

According to Morgenthau, the balance of power system reduced the incidence of warfare and ensured the continuing survival of the states who made up the system. In doing so it prevented any one state from reaching a position where it could establish hegemony over the system. Thus, in the reasoning of both Morgenthau and Waltz, the balance of power system is maintained through the foreign policies of states pursuing their own interests – indeed, Waltz argues that it is not necessary for any of them to actually desire the creation or maintenance of such a system.

However, as Claude (1962: 26–37) has pointed out, Morgenthau does not clearly define the elements which must be present for a balance of power system to be said to exist. It was left to later writers such as Kaplan to attempt to repair this deficiency.

A balance of power system has been defined in terms of a 'stable equilibrium' by Reynolds. Thus, in the anarchy of international relations, states and alliances will interact in such a way that the system as a whole maintains itself in equilibrium. The equilibrium in this instance is not between states or groups of states in the system, but rather of the system itself (1971: 202). Therefore, a disturbance in the system will be countered by compensating changes in the nature of the interactions among the units. If the challenge to the existing balance of power is defeated and the original situation restored, the equilibrium is deemed stable; if the struggle to prevent hegemony produces a new balance of power with the system in a different condition, then this reflects an unstable equilibrium. Reynolds argues that the phrase 'balance of power' carries with it the implication of a stable equilibrium. In practice, however, this is rarely achieved. The historical experience indicates that although statesmen's objectives reflect the desire to maintain a stable equilibrium, the practical difficulties involved in maintaining an international equilibrium are such that following major challenges, such as those of Napoleon or Kaiser Wilhelm II, a new balance evolves, significantly different from its predecessors, so that the pattern is more characteristic of an *unstable* equilibrium.

Such an unstable equilibrium is what ought to be expected given the nature of international relations. The stability of balance of power systems needs to be seen in this sense. There is a difference between stability and stasis. As shown by the definitions at the start of Chapter 1, the 'equilibrium' aimed at by balance of power systems is not one composed of a number of states all equally powerful, rather it is a *system* in balance, with that condition defined in terms of the inability of any one state or alliance to overthrow the system and establish a hegemony or empire. Thus, there are always elements of disequilibrium present, and adjustments taking place. Stability exists not at the level of particular interstate relations, but at the level of the system as a whole, where the changes occurring are within tolerable limits, that is, not threatening the overall equilibrium. There may still be aggressive attempts by states to enhance their power, there may even be wars, but as long as such wars do not undermine the ability of states within the system to resist and defeat a hegemonic aspirant, the system as a whole is an equilibrium.

It is in this sense that it can be argued that a theory such as Kenneth Waltz's structural realism predicts *balancing* of power rather than particular *balances* of power. The question of system structure is an important one because there are many forms which a balance of power system can take. In Waltz's 1979 study, system structure is composed of three elements, the first of which is the principle according to which the system is organised or ordered. For example, a balance of power system may be bipolar or multipolar in form. The differences are of more than passing interest, because there exists a major debate within the literature of international relations as to which particular form of the balance of power produces the greatest stability and the least war within the system. Kenneth Waltz, for example, argues that systemic stability (defined as the absence of system-wide wars), is greatest when the number of great powers is smallest, and that the best system is one dominated by only two great powers, a bipolar system. Morton Kaplan, in contrast, argues that the minimum number of great powers (of approximately equal power) required for a system to be stable is five.

A 1972 study by Singer, Bremer and Stuckey looked at the international system during the nineteenth and twentieth centuries. The study indicated that during the nineteenth century the amount of war in the system increased as power capabilities became concentrated in fewer states. However, in the twentieth century, the same process led to a decline in great power war. Clearly different factors were also at work; the emergence of the 'superpowers' and the advent of nuclear weapons are two obvious reasons why the centuries appear so different.

The key feature of the systemic balance of power theories is that state behaviour is seen as being governed by the nature of the system. Regardless of individual differences between states in terms of culture or ideology, all states must act in a similar way, selfishly seeking to increase their own power. Martin Wight saw power politics as an inevitable feature of a political system which was an anarchy, without a central authority, and he thus made the two almost synonymous. He declared that 'power politics means the relations between independent powers' (Wight, 1946: 7).

This interpretation of the balance of power is as old as the concept itself. In 1605 the Venetian Giovanni Botero described the balance of power as arising incidentally from the efforts of the constituent states in the system to gain an advantage, 'from the plurality of Princes it follows that the balance (*contrappeso*) is useful and good, not from its own nature but by accident' (Anderson, 1993: 154).

The 'system' argument put forward by realists such as Waltz argues that the nature of the system does not provide the state with protection or help.

> The contribution of the realists' beliefs about the lack of harmony of interest in the world and about man's capacity for evil and his thirst for power is, therefore, to reinforce the system argument:

not only do states not have protection, they are also in danger and so need it.

(Taylor, 1978: 130)

The normal process of international politics should produce a rough equilibrium. In Gellman's words, 'beyond the plurality of national wills exists a logic intrinsic to the system' (1989: 161). This is not because any state is necessarily enamoured of the idea of equilibrium. Statesmen would much prefer their state to be more powerful than all its rivals. Unfortunately, the costs of attempting to achieve such a dominating position are prohibitive, beyond the resources of most states in most periods of history.

Not all states would even seek such dominance. As Kenneth Waltz has noted, no set of rules can specify how important the game should be considered (Waltz, 1959a: 206) and cultural factors can impose self-restraint. Most states pursue the lesser objective of avoidance of being dominated, a key part of which is remaining alert to take action against states which seem to be seeking a dominating position. This objective, when pursued by most states most of the time, tends towards the creation of a balance of power in the system.

The emergence of a balance of power can therefore be seen as being simply a result of a process, rather than the attainment of a goal being pursued by the state actors. In this sense, the system normally protects itself. As Butterfield put it, 'if there exists an international order, it tends to be mechanically self-adjusting and self-rectifying. As soon as the equilibrium is disturbed at any point, compensatory action automatically emerges in some other part of the system' (1953: 89–90). States with less than overwhelming power will tend to ally against a state or alliance which threatens to overturn the system. Lord Brougham in 1843 described as an 'obvious principle' the idea that a threatened state ought to call on its allies or form alliances and that other states, neither attacked nor threatened ought to make common cause with the endangered state, since

> its overthrow will further increase the power of the aggressor and expose them to the risk of afterwards being assailed and conquered. So far from being a refinement of policy, this is simply yielding to the common instinct of self-defence.

(Gareau, 1962: 70)

This is the essence of the mechanical view of the balance of power, a self-regulating system based on the dictates of common sense. This is the view held by Craik and Waltz, quoted in Chapter 3.

The way in which thinking about the balance of power developed through the use of analogy and metaphor undoubtedly played a part in reinforcing this view of the balance. Seventeenth- and eighteenth-century commentators on the balance of power were fond of comparing its workings to the mechanical precision of clockwork or the orbital movements of planetary bodies in the solar system. Thus, for example, Brougham in 1803 argued that the solar mechanics and balance of power both induced order in their respective systems and that, just as newly discovered planets were found to obey the celestial laws common to all heavenly bodies, 'so the powers, which frequently arise in the European world, immediately fall into their places, and conform to the same principles that fix the positions and direct the movements of the ancient states' (Anderson, 1993: 168).

This was by no means a conception confined to eighteenth-century thinkers. The twentieth-century British historian A. J. P. Taylor clearly had such a perspective in mind when he wrote that in the nineteenth century British statesmen saw the balance of power, 'as something that worked itself without British intervention' (Taylor, 1954: 284).

The distinguishing element in this conception, according to Claude, is the assumption that 'equilibrium may be produced or preserved without actually being willed by any state' (Claude, 1962: 46). Kenneth Waltz goes further and criticises those writers who advocated policies designed to preserve a balance, on the grounds that it has proved to be 'an unfortunately short step from the belief that a high regard for preserving a balance is at the heart of wise statesmanship to the assumption that states must follow the maxim if a balance of power is to be maintained' (Waltz, 1979: 119–20). Hans Morgenthau went so far as to assert a determinist view of the balance of power, arguing that statesmen have no choice but to follow balance of power policies, that 'the balance of power and policies aiming at its preservation are not only inevitable but are an essential stabilizing factor in a society of sovereign nations' (1978: 173). For Waltz, this is the key contribution made by the balance of power concept to international relations theory. The balance of power is what gives the international system its coherence. This was, in essence, the view of the nature of the European balance of power system that emerged at the end of the seventeenth century.

During the 'classical' period of the balance of power from 1700 to 1918 states were generally not content to rely upon the workings of an automatic balance of power. British politicians, for example, believed that all states should watch their rivals so that no state or alliance should become dominant through the inertia of others. However, they realised that not all states would be vigilant enough, that mistakes would occur, actions would be deferred until too late and so on, and they were therefore prepared to adopt a watchdog role, drawing other states' attentions to threats to the balance as they perceived them.

Most statesmen's views conformed more closely to conceptions of the balance of power system which Inis Claude has termed the 'manually-operated' and 'semi-automatic' conceptions (1962: 47–9). The 'manually operated' balance of power system is one in which the equilibrium is consciously sought by the leading statesmen, who conduct their states' foreign policy with this end in view. In this system the balance is not produced by the automatic process of the system or by the efforts of a 'balancer' state, but by skilled multi-lateral diplomacy. The balance of power is something which statesmen 'scheme for and contrive', it is not a gift of the gods or something that occurs accidentally. States cannot wait for it to 'happen' (Palmer and Perkins, 1954: 308).

For a system to be said to exist four conditions must be satisfied (Luard, 1992: 342). In the first place 'there must be a clear *inter-connection* between the parts to make it a coherent and interrelated whole'. Secondly, the constituent parts must be in regular *commu-nication*. Thirdly, there should exist a history of predictable interaction such that there are common expectations among the members of the system. Finally, the pattern of relationships should demonstrate regularity. This would include the existence or pursuit of an overall equilibrium among the states, in the sense defined at the start of Chapter 1, that is, the absence of a hegemonic state or group able to dominate and give the law to the other states in the system. For a balance of power 'system' to be said to exist, the pattern of interaction among the constituent states would have to characterised by the formation of regular combinations designed to block the emergence of a hegemonic power.

VARIETIES OF BALANCE OF POWER SYSTEMS

It is possible to distinguish a simple balance of power from a complex one, that is to say, a balance made up of two powers from one consisting of three or more. The simple balance of power is exem-plified by the clash of France and Habsburg Spain/Austria in the sixteenth and seventeenth centuries, and by the confrontation between the United States and the Soviet Union in the cold war.

The complex balance of power is illustrated by the situation of Europe in the mid-eighteenth century, when France and Austria were joined as great powers by Britain, Russia and Prussia. A. F. Pollard noted the crucial difference between a two-state system, which he called a 'simple' balance, and a five-state system, which he called a 'multiple' balance. In a two-state system the power of the states needs to be equal. In a five-state, or more, system the states no longer need to be equal in power for the system to remain a balance of power (Pollard, 1923: 60).

For most writers there is a minimum number of actors who need to be involved if a balance of power system is to work effectively. According to Stanley Hoffman (1972) the number must be more than two, and historically has been five or six, with these actors being of comparable if not equal powers. Morton Kaplan (1969: 35) also argued that the number must not fall below five. P. A. Reynolds (1971: 203) argues that a system involving less than five states is likely to break down. A bipolar balance will be characterised by mutual suspicion, enmity and competition. It is a 'zero-sum' conflict in which one side's gain is automatically the other side's loss and if there is indeed a fine balance between the two sides, than a relatively minor gain for one side may give it the margin of advantage it is seeking. This is a brittle system likely to break down into war.

For Reynolds, where there are three states in the system, if any two combine against the third they are likely to gain a significant advantage. A four-state system is likely to resolve itself into a two-against-two simple balance during crises. Thus, only when five states are reached is a sufficient degree of flexibility present. Even a five-state system can break down, but it is far less likely to do so than the others, because it offers a greater number of possible combinations and therefore a flexibility in terms of possible responses.

The advantages of a multi-state balance system based upon flexible alliances, over a simple bipolar balance can be seen through Richard Rosecrance's concept of the 'regulator'. Rosecrance (1963: 220–1) argued that any international system which has stability as a goal is composed of a number of elements – a source of disturbance, a 'regulator', and an array of environmental factors which translate the interaction of the first two into outcomes. For the regulator to produce stability it must produce outcomes regarded as acceptable to the major participants in the system and it must have a number of options at least equal to the number of potential disruptive forces. 'Only by increasing the variety of the regulator states is it possible to reduce the variety of the outcomes. This is the law of requisite variety. Only variety can destroy variety' (ibid.). Regulative forces may be institutional, such as an international organisation, or informal, as would be the case with states acting within a multipolar balance of power system.

A simple bipolar balance system severely limits the potential variety of response, whereas a multipolar system, particularly one based upon flexible alliances, tends to maximise the number of potential responses to a threat to stability. One state may be approximately balanced by an alliance of several lesser states, which together produce a rough equivalence of power. Another form of balance system is one in which allied groups, the members of each group being roughly comparable to each other, may be in balance. This is essentially a variant of the bipolar balance, with all its advantages and disadvantages.

A 'chandelier' type of balance may exist. Here states of comparable power confront each other, their weapons turned impartially in all directions. The great power 'balances' of the eighteenth and nineteenth centuries were very broadly of this type. Alliances which are formed in the maintenance of this kind of balance tend to be comparatively short-lived, and not to be coloured by strong ideological congruences among the allies or ideological cleavages with the states against which alliances are formed.

Dina Zinnes listed six possibilities of power distribution and alliance configuration that could be deemed a balance of power. The examples assumed a five-state system and were neither exhaustive nor mutually exclusive.

---

1   There are no alliances and all states have equal power.
2   All states belong to one of two alliances and the power of the two alliances is equal.
3   There are two alliances equal in power and one non-aligned state.
4   There are two alliances and a third non-aligned state, such that the power of either alliance plus the non-aligned state is greater than the power of the other alliance.
5   There are no alliances and the power of each state is less than the summed total power of all the remaining states.
6   There is one state or alliance which is more powerful than any other unit in the system, but such that condition 5 is still met.

(Zinnes, 1967: 273)

SYSTEMS AND THE BALANCE OF POWER

A feature of the academic study of the balance of power has been the tendency of theorists to derive 'rules' for the balance of power game. Morton Kaplan took this tendency furthest in a book published in 1957 which identified a number of possible international systems, one of which was the balance of power system. Kaplan defined his system in terms of the behaviour of the states operating within it, so that a system could only be identified as a balance of power if the states operated according to Kaplan's rules.

The problem with this approach is that it makes the balance of power system appear far more mechanistic than has historically been the case. Indeed, the beauty of balance of power politics lies in its very flexibility, in the variety of power distribution that can legitimately be termed a balance of power, and in the freedom of manoeuvre available to states within a balance of power system. Ziegler (1977: 173) uses Kaplan's model to describe the balance of power and declares that 'the system operates according to a set of principles or rules'.

Statesmen involved in a balance of power system are unlikely to follow all the prescribed 'rules'. They may not automatically support the weaker side; inhibited perhaps by recent animosity or religious bitterness, they may not feel that the most powerful state in the system is necessarily the one most to be feared. For this reason, Inis Claude urged caution 'when academic theorists succumb to the urge to codify the operations of the balance of power system ... the theorist misleads when he undertakes to reduce to rigid patterns what is in reality a fluid process' (Claude, 1989: 81). There was nevertheless always the danger of rigidity entering the balance of power system. There has always been a historical tendency to regard the current system as being stable and to prefer to keep things as they are.

Nevertheless, the appeal of the balance of power has always lain partly in the fact that it appears to make international politics systematic. As Lord Brougham put it in 1803,

> the grand and distinguishing feature of the balancing theory is the systematic form to which it reduces those plain and obvious principles of national conduct ... the general union which it has effected, of all the European powers in one connected system – obeying certain laws, and actuated in general by a common principle.
>
> (Forsyth, Keens-Soper and Savigear, 1970: 269)

The 'rules' set out by writers such as Kaplan are still useful if they are seen more as the identified recurrent behaviour patterns of members of a successful system rather than as rigid prescription. Seen in this way, they can provide a useful outline of the key features which helped to make the system work.

Morton Kaplan's rules are looked at below. They are based upon 'realist' assumptions about the objectives and methods of the states comprising the system, that is, that states wish to increase their power (their capability to influence outcomes) and this brings them into conflict with other states in a political environment which is essentially anarchic.

Kaplan's balance of power model makes certain key assumptions:

1 The only relevant actors are nation-states.
2 The major powers seek security as their primary goal.
3 The weaponry in the system is not nuclear.
4 Because some power factors are unpredictable and hard to measure, each seeks a margin of security higher than its current capabilities.
5 There must be at least five major powers in the system.
6 Each state, even a great power, is likely to need allies to achieve its goals. This explains the willingness to preserve the existence of possible future allies.

(Kaplan, 1968: 389–90)

The third assumption limits the utility of the model somewhat, since it rules out consideration of the nuclear 'balance of terror', which dominated relations between the superpowers during the cold war. This variant of the balance of power approach is an interesting one and is examined in Chapter 8. Kaplan's requirement that there should be at least five great powers would in addition have ruled out consideration of the early cold war period, because of the bipolarity characteristic of that era.

These assumptions lead to six fundamental 'rules'.

---

1 Act to increase capabilities, but negotiate rather than fight.
2 Fight rather than pass up an opportunity to increase capabilities.
3 Stop fighting rather than eliminate an essential national actor.
4 Act to oppose any coalition or single actor which tends to assume a position of preponderance with respect to the rest of the system.

5   Act to constrain actors who subscribe to supranational organ-
    ising principles.
6   Permit defeated or constrained essential national actors to re-
    enter the system as acceptable role partners or act to bring some
    previously inessential actor within the essential actor classifica-
    tion. Treat all essential actors as acceptable role partners.

The first two rules flow from the need to allow states to pursue a
margin of security when they are operating in a world in which the
unpredictable has an important effect on outcomes. Rule 3 is based
on the realisation that the balance of power is a system based upon
the operation of alliances and therefore potential future alliance
partners must be preserved. The fourth and fifth rules represent
the requirement to take action against any alliance or state which
seeks to overthrow the system. The final rule, like rule 3, reflects
the need to allow maximum choice of potential alliance partners
(Kaplan, 1968: 31).

Kaplan argues that a balance of power system exists only when
all these features are present. They are the 'essential rules' of the
system. The logic of his argument is that if the historical record
shows a high correlation between the actual behaviour of states and
the predictions of the theory in terms of the rules to be observed,
then the 'theory' can be held to be correct. However, Kaplan's model
is not really a theory, but simply a systematic presentation of the
traditional view of the way in which the eighteenth-century balance
of power system worked.

Because the system is held to define and determine the behaviour
of the states within it, the rules identified by Kaplan are specifically
described as being prescriptive rather than descriptive, that is, states
must follow these rules if they are to gain the maximum amount of
security possible within the limitations of the system.

It is important to note that Kaplan's rules derive from a model.
They are not meant to be a description of an actual balance of power
system based upon a historical example. Rather, they derive from
an attempt to narrow the criteria down to the minimum required to
allow generalisation. For the construction of a model of a *particular*
balance of power system it would be necessary to build in far more
detail about capabilities, history, logistics, military technology and
tactics, the amount of information available to governments, the
role of individuals, technology, domestic politics, and so on. All the
factors that are specific to one particular system would prevent it

from being used to analyse other examples. However, a criticism that can be levelled at Kaplan is that while his model is insufficiently detailed to serve as a description of any particular system, nevertheless it shares so many distinctive features with the eighteenth-century European system that it is clearly largely based upon it, which weakens its claim to universality.

Kaplan's approach is still a valuable one, however, because it can be used to look at other examples of actual or suggested balance of power systems and compare them with Kaplan's norm. This was done by Chi (1968) and Franke (1968). Alternatively, the general approach of attempting to systematically outline the key features of a balance of power system can be adapted to build in more assumptions or a larger number of variables. An example of this latter approach is that of Pelz (1991).

Pelz modifies Kaplan's systems to allow for variations in key features of the balance of power in different periods. He identifies three systems in the period since 1776. System I is a representative example of his approach. It overlaps with the period which inspired Kaplan's model, but goes into greater detail in identifying key features. Unlike Kaplan's model this is clearly an attempted description of a perceived historical reality.

System I 1776–93, 1815–92

A *Great power relations with other great powers*
1 Each power maintains or increases capabilities relative to those of its opponents;
2 each power opposes any single actor or coalition that tries to dominate the system.

B *Great power relations with smaller powers*
1 Major powers try to dominate or heavily influence smaller powers, particularly those that occupy strategic positions or possess important resources;
2 in times of change in the balance of power, the weaker coalition of great powers bids for the support of the smaller powers.

C *Conduct of small powers*
1 In peacetime small powers try to play great powers against other great powers in order to maintain independence or gain concessions;

2   in times of tension or war, small powers try to extort disproportionate concessions for their neutrality or their participation in wars that are threatened or are in progress.

D   *Diplomacy*
1   Each great power tries to join or construct the preponderant
coalition;
2   frequent or businesslike diplomatic conferences adjust the
balance of power by distributing monetary and territorial
compensation, but usually without resort to war.

E   *Military action*
1   The powers use limited amounts of force to adjust the balance
of power or to oppose potential hegemons;
2   each power goes to war rather than pass up a chance to
increase its capabilities.

F   *Constraints on use of force*
1   Each power has to rationalize the war as necessary for maintaining or adjusting the balance;
2   each power permits defeated actors to re-enter the system as
acceptable alliance partners on terms that do not greatly
alienate them.

G   *Military assets, technologies and doctrines*
1   Economic: most belligerents rely on limited national taxes,
merchant ship prizes and forage and loot;
2   troops: most belligerents use professional standing armies and
some conscripts;
3   technology: most belligerents use muskets, light field artillery
and ships of the line;
4   strategy: most belligerents use incremental encirclement, attri-
tion and limited campaigns.

H   *Ideology*
1   Each power opposes any actor or coalition that engages in
supranational activities, such as subversive appeals, religious
or revolutionary campaigns, or collective security operations.

I   *Risk-taking*
1   Major powers risk wars of adjustment fairly frequently;
2   major powers attempt hegemonic wars very rarely.

J   *Domestic politics*
1   Elites are able to make foreign policy decisions with little
interference.

The rules above (system I) are those which policy-makers tended to follow in the classical multipolar balance of power system. States tried to increase their security by choosing policies that provided a high probability of survival rather than take risks that might yield either hegemony or annihilation. Each state was free to pursue its national interests amorally, as long as it did not try to overthrow the system. Unlike their counterparts in other systems though, decision-makers tended to take the social norms of system I fairly seriously.

The greater detail involved in Pelz's system I brings out Kaplan's point that the more detail involved, the more historically specific it becomes, and the more difficult it is to use it as the basis for generalisations about the balance of power as a system. Unfortunately, in this sense Kaplan's own model falls between two stools. It is not sufficiently detailed to serve as a model of the eighteenth- or nineteenth-century balance of power systems in Europe, yet the similarity between the model and the eighteenth-century system is such as to leave it with little general predictive capability. Little (1978: 192) points out that there is no obvious theoretical logic behind the selection of Kaplan's particular six variables. The first three reflect the practice of the eighteenth-century system, while the last three are additions designed to add rational guidelines for the maintenance of the system.

SUB-BALANCES AND THE GENERAL BALANCE

According to Kaplan, 'the balance of power international system is an international social system which does not have as a component a political subsystem' (1969: 35). However, this definition flies in the face of the historical record, which provides a number of examples of functioning balance of power systems that have been characterised by the presence of sub-systems within the larger whole. This is what one would expect. Since the state system was diversified by geography and the difference in calibre between its members, there were likely to be local and regional distributions of power, distinct from but needing to be comprehended in, the general distribution of power.

A balance of power system may be composed of a number of sub-systems that interrelate to form the larger balance, but which are themselves composed of a number of states who form a regional balance. Usually, the interrelationship between the different systems is one in which the lesser systems are subordinate to the greater, because of the greater capabilities of the states and alliances forming the larger balance. However, though each of the sub-balances represents a separate individuality, they are united to the whole. It has been characterised as the 'wheels within wheels' of the complex machine that was the European balance of power. In the eighteenth century in Europe an overall balance of power existed composed of Austria, France, Britain, Russia, Prussia and Spain, but in addition there were distinct regional sub-balances in the Baltic and Mediterranean, while a highly complex equilibrium existed within the Holy Roman Empire.

The German sub-balance is unusual historically because it existed in the area which was the geographical heart of the general European balance of power. The more usual situation, as Hans Morgenthau (1978) noted, is for the autonomy of such sub-systems. The closer a regional balance of power is to the core area of the central balance, the less opportunity it has to operate autonomously and the more it tends to become merely a localised manifestation of the dominant balance.

The relationship between a general balance of power and any sub-balances is not a clear one. M. S. Anderson (1970: 185) has noted with regard to contemporary thinking about the eighteenth-century system that

> there was little attempt to show with any exactitude what role these 'particular' or 'inferior' balances played within the European one. A connection between the two was, rightly, assumed; but hardly any effort was made to analyse or even to illustrate it.
>
> (Anderson, 1970: 185)

An exception to this was Alexandre Maurice, who wrote in 1801 that there was a general European balance of power and that

> there are besides, in some parts of Europe, partial equilibriums formed from the agreement of the relations of states placed in almost immediate connection with each other; in like manner as the general equilibrium is formed from the agreement of all the particular equilibriums. These last are more easily formed than the general equilibrium and once established, are more susceptible of duration.
>
> (Gareau, 1962: 43)

Writers on the balance of power closer to the present day have done little to make up for this deficiency. Martin Wight (1973: 108) described the minor balances as being 'distinct from but comprehended in the general distribution', but he does not elaborate. Frederick Hartmann argued that the sub-balances were clearly inferior to the general balance,

> swallowed up within the larger general balance they reemerge after a war or when the danger of a war recedes ... the extent to which most of the local balances remain stubbornly unintegrated into a general balance is indicative of the relative lack of expectation of general war, just as their subordination within the general balance is a clear sign of increasing tension.
>
> (Hartmann, 1973: 315)

Hedley Bull (1977: 103) confused the issue still further by distinguishing between (a) the general balance of power as opposed to local balances, and (b) the dominant (or central) balance compared with subordinate balances. According to Bull, the dominant balance is still only a particular balance of power and therefore is a 'local' balance as far as the general balance is concerned. The central balance should not be identified with the general balance or equilibrium of the system as a whole.

This is true, but seems to be an unnecessary over-complication of an already complex distinction. In any event, it is clear that modern writers are not more lucid on this question than their predecessors. In fact the eighteenth-century writers were far more clear in their writings, and British statesman eventually succeeded in developing a policy which successfully established a relationship between the balances, despite the difficulties involved.

It was only in the eighteenth century that the idea of comprehending Europe as a whole with regard to interstate relationships began to take hold. The Thirty Years War (1618–48) had, it is true, involved virtually all the European states at one time or another, but the European state system only really emerged into maturity *as a result* of that great struggle. It required the intellectual revolution of the second half of the seventeenth century and the satisfactory resolution of the general crisis of authority, to enable a stable system to emerge. By 1800 writers such as the Abbé de Pradt spoke of Europe forming 'a single social body which one might rightly call the European Republic' (Gulick, 1955: 11), but at the start of the eighteenth century the European political system was not the unified framework which it later became. Several 'inferior balances' were recognised, with the Baltic and Italy being regularly seen as such, and the Holy Roman Empire also frequently being described as a 'minor balance', for example by the anonymous authors of *A Defence of the Measures of the Present Administration* (London, 1731: 23) and *The Present State of Europe* (London, 1750: 26–7). The powers of northern Europe in 1700 had little to do with those in the extreme south, and *vice versa*. This separation was reflected in the organisation of the British government, which included two foreign ministers – the Secretaries of State for the Northern and Southern Departments – who dealt with matters relating to northern and southern Europe respectively. This practice was also followed by Prussia.

By 1714, however, Britain was certainly one state which had developed a habit of looking at Europe as a single political system, and this raised problems in dealing with the minor balances. There were two possible ways of looking at the sub-balances, and either approach would have been compatible with a commitment to the general balance.

The first option was to give priority to the general balance. In following this policy, the argument would be that the European equilibrium was produced by the balanced interaction of a number of major powers. However, in order to be 'major' powers and to be strong enough to play their part in maintaining the general balance, these states would have to draw their strength from their regional dominance, for example Austria dominating southeast Europe, Prussia dominating north Germany, Sweden dominating the Baltic, Britain being the major naval power, and so on. In this conception, if a balance at the regional level existed at all, it could only exist by an equality of the combined regional actors with the local dominant power. In other words, the regional 'power' would be too strong to be overthrown by the second-rank states in that region. Following this policy, therefore, intervention would only be triggered if *another* great power intervened in the region, threatening to overthrow one great power's power base, and with it the general equilibrium.

One writer who described such a system was Alexander Maurice, quoted earlier. Maurice believed that the equilibrium in the sub-balances should arise from a tension of forces between a dominant local power and the other states in the sub-balance. He felt that it was the duty of the local hegemonic power to maintain regional stability and that these local balances would then produce an overall general balance (Gareau, 1962: 43).

The second option was to follow a policy of supporting balances *at all levels*. A state could act so as to encourage regional balances of power. This would be both good in itself, since it would keep these regions open to access by other states, and it would also contribute to a balance of power at the general level supported in a complex fashion by the sub-balances. The effect of this system would be to produce a general equilibrium in which the offensive inclinations of the great powers would be greatly inhibited, more so than in the alternative balance system. The reason for this would be that since balanced power is neutralised power in the first conception, if one state dominated a region it would have a margin of disposable power. However, such power could be used to threaten the general balance as well as to defend it.

In the complex multi-balance system, however, constraints were more marked. The great powers would derive their power and prestige from their diverse areas of interest. Yet in several of those areas their room for manoeuvre would be limited. Thus, for example, Austria would be one of the actors in the Italian sub-system and also one in the German sub-system. Should however she attempt aggression by concentrating her resources in one area, she would weaken her influence in the other. Thus, involvement in the regional balance would involve constraints as well as opportunities.

This concern with sub-balances may have been the result of the fact that in the early period of balance of power politics, Europe did not in fact form a single political system. During the eighteenth century, as the sub-systems were steadily integrated within the larger concept of the European system, they gradually ceased to be of such concern to commentators on the balance. The major exception to this general trend was the German-speaking world, where the positions of Prussia and Austria, at the margins of East and West Europe, together with the conception of Germany forming a particular kind of balance in itself, led German thinkers to continue to study the question of inferior balances. The difference in approach to the balance of power this engendered would become significant during the nineteenth century.

SYSTEMS IN PRACTICE

Morton Kaplan and Richard Rosecrance both saw eighteenth-century Europe as a model for their systems approach to the balance of power. However, Evan Luard, in his 1992 study of that system was sceptical about the extent to which it truly functioned as a balance of power system. In a broad sense the system can be held to have worked. Regular responses did occur to curb the expanding powers within the system. The major challenge, that of France under Napoleon, was successfully overcome.

However, a number of caveats can be entered. The system protected only the *major* powers; lesser states disappeared or were substantially reduced. Moreover, on these occasions states engaged in a territorial feeding frenzy, rushing to join in the land-grab, rather than coming to the aid of the victim. Austria was a victim of such bandwagoning in 1740, as was Prussia in 1756. Even during the 'Great War' against France from 1792 to 1815, there was no consistent pattern of resistance to France. States combined not against aggression or expansion on principle, but against specific threats to their particular interests. For Luard, therefore, 'though there was a frequent *tendency* to combine against threats to the peace, it did not have the regularity and consistency which an effective system would have required ... actions were reactive rather than planned: a response to a domination already secured rather than a deliberate "systematic" attempt to prevent domination being won in the first place' (1992: 348).

It was not so much that a system did not exist in eighteenth-century Europe, but rather that it was far less coherent a system than was suggested at the time or subsequently. The century represented an important period in the political evolution of European international relations and is worthy of study for that reason.

5 The eighteenth century: 1700–1815

INTRODUCTION

The eighteenth century has been called 'the golden age of the balance of power', in theory as well as in practice (Morgenthau 1978: 196). It is certainly true that it was in this century that the greatest volume of literature on the balance of power appeared and that European diplomacy was characterised by a constant attention to the balance of power. According to Palmer and Perkins, 'the balance of power was a kind of thread running through the maze of alliances and counter-alliances, the frequent shifts in alignments, and the devious manoeuvres which marked the foreign policies of the great powers of that century' (1954: 318).

M. S. Anderson is even more forthright, declaring of the balance of power concept in the eighteenth century that,

> never before or since has it been the object of so much generally favourable discussion by so many different writers. Never before or since has a single idea been so clearly the organising principle in terms of which international relations in general were seen.
>
> (Anderson, 1993: 163)

Governments in this era assumed that states were driven by an urge to expand unless they were countered and increasingly the balance of power acquired strong positive moral connotations. Proponents of the principle argued that states had a positive moral duty to oppose the expansionist tendencies of aggressive states. The British government, having embraced this doctrine, projected an image of it as an onerous burden. The King's speech opening Parliament in 1732 spoke of 'perfecting and finishing this tedious work, conducted through a series of infinite changes and vicissitudes and encumbered with all the different views of interest and ambition ... calculated purely for preserving a due balance' (Cobbett, 1806–20, VIII: 868).

Historians and theorists of international relations have long argued that there were particular reasons why the balance of power flourished in eighteenth-century Europe. Perhaps the most systematic exposition of these reasons was given by Richard Rosecrance. Rosecrance identifies a number of key features of international relations in eighteenth-century Europe which he believed enabled the balance of power system to work effectively.

A key element was the absence of nationalism as a determining factor in foreign policy. There were a few nation-states, such as Portugal and the Dutch Republic, but these were very much the exception. Some states, like Britain, were still in the process of becoming nation-states, and the series of Jacobite and Irish risings during the century show that this process was far from complete. Many states, such as those in Italy and Germany, were sub-national – Bavaria, Württemberg, Saxony and Hanover mistrusted each other as much, if not more than they did non-German states like France, Britain and Spain. Other states, such as Prussia, Austria, Spain and Russia were multinational. These were large, sprawling political entities whose boundaries encompassed peoples of very varied national, religious and linguistic background. Because of this, the decision for or against allying with any particular state was largely uninfluenced by the prejudices of nationalism.

Indeed, among the European ruling classes the eighteenth century was characterised by a high degree of cosmopolitanism. Spain was ruled by a French monarch, Britain by a German, Prussia and Bavaria by Francophiles. All the continental armies contained large numbers of foreign troops, often whole regiments or corps, such as the Scots brigade in the Dutch Army and the Irish brigade of France. By the later stages of the Seven Years War a majority of soldiers serving in the Prussian Army were actually foreigners.

These factors were important because a balance of power system requires moderation in the pursuit of foreign policy objectives and the eighteenth century was characterised by such moderation. In comparison to the ferocious era of religious warfare seen the preceding century, and the turmoil of the revolutionary and Napoleonic wars which followed, the period between 1700 and 1792 seems restrained. The struggle for power was characterised by limited warfare and compromise peace settlements. It should be noted, however, that some of the later writers who heaped praise on the eighteenth-century balance of power, men such as Brougham, von

Gentz and Vattel, were writing during the Napoleonic era. Some of their arguments were coloured by an exaggerated view of the moderation inherent in the eighteenth century. The earlier age certainly seemed moderate in comparison with the turmoil of the age in which they wrote, but its moderate qualities should not be overplayed. The Austrian Succession and Seven Years Wars were bloody conflicts, in which the dismemberment of major powers was sought by some of the warring partners.

LIMITED WARFARE IN THE EIGHTEENTH CENTURY

One reason for the limited nature of the warfare, characterised by manoeuvre and siege rather than sanguinary battlefields, was that the armies of the day were expensive and brittle instruments. Most governments, operating from a limited tax-base (certain wealthy groups such as nobles and the church paid little or no tax) could afford only comparatively small armed forces. These were difficult to equip and train, and extremely expensive to replace. In order to avoid the destruction of these vital assets therefore, wars were fought for advantage, but were in no sense total wars.

The enormous expense involved in wars meant that whenever possible, states tried to achieve their aims without resort to war. The bribing of foreign ambassadors and the maintenance of elaborate intelligence networks was a feature of the age. Since, by its very nature, the system pursued the balancing of power, accurate information about the intentions of states and about their military capabilities, economic resources, political divisions and key personalities became a crucial requirement. It was an era of secret diplomacy and the widespread use of highly developed spying networks, and of diplomatic couriers and codes designed to ensure secrecy. However, since *all* the great powers were simultaneously engaged in activities of this sort, in practice no significant military or diplomatic development could be kept secret for long. Richer states subsidised poorer allies in order to allow them to maintain larger armies than would otherwise have been the case. Enormous sums were spent on bribes for critical elections, such as those for the King of Poland in the 1730s and the heir-apparent to the Holy Roman Emperor in the 1750s.

For Rosecrance

the conditions of social organisation, diplomacy, militarism and statesmanship in the eighteenth century led to the creation of a system of international relations which was unique in the history of statecraft and unlike any system functioning today. These conditions filled almost completely the ideal precepts for a balance of power mechanism.

(Rosecrance, 1963: 25)

This was so because a balance of power could not function without the existence of a state system, that is, in Gulick's words 'a group of independent neighbouring states more or less connected with one another' and of approximately equal power. It could not operate unless there existed a common outlook in terms of political attitude among the leaderships of the states in the system and a common concern to protect the system. It also required a limitation of warfare in order to preserve the key states making up the system. The eighteenth century met the requirements for a balance of power mechanism in all these ways and, as noted at the start of this chapter, the maxims of balance of power theory were seen as guiding principles to a greater degree than in any other era.

A further factor making for moderation in this era was the fact that ideology was not a driving force. There was nothing comparable to the religious intolerance and ruthlessness of the preceding century which spawned the ferocious Thirty Years War. Religious sentiment certainly existed, and governments such as Britain occasionally played on it in order to reinforce domestic support for their alliances, as they did, for example, with the Prussian alliance during the Seven Years War of 1756–63. But religious differences had not prevented Britain's alliance with France (1716–31) or with Austria (1702–56) throughout the period. The absence of such ideological prejudices did not reduce the energy devoted to the struggle for power in Europe, but it gave it a quite different character, in which restraint was imposed both by the conservatism of the major actors themselves and also by the workings of the balance of power system. War in this era was war between governments, not the total war, the war between peoples, of later centuries. It tended to be fought for concrete practical gains or for prestige, which was an important consideration in this era, not for ideologies or national survival. This was important because where war was not total, peace was easier to make. For Anderson, the balance of power concept was very much 'in tune' with the prevailing intellectual ethos. Its characteristic features such as the stress on rationality, calculation, moderation and adjustment, were 'congenial' (Anderson, 1993: 167).

According to Rosecrance, the spirit of internationalism which was so characteristic of the eighteenth century was itself reinforced by the working of the balance of power system. Under this system power was constantly fluctuating within the system and states were not limited in choosing diplomatic alignments with which to maintain the equilibrium. The regular changes in alliance partners encouraged a sense of belonging to a European international state system of which that state was only a single member. In addition, this sense of being part of a fluid system encouraged a recognition of the importance of the other states who made up the system.

Eighteenth-century writers suggested that many factors contributed towards the evolution of Europe into a single political 'system'. The British pamphleteer John Campbell, for example, believed that the European system was fundamentally based upon the complexity of the trading bonds between the European states, which had led to such a degree of economic interdependence that European states were forced to concern themselves with the fate of their neighbours and trading partners (Campbell, 1750: 24).

The eighteenth-century system had its limits, however. Unlike its nineteenth-century successor, it never developed into anything resembling a European concert of states. The conference which did take place at Cambrai in 1724 and which ran for four years in an attempt to resolve the differences between Austria and Spain, was unsuccessful. This was a major failing, for as contemporary commentators such as Bolingbroke pointed out, no balance of power could ever be permanent. It would always be subject to evolution brought about by dynastic failures or marriages, internal reforms, economic improvement or decay, none of which could justify a preemptive war. Therefore, in order to allow for occasional adjustments to the system, the self-help basis of the system really needed to be supplemented by some form of periodic international negotiation and by a degree of flexibility in allowing the major actors room for limited gains in influence or territory. Since it lacked the systematic conferences of the nineteenth century, the eighteenth-century system sought to avert general warfare by resort to a perplexing quadrille of minor wars, treaties and negotiations, supplemented by occasional regional conferences, but without ever evolving a degree of organisation comparable to the nineteenth-century Concert of Europe.

Although the states of Europe were frequently at war during the eighteenth century, it was a generally stable period in international relations. The balance of power system did not prevent war, indeed it was not part of its objectives to do so, but it did help to produce an era of limited wars. The outcomes of international politics remained within boundaries that were acceptable to the great powers. There were no *permanently* dissatisfied key actors in the European state system.

However, war did bring about important changes in the system. Prussia's attack on Austria in 1740 led to her acquiring great power status and similarly Russia's involvement in the mid-century wars in Western Europe gave her a place in the list of great powers. There was no hegemonic threat comparable to Louis XIV or Napoleon, but it was nevertheless an era characterised by wars which produced important changes in the fortunes of the major states of Europe. Spain and Austria were in fact deeply dissatisfied with the territorial arrangements for long periods in this era. Placid stability remained elusive. Change, not stasis, was the characteristic of the age.

In the eighteenth century war was very much an extension of politics. It was significant also that anti-militarist sentiment was quite marked in these decades, producing the great projects for universal peace proposed by the Abbé St Pierre and Kant and governments, such as those of Walpole in Britain and Fleury in France, which sought to avoid war rather than embrace it.

However, because the balance of power itself was increasingly seen in terms of natural rights and moral good, it was easy to justify going to war if doing so could be described as a defence of the balance. So frequently were particular wars defended in these terms, that for critics of the balance concept it became almost synonymous with war. Réal de Curban despaired of the 'streams of blood the balance of Europe, this new idol, has caused to be shed' (Anderson 1993: 176).

The need for moderation was emphasised in much of the theorising on the balance of power which appeared during the eighteenth century. Lord Bolingbroke, for example, called for restraint in entering into armed conflicts and moderation in the formulation and pursuit of war aims. Bolingbroke pointed out that not every conflict between European states was a threat to the balance of power and noted also that the exact state of equilibrium was, for practical reasons, never perfectly attainable.

Some of the criticism levelled at the balance of power concept in the eighteenth century was based on a failure to understand or accept this fundamental point. For some, the balance was something which ought to be attainable, and which would then maintain itself

indefinitely. The critics charged that if this was not possible, then the pursuit of the balance was a chimera, 'even more ridiculous than Crusades and combating Saracens for recovering the holy Sepulchre', because it could not be achieved (Shebbeare, 1755: 32–3).

Critics on these grounds looked always for the definitive treaty that would settle the balance for ever. But this was an impossibility. The dread behind these arguments was the fear that Europe might never again know peace. The British Member of Parliament William Wyndham expressed the fear most eloquently when he compared Britain as balancer to the mythical Penelope,

> continually weaving and unravelling the same Web; one time raising up the Emperor to depress France, and now we were for depressing the Emperor, which could not be done without aggrandising France, which, in the End, may make the latter too powerful: so that at this rate, under Pretence of holding the Balance of Europe, we should be engaged in continual Wars.
>
> (Chandler, 1742, VI: 377)

Bolingbroke clearly thought in terms of there being a European 'system', noting of the continental powers that their alliances were governed by circumstance and were therefore subject to change, 'and therefore, as a change in some of the parts of one system necessarily requires a change in all the rest; so the alteration of one system necessarily requires an alteration of the others' (Maurseth, 1964: 125). It was Bolingbroke also who pointed out that the pursuit of political equilibrium could never be an exact science, for

> the scales of the balance of power will never be exactly poised, nor is the precise point of equality either discernible or necessary to be discerned. It is sufficient in this, as in other human affairs, that the deviation be not too great. Some there will always be.
>
> (Maurseth, 1964: 125)

This particular interpretation of the balance of power reflected similar ideas prevailing in other fields of thought. For example, in 1776 Adam Smith in his *Wealth of Nations* argued that in the free market, competition between producers would create benefits to consumers. Smith's ideas were profoundly influenced by the earlier work of Bernard Mandeville, who had argued in 1714 that there was no necessary incompatibility between behaviour originating out of purely selfish motivations and the pursuit of a virtuous society (Kaye, 1924: xlvii). Mandeville's argument that something which produced benefits for all was inherently good, however selfish the original purpose, had a major impact upon British moral philosophy and economic theory during the eighteenth century. British advocacy of the balance of power system was grounded in a similar rationalisation of the benefits of the end result to the entire system.

This is a feature of thinking about the balance of power demonstrated in all eras. The concept is in a sense itself a metaphor, it is certainly continually expressed through analogy and metaphor. The seventeenth-century obsession with balance mechanisms and the British ideas about the benefits of competition show that the balance of power idea may have helped to shape the eras in which it was present, but it was also shaped by the thinking that was characteristic of those different eras.

Michael Mandelbaum (1988) has argued that the eighteenth-century balance of power was not overtly sought by the states involved in the system, but rather arose from 'the uncoordinated pursuit by each power of its own interest, which was defined, even above self-aggrandisement, as independence. The balance of power was the unintended outcome of these individual strivings' (Mandelbaum, 1988: 8). Independence, even with the concurrent risk of war, was seen as being preferable to peace through subservience.

Yet the concept of the balance of power was well understood throughout Europe during the eighteenth century and was referred to as a positive feature in important documents such as the Treaty of Utrecht of 1713 and the French guarantee of the Pragmatic Sanction in 1735 by the Treaty of Vienna. By mid-century the term 'balance of power' had become so well understood that it could be incorporated in a humorous turn of phrase in the British Parliament (Cobbett, 1806–20, XII: 319) or used as a vehicle for satire (Anon, 1741). In fact, as Anderson has noted, by the middle of the century pamphleteers and historians were agreed not only that the balance of power safeguarded the peace and freedom of Europe and should therefore be the objective of intelligent statesmanship, but also that the system was of a certain antiquity, having existed since the French invasion of Italy in 1494. In this latter belief they were mistaken, but it is evidence nevertheless of the esteem in which the balance of power idea was held, that thinkers should seek to identify it in earlier eras.

This is not to say that the concept held a concrete and unambiguous meaning for all its users or that the implications of the theory had been fully investigated and understood. In important areas the ambiguities of the concept were not properly explored or reconciled. An example of this is the question of the minor or local balances which were felt to be an important element in the overall balance.

But as noted in the previous chapter, little effort was made to show what role these 'particular' or 'inferior' balances played within the overall European one.

Nor was much thought given to the contradiction between the eighteenth-century attitudes to balance of power as a system and as foreign policy. The former was self-sustaining, essentially a product of nature and morally neutral. The latter had positive moral connotations and was seen as something which *ought* to exist and *ought* to be worked for. For the most part it was the latter conception which was the more strongly held. The balance was too vulnerable to chance and the random effects of government policies for its maintenance to be left to natural forces (Black, 1983: 57).

THE WAR OF THE SPANISH SUCCESSION

The War of the Spanish Succession which opened the eighteenth century was essentially a 'coalition' war with the object of containing French expansionism. It also provided the stage for the emergence of Britain as 'balancer' of the European system. Though the utility of being the holder of the balance had been discussed in earlier writings, so long as Britain was simply one part of an alliance engaged in a deadly struggle with powerful France, ideas of this sort were simply speculations, since Britain had no actual room for diplomatic manoeuvre. It was the accession of Charles VI as Holy Roman Emperor at a time when war-weariness was becoming strongly evident in Britain that made it possible for Britain to adopt a genuine balancer role. Britain, in its stated war aims, was fighting France on the grounds that only one sickly youth stood between Philip V of Spain and the French throne. A unified Franco-Spanish kingdom was seen as being overwhelmingly powerful and therefore the allies were committed to supporting Archduke Charles, the younger brother to the heir to the Austrian throne, as King of Spain.

In 1705 Emperor Leopold died and was succeeded by his son Joseph. However, in 1711 Joseph died without having produced an heir and was therefore succeeded in turn by his brother, the Archduke Charles. Britain and the other minor allies now found themselves fighting to place the Austrian Emperor on the throne of Spain, a prospect no more pleasing than having France and Spain united. Jonathan Swift's *Conduct of the Allies* was published in 1711 to help persuade the nation to support the idea of a separate peace with France. Swift described the possible union of Spain and the Austrian empire as 'a dreadful consideration and directly opposite to that wise principle on which the Eighth Article of the Grand Alliance is founded'.

Austria's emergence as a potential threat to Europe's liberty produced a re-evaluation of the balancer role in Britain, and encouraged a more profound analysis of the balance of power as a guiding principle. Daniel Defoe, for example, amplified Halifax's explanation of power drives originating in the nature of the state system. Unlike most writers on the balance of power, Defoe believed that it acted as a deterrent to war by making the costs disproportionate to the gains.

Defoe's major contribution to the development of thinking about the balancer role, and a crucial contribution as far as British experience in the following half-century was concerned, was his insight into the need to remain *permanently* devoted to the maintenance of that position, which could only be done by regarding *all* attempts to disturb the balance with equal hostility, no matter what quarter they came from. This would mean not only, as Halifax and others had noted, that there could be no permanent friends or permanent enemies, but also that the very nature of the balancing process would tend to turn Britain's hostile attention towards her most recent allies. Once the aggressive state or alliance of the day had been defeated,

> it ceases to be any more the object either of Jealousy or Resentments of the rest, but if any of the united Powers erect themselves upon the ruin of that or by any other method set themselves up too high, the Nuisance is transposed to that Power, which before it was thought convenient to assist, and it becomes as necessary to the rest to reduce that Power or Prince, as it was before to reduce the other.

> (Wright, 1975: 49)

This was written in 1706, and in the same piece Defoe goes on to warn of the danger of one of the Grand Alliance states assuming such a position once France was defeated. By 1711 the danger had arisen, but Defoe's warning was also to be appropriate in the later crises of the middle 1720s and early 1730s and between the two great mid-century wars. The change of circumstances in 1711 meant that Britain no longer felt committed to the war aims developed before 1705, since from a balance of power perspective, supporting Charles VI of Austria's claims to the Spanish throne was little or no better than supporting those of Philip V.

The Peace of Utrecht of 1713 brought into being a balance of power system in Europe. Despite Spain's hostility to the Utrecht arrangements, they provided the basis of a balance which was sustained, largely through diplomacy rather than war, for a generation. In the first half of the eighteenth century, despite the multiplicity of states there was an essentially bipolar balance between France and Austria. After 1740 however the emergence of Prussia and Russia as European great powers made the balance far more complex. It was indeed the irruption of Prussia into the group of major powers and the aggression and desire for territorial expansion of its ruler Frederick II, which was the prime factor in the destabilisation of the state system in mid-century, when Europe was rocked by the War of the Austrian Succession (1740–8) and the Seven Years War (1756–63).

The peace treaties of 1713–14 sought to contain France and Austria by promoting a series of buffer states in Germany, Italy and the low countries. But these buffer states were powerless without the support of one of the two leading powers or of Britain, which had assumed the role of 'balancer' of the system. Indeed, in 1727 the British government, in the annual Mutiny Act, described the purpose of Britain's army as being 'the preservation of the balance of power in Europe', a formula that was retained until 1867 (Wight, 1973: 98).

European diplomacy in the eighteenth century is a tortuous maze which is extremely difficult to navigate without a guiding thread. The feature which gives meaning and pattern to the complex diplomacy of this era is the balance of power principle. The balance of power idea appealed to many eighteenth-century statesmen and thinkers precisely because it appeared to provide a method of systematising foreign policy and of comprehending the complexities of European international politics. In an age which believed in progress and enlightenment, it was not surprising that there was a desire to obtain the same certainty and predictability in the study of international politics as had increasingly become the case with the natural sciences. Moreover, the balance of power could be seen as taking 'the Government of the World out of the hands of Providence, and Entrust it to our own Skill and Management' (Anderson, 1993: 180) an attractive idea for the Age of Reason.

THE EIGHTEENTH-CENTURY SYSTEM IN OPERATION

In 1716 Britain began negotiations with France for the conclusion of an alliance. The negotiations were successful and the treaty was signed in December 1716. When the Dutch United Provinces acceded in January 1717 this became the Triple Alliance. The Anglo-French alliance represented a dramatic change of policy for both states.

England and France had been traditional enemies for centuries; England under William III had been the focus of the coalitions against France during the War of the League of Augsburg and the War of the Spanish Succession. Only the previous year France had given material aid to the Jacobite rising in Scotland. The agreement was therefore highly controversial in both countries.

Nevertheless, both Britain and France had much to gain from the agreement. Each had been isolated by the negotiations which led to the signing of the Treaty of Utrecht, and both had dynasties whose hold on power was uncertain. Britain was threatened by the possibility of another Jacobite insurrection, for which French support would be crucial, while France itself was ruled by a regent, because the sickly Louis XV had succeeded to the throne in 1715 at the age of only 5. In fact, the Anglo-French alliance lasted as a genuine factor in international politics until 1731, by which time Louis XV was 21 and had produced an heir. The Anglo-French alliance was described by Richard Lodge as 'quite as deserving to be called a diplomatic revolution as the Austro-French alliance of 1756, to which the term is usually applied'.

The Anglo-French alliance of 1716–31 was instrumental in developing the 'European' foreign policy views of Britain and France in this period. During the long wars with Louis XIV virtually every state in Europe had eventually become either susceptible to French influence or hostile to it. As Britain had attained a leading position in the Grand Alliance, she had pursued a policy of active diplomacy aimed at the anti-French states. Thus, by 1716 virtually every state in Europe was susceptible to some degree of influence by *either* Britain *or* France.

In seeking to construct a European system and integrate the sub-balances into it, therefore, the French diplomatic network almost perfectly complemented the British. Moreover, since British military power was essentially sea-based, while French power was land-based, their military resources were also complementary.

In 1717 the Triple Alliance came into being between Britain, France and the Dutch Republic. A year later the accession of Austria transformed it into the Quadruple Alliance. The terms under which the Quadruple Alliance was formed effectively attempted to tie up the diplomatic loose ends left by the Treaty of Utrecht and, moreover, the governments involved agreed to meet at a congress to be held at Cambrai to finalise the details. In the first half of the eighteenth century the balance of power was envisaged in what a later century would call 'bipolar' terms. On the one side was France and her allies, on the other was Austria and her allies. The Quadruple Alliance was itself a diplomatic revolution, because it attempted to transcend this bipolar model and create an overwhelming preponderance for the post-Utrecht *status quo*. When Spain challenged the Utrecht settlements in Italy in 1718–19, the Quadruple Alliance defeated her with overwhelming force and obliged her to agree to the holding of a congress to produce a permanent settlement based on the terms laid down by the Quadruple Alliance. The Anglo-French undertaking which lay at its heart produced diplomatic settlements to a number of other outstanding disputes. The Anglo-French alliance made possible the series of treaties which brought peace to the Baltic, ended the Austro-Turkish war and crushed the Spanish attempt to undermine the Utrecht settlement in Italy.

The eighteenth century offers some parallels to the nineteenth, therefore. In both, a major coalition war against a state deemed to have hegemonic aspirations resulted in the defeat of the expansionist state and the international community affirmed the desirability of maintaining a balance of power. A major treaty attempted to create the basis for such a system. The former danger state was then re-admitted to the international community which subsequently attempted to fine-tune the arrangements by consensus through periodic congresses. The eighteenth-century version was neither as structured nor as long lasting as its nineteenth-century equivalent, but nevertheless the parallels are there. With the Treaty of Nystadt in 1721, which ended the Great Northern War in the Baltic, Europe was stabilised and at peace and her peace was founded on a balance of power in the sense that none of the major powers was significantly more powerful than its rivals.

France had been saved from a catastrophic peace in 1713–14 by Britain, which had abandoned its Austrian ally because of her pretensions to the Spanish Empire. Britain had felt no desire to revive the empire of Charles V for Charles VI. The settlement arrived at by 1721 limited this danger by dividing the Bourbon house into a French and a Spanish branch and by ending the Habsburg claim to Spain. Nevertheless, the period between 1715 and 1740 was characterised by a series of crises and minor wars, produced by the absence of a true 'Concert of Europe'.

Thus, according to Penfield Roberts, in order for the balance of power to function effectively it needed to be

supplemented by some form of periodic consultation and negotiation among the great powers, and by some degree of willingness to allow every strong power at least a little scope for its ambition to add to its territories and its influence. The perplexing series of minor wars, negotiations, conferences, congresses and treaties between 1715 and 1740 merely reflected an unorganised and chaotic effort to achieve a Concert of Europe which might avert another *general* conflict by a more or less tacitly agreed upon division of the available spoils among the strong powers.

(Roberts, 1947: 3)

Pollard argued that it was not

a balance of power so much as a community of power which ordinary monarchs needed to express their common interest against the aspirant to monopoly; and early in the eighteenth century this common interest attempted to express itself in a series of European Congresses.

(Pollard, 1923: 54)

The notion of a 'community of power' expresses the idea well. It was this Grotian conception which was still largely current during the years immediately following the War of the Spanish Succession.

The statesman who continued the Quadruple Alliance, notably the British and French premiers Stanhope and Dubois, were seeing the 'European equilibrium' less as a mechanism which guaranteed opposition to a preponderant power and more as a device for preserving a general *status quo* amenable to evolutionary change. It was a conception close to that put forward by Friedrich von Gentz in 1806 – that the balance of power is a

constitution subsisting among neighbouring states more or less connected with one another; by virtue of which no-one among them can injure the independence or the essential rights of another, without meeting with effectual resistance on some side, and consequently exposing itself to danger.

(Forsyth, Keens-Soper and Savigear, 1970: 281)

Von Gentz also noted that such a system of balance would be better described as one of *counterpoise*, 'for perhaps the highest of its results is not so much a perfect *equipoise* as a constant vacillation in the scales of the balance, which from the application of *counterweights* is prevented from ever passing certain limits' (ibid.: 284).

But there were clear limits to what constituted a reasonable extension of territory or influence. Prussia's hunger for major territorial expansion under Frederick II, which struck both at the Habsburg

Empire and the smaller German states was the major factor in disrupting the balance of power established by 1721.

The balance of power system was attractive to British statesmen such as Stanhope and Townshend, with their boundless energy and combative characters, and this might have owed something to the influence of the contemporary British political system where there was antagonism and struggle in everything, where check and counter-check was the principle of the constitution. However, to work it required engaged, energetic diplomatic leadership, and in the 1730s with the advent of more cautious leaders such as Walpole in Britain and Cardinal Fleury in France, it could not be sustained.

There were no major European wars between 1715 and 1740, but a number of wars did take place which exemplify the vulnerabilities of the eighteenth-century balance of power system. In 1733 war broke out between Austria and France over the issue of the succession to the elective throne of Poland. Austria and Russia were able to ensure that 'their' candidate, Augustus III of Saxony, became king rather than Stanislas Leszczyski, the French favourite. This was a blow to French prestige. However, in the campaigns in the West an alliance of France, Spain and Sardinia inflicted a series of defeats on the Austrian forces in Italy. France also had the better of the fighting on the Rhine, though it won no striking successes. The war was eventful in that for the first time in history, Russian troops appeared in Western Europe, fighting alongside the Austrians. The Polish Succession War ended in 1738. Even before it was over, Austria became embroiled in a second important conflict, this time with the Ottoman Turkish Empire.

The war between Turkey and the Austro-Russian alliance lasted from 1736 till 1739. Its course demonstrated the increasing interdependence of Eastern and Western Europe, the growing power of Russia and the vulnerabilities of Austria. Austria and Russia had concluded a military alliance in 1726. By 1736 both states were keen to make territorial acquisitions at the expense of the Turks. Russia attacked at once, while Austria waited till 1737. Though the Russians, after early setbacks, eventually made significant gains, Austria endured a series of military disasters, which led her to conclude a separate peace with the Turks, at which she surrendered many of the gains she had made in the previous generation.

The Polish Succession War had demonstrated that the balance of power established between 1714 and 1721 was becoming steadily more difficult to sustain. It lacked the structured basis to cope with the strains produced by a dynastic succession crisis in one of the major states. A crisis in a minor actor such as Poland could be coped with without a general war, though even Poland had produced campaigns on the Rhine, in Italy and in the Baltic region. A succession crisis in a major actor, however, would produce a major war, as the failure of the Habsburg line in Spain produced the War of the Spanish Succession. In 1740 the death of Emperor Charles VI plunged Europe into a new succession crisis and revealed for the first time the new power of Prussia.

The international system in 1740 was anarchic, with powers left free to expand until checked by the mechanisms of the balance of power. Prussia in 1740 was not a recognised great power and her expansion to that point had raised no fears among the major powers in Europe. Her *Blitzkrieg* attack on Austria in 1740 raised fears, not so much of Prussian expansionism as of the damage being done to Austria, which was seen as one of the two pillars of the traditional European balance of power. The emergence of Prussia, and within a few years, of Russia, were to decisively shatter that bipolar concept of the balance and replace it with a much more complex multipolar one.

On 20 October 1740 Emperor Charles VI died. Despite having signed the Pragmatic Sanction guaranteeing the succession in the Habsburg territories to Maria Theresa, the late Emperor's daughter, Prussia, Bavaria and Saxony soon found excuses for repudiating their engagements. On 23 December 1740 Prussia invaded the rich Austrian province of Silesia. France promptly began seeking allies for the purpose of partitioning Habsburg territories in Germany, while Spain laid claim to the Austrian possessions in Italy.

Frederick II of Prussia believed that expansionism was forced upon Prussia by her exposed strategic position. Silesia was a richer province than any of Prussia's existing ones and its acquisition would materially strengthen the state. Frederick calculated (correctly as it turned out) that the other great powers would not object to Austria losing territory, so long as it did not go to one of the existing great powers. In a debate in the House of Lords in November 1740, the Duke of Newcastle declared that the maintenance of the balance of power in Europe depended, not so much on the preservation of the Habsburg territories intact, as on ensuring that no powerful state in Europe gained too large a proportion of them. The Prussian victory at Mollwitz in April 1741 led to Bavaria, Saxony, Savoy and Spain putting forward territorial claims against the Habsburg Austrian Empire. By the end of 1741 French and Bavarian forces had overrun and occupied Bohemia and Upper Austria. The political impact of their presence meant that in early 1742 the Electoral Duke of Bavaria, Charles Albert, was elected King of Bohemia, recognised as Archduke of Austria by the estates of Upper Austria and unanimously elected Holy Roman Emperor, as Charles VII on 24 January 1742. Even George II of Britain, in his role as Elector of Hanover, signed a neutrality agreement with France and voted for Charles Albert as emperor.

However, the French-led alliance soon began to break up, riven by mutual suspicions. In return for Silesia, Prussia made peace with Austria in 1742. Austria reorganised her forces and drove her enemies from Bohemia. However, in 1744 Prussia re-entered the war and forced Austria to re-affirm its loss of Silesia. In the same year Charles Albert died. His successor made peace with Austria and Empress Maria Theresa's husband was elected Holy Roman Emperor. However, despite this, Prussia was clearly the main victor in the war, reducing Austria's power and greatly increasing her own.

The rise of Prussia was not just the result of Frederick II's aggressive nature. It was due also, in very large part to the reforms within Prussia carried out by his predecessors over the previous century, and particularly during the reign of his father Frederick William I. Frederick William had created a strong, centralised state and a powerful, well-trained army, four times the size of Britain's. Through his careful husbanding of the state's resources, Frederick William also bequeathed his son a healthy budget surplus. It was left to Frederick II to complete his father's work by using the powerful state and army he had inherited to establish Prussia among the first rank of the European powers, a process that was completed between 1740 and 1763 in the course of two major European wars. Nevertheless, the largely unnoticed rise of Prussia between 1700 and 1740 demonstrates a feature of the balance of power system in this and other centuries, that the balance of power is constantly dynamic, not just because states can expand and contract in terms of territory, but also because, through their own efforts they can develop and prosper or decay and decline internally. While Prussia developed, the historic power of Spain was in steady and irreversible decline. This reality is important, because while territorial changes produce clear diplomatic responses in the balance of power system, it was and is by no means clear whether the 'rules' of the balance of power justify intervention against a state whose growing strength is due entirely to *internal* development. The *logic* of the balance of power approach says it does, but this would imply a right of interference in the internal affairs of other states which goes against one of the fundamental precepts of international law as it has evolved since 1648.

This uncomfortable problem was largely ignored by eighteenth-century writers on the balance of power, or finessed by suggesting that internal reform was somehow inherently less threatening than a power growth based upon territorial expansion. Eighteenth-century writers and diplomats were well aware of the importance of internal factors, however, and argued that they had to be taken into account in international relations. Power assessments based upon a state's ability to mobilise power through reform or by over-coming internal political strife were seen as being highly significant (Black, 1983: 58–9).

Prussia's successes in the Austrian Succession War had made her many enemies, including some of her erstwhile allies such as France, which had twice been deserted by Prussia during the war. Austria and Saxony were determined to gain revenge on Prussia, while Russia was increasingly hostile and was interested in making terri-torial gains at Prussia's expense.

The most dramatic result of the diplomacy of this period was the alliance between France and Austria. This was a most surprising development, since for nearly a century France and Austria had been the two poles of a bipolar balance of power system. Each sought the alliance to insure themselves for a struggle against the state which each saw as its real enemy. In the case of France this was Britain; in Austria's case it was Prussia.

The alliance was difficult to achieve, since Prussia had been an ally of France for decades, while Austria had been an ally of Britain for seventy years. It was only when France decided in May 1756 that war with Britain was inevitable that she overcame her doubts and concluded an alliance with Austria. Since she was unwilling to be dragged into an aggressive war for the recovery of Silesia, France sought to make this a defensive alliance only. Austria, already allied with Russia and Saxony, was now in a position to gain revenge upon Prussia (Luard, 1992: 80). In the war which followed, the newly allied Britain and Prussia were the clear victors. Prussia with British aid fought its enemies to a standstill, suffering enormous losses in men and material, but emerging with her earlier territorial gains intact. Outside Europe, Britain made huge gains, acquiring Canada, new possessions in the Caribbean and Africa and securing a dominant position in India.

The sweeping British colonial gains in the Seven Years War high-light a feature of eighteenth-century balance of power thinking. As the century progressed, increasing attention began to be paid to the question of the colonial and commercial empires of the great powers. It was clear that the wealth derived from their trade and colonies was a crucial element in the ability of states such as Britain to exercise their role in the European balance of power. The question this begged, however, was that of whether or not balance thinking should be applied directly to colonial questions. In other words, should there be a balance of power overseas as well as in Europe?

In this context Liska (1977: 12) has argued that the balance of power tends to operate one-sidedly in favour of a sea power endowed with strategic security. This is because over the course of a protracted conflict the disposable resources of land powers tend to become stalemated. By contrast, naval superiority tends to advance almost to the point of monopoly.

It was to just this tendency that France, so often the victim of Britain's balancing policies, tried to draw attention. French ministers argued that if 'universal monarchy' was a possibility, then it was most likely to appear through the application of overwhelming naval strength. Yet, as the Duc de Choiseul noted bitterly, 'the English, while pretending to protect the balance on land which no-one threatens, are entirely destroying the balance at sea which no-one defends' (Parkinson, 1977: 51). French writers therefore called for a colonial and maritime balance of power to complement the territorial balance of power in Europe (Anderson, 1993: 172).

The absence of any sustained debate over the issue of a naval and colonial balance is interesting. One of the features of the international system over the past 500 years has been the steady advance of the process of 'globalisation'. As a phenomenon it is a feature which commands attention. Yet the voluminous balance of power literature is almost completely silent on the issue. The balance of power concept for some 200 years after its confirmation as the basis of the European state system remained a purely European phenomenon. Its logic was not applied beyond the boundaries of the European continent. This may have been because the strongest proponent of the theory, Britain, had the most to lose from such a development. It may also have been related to the fact that that the European balance of power idea was, in terms of its origins, part of a peculiarly European solution to the problems afflicting the European imagination. Its extension beyond the frontiers of Europe was therefore by no means as obvious a development as it might have seemed to a later century.

In 1763, as in 1715, Europe reverted to a situation of fairly stable peace. But this period saw a crucial development in relations between the great powers which was highly controversial, both to advocates and opponents of balance of power policies. In 1770 discussions occurred between Russia and Prussia concerning the acquisition of territory by both at the expense of the Kingdom of Poland. The proposal was acceded to by Austria and led in August 1772 to the First Partition Treaty, by which Poland lost 30 per cent of her territory and 35 per cent of her population to her rapacious neighbours. The first Partition of Poland fatally undermined the claim that one of the advantages of the balance of power system was that it maintained the independence of all the states in the system. As Sorel noted, its true nature was now revealed, for if the balance of power system 'often required that the powerful states which were aggressive should be contained, it seldom suggested help for the weak states which might be despoiled' (Sorel, 1969: 60). While at first Prussia was indifferent, Frederick II noted of the territories seized by Austria and Russia 'if they pretend to keep them, they surely authorise the other neighbours of Poland to think about declaring their rights to do the same'. Prussia joined in the partition on 25 July 1772. Neither Britain nor France attempted to intervene on Poland's behalf.

THE CHALLENGE OF NAPOLEON

The revolutionary and Napoleonic period does not fit neatly into a study of either the eighteenth- or nineteenth-century balance of power systems. Yet it was the agent of the change from one system to the other. During the revolutionary period the classical eighteenth-century balance of power was overthrown. France's territorial gains were significant but not outrageous. She surrounded herself in addition with a cordon of client states covering northern Italy, Switzerland and Holland.

Opposition to France by the other great powers was based not just upon eighteenth-century balance of power considerations, but also upon the conservative states' fear of the ideological threat represented by the French Revolution. These considerations prompted the creation of a number of anti-French alliances, orchestrated by Britain in an attempt to limit or even reverse France's gains.

In January 1805 Britain and Russia were engaged in negotiating the construction of a third coalition against Napoleon. The British

Prime Minister, William Pitt wrote to Vorontsov, the Russian envoy, outlining his views on the construction of an alliance and on the post-war security order he hoped to see in Europe once Napoleon was defeated. His views were extremely radical, particularly given that at this date Napoleon had not yet even begun the campaign of 1805 which would eventually lay Europe at his feet.

Pitt called for France to be

> returned to her old boundaries, Holland strengthened, Prussia brought forward in Western Germany to act as the main rampart in the barrier against France, and a general strengthening of Austria and Prussia in order to equip them to serve as a solid core in the centre of the continent, able to resist aggression from east or west.
>
> (Gulick, 1955: 142)

Pitt felt that, even with all these territorial revisions, Europe would not become secure unless some mechanism could be devised for making the new equilibrium permanent. To make it secure, he proposed accepting an earlier Russian proposal for making the wartime alliance a permanent institution. The major powers' alliance would commit them to protect and support each other against any attempt to infringe their rights and territories. The alliance would act as what a later century would call a 'collective security system', responding together against any member which committed an act of aggression. This proposal represented a major refinement of the haphazard alliance system used to maintain the balance of power during the eighteenth century. It demonstrates the degree to which statesmen using the phrase 'balance of power' in Europe frequently had in mind a much more complex social equilibrium than that represented by a simple military balance. In this sense, the term should be seen as comprehending a number of points along the spectrum from true anarchy to an effective collective security system.

Under Napoleon's leadership France dramatically extended its dominance of Europe, expanding its territory and those of its client satellites on a major scale. French control extended from southern Spain to the Baltic, and the major powers who had made up the eighteenth-century balance of power were beaten into submission. Austria was defeated in two wars and turned into an unwilling French ally, with its territory dramatically reduced. Prussia suffered catastrophic defeat in 1806–7 and lost the greater part of her territory. Spain was occupied by French armies and Napoleon's brother Joseph sat on the throne in Madrid. Only Britain and Russia, on the periphery of the continent, remained capable of challenging French domination. Napoleon's empire was the gravest threat to the European state system since the sixteenth-century Habsburg empire of Charles V. The European balance of power system was destroyed in the dramatic French victories of 1805–7 and it was left to Britain to attempt to construct a coalition capable of defeating France and restoring the balance of power system in Europe. Such a coalition only became feasible after the disastrous failure of Napoleon's invasion of Russia in 1812. The French army was destroyed in Russia and Russia's armies pursued the broken French beyond Russia's borders and into Western Europe, giving Prussia and Austria the confidence to declare war on France once more and to form, with Britain, a new coalition aimed at defeating Napoleon's hegemonic France and restoring a balance of power in Europe. Russia's policy in 1812–13

> was impeccably equilibrist in nature: it was calculated to overthrow the preponderant power of France which threatened the survival of the state system; it was directed toward a reduction of that power to a size compatible with the safety of neighbouring states; and it was based, consciously or unconsciously, on a concern with the preservation of the state system as a means toward achieving a balance of power in Europe.
>
> (Gulick, 1955: 106–7)

The initial peace proposals to France called for dissolution of the Confederation of the Rhine and the Duchy of Warsaw, the enlargement of Prussia and Austria and the loss by France of her territories in northwest Germany. Russia felt that the proposals did not sufficiently reduce France and that she would remain a dominant first-among-equals. The allies were in agreement that French power needed to be reduced and a new overall equilibrium established, but they found it much harder to agree upon the particular form that the equilibrium should take. In the event, Napoleon rejected the peace proposal. In June 1813 the Treaty of Reichenbach between Russia, Austria and Prussia defined the objective of the alliance as being 'the re-establishment of a state of equilibrium and lasting peace in Europe'. The separate treaties between the various alliance partners echoed these sentiments.

Gulick makes the interesting point that, in drawing up these war aims, the allied statesmen hoped to elicit public enthusiasm and support and they were published with that aim in mind. Clearly, it was thought that the appeal to the balance of power principle would be received in a positive way by the peoples of Europe. This is evidence that in this period the balance was a vehicle for idealism. 'Later in the nineteenth century, support of balance-of-power theory was more likely to be interpreted as evidence of cynicism or a harsh "realism" ' (Gulick, 1955: 129).

Indeed, France, recognising the centrality of the balance of power concept in allied thinking, attempted to play upon this in its diplomatic response to the allied peace proposals. France insisted that it too believed that any eventual peace settlement should have as its objective the establishment of an 'equilibrium' in Europe that would prevent the preponderance of any state.

Napoleon was an imperialist, and the French note, which was echoed in subsequent French diplomatic correspondence, reflected not Napoleon's personal beliefs, but rather his understanding of the objectives and value-system of the allied statesmen with whom he was dealing. The allied objectives were clearly equilibrist in character and are demonstrated in the Declaration of Frankfurt of 1 December 1813, which was a classic example of balance of power thinking. The allies stated that their struggle was not against France, but against French preponderance outside France. The British Foreign Minister, Castlereagh, believed that France should be given a moderate peace, one which paid full respect to France's legitimate interests as a great power, and a vital component of the European state system (Derry, 1976: 155).

In March 1814, in the Treaty of Chaumont, the Allied Powers took the step which William Pitt had suggested a decade earlier. Under Article 16 of the Treaty, the wartime alliance against Napoleon was turned into an alliance which would last for 20 years and could be renewed for further periods before it expired. This treaty created the framework for a peacetime great power coalition to maintain the balance of power.

As Gulick has argued, such an idea was not new in Europe, indeed, balance of power theorists had been commending it for over a century.

> Fénelon, the Abbé de Saint Pierre, de Réal, Ségur, Vattel and Wolff had all described it in the eighteenth century. More recently, Brougham, Koch, Vogt and von Gentz had discussed it in their books. In short, the idea had been alive for a century. Nevertheless its practical application was new. While there are earlier expressions of the theory of an automatic peacetime coalition to

preserve the balance of power, there are no earlier treaties in European history which embody it, and in detail.

(Gulick, 1955: 155)

As is often the case, the statesmen of 1814–15 constructed a post-war order designed with a greater regard to the past than to the future, strongly influenced by the experiences of 1792–1815. But they also sought to correct the weakness of the pre-1792 system.

The lesson statesmen had learned from a quarter of a century of warfare was that Europe needed a mechanism for creating an automatic coalition against aggression in the post-war order. The post-war alliance and 'concert' system can be seen as representing an evolution of earlier equilibrist theory and practice. The eighteenth-century system had been characterised by loose coordination. The new post-Napoleonic order would be characterised by a significantly greater degree of organisation.

6 The nineteenth century: 1815–1914

INTRODUCTION

The final defeat of Napoleon I in 1815 ended the greatest threat to the Westphalian state system that it had faced since its birth in the mid-seventeenth century. Napoleon's downfall had been encompassed by a wartime alliance, the Fourth Coalition, which had proved remarkably effective in combining and coordinating the military and diplomatic efforts of France's enemies and directing them towards a common end. The great issue facing the allied statesmen in 1815 was the desire to create a post-war system of international relations which could serve to constrain international violence and prevent the emergence of a new threat as menacing as Napoleonic France had been.

In this they were surprisingly successful. The nineteenth century stands in stark contrast to the revolutionary period which preceded it and the era of global 'total warfare' which followed it, in that it was characterised by an underlying stability and an absence of systemic warfare. The wars of the period were fought for limited objectives and were geographically localised. When in 1848–9 Austria came to the edge of disintegration, it was Russian support which enabled her to survive. In 1871 when Paris was under the control of the revolutionary commands, the victorious Prussian forces stood back and allowed the French government's troops to suppress the revolution with brutal force.

The nineteenth-century system was multipolar in form, dominated by a small group of great powers, numbering five for most of the period. The leading states were Austria-Hungary, Britain, Prussia/Germany, Russia and France. This group of states were clearly distinguished from the second- and third-rate powers of the period. Their status reflected their perceived economic and military strength.

The criteria for great power status remained that of the ability to wage war against other great powers with a reasonable prospect of success. In assessing power with a view to establishing balances, statesmen continued to think overwhelmingly in terms of population and territory, the two being related.

The great powers were keen to preserve their distinctive status and were reluctant to accept the claims of new states aspiring to this ranking. At the end of the century Italy wished to be accepted among the ranks of the great powers, but was never truly successful in this regard, while throughout the period the Ottoman Empire was never fully accepted as a member of the European system, despite the fact that the 1856 Treaty of Paris described her as being part of the Concert of Europe.

Some writers have argued that the nineteenth-century concert system was not a development of balance practice but rather represented a quite different approach to international security. Fay for example, argued that 'the idea of the Concert of Powers is fundamentally different from the balance of power principle. The Concert aims to secure harmony and cooperation by conciliation and by minimising the tendency of the powers to group into opposing combinations' (Fay, 1937: 153–4).

However, this interpretation ignores the attitudes and objectives of the statesmen who designed the concert system. They did so with the explicit and publicly announced objective of creating and sustaining an effective balance of power system. It was 'deeply rooted in the balance of power tradition of Europe' (Gulick, 1955: 157).

The experience of the previous thirty years had demonstrated to the statesmen of Europe, not that the balance of power system should be abolished or replaced, but rather that it needed to be refined and modernised in the light of new conditions. However, there is no doubt that the Concert differed significantly from the balance policies of the previous century.

Joseph Nye has argued (1993: 57–8) that the nineteenth-century balance of power system can be sub-divided for analytical purposes into five reasonably distinct periods, based on process. The first period, 1815 to 1822 was the true 'concert' period, based upon great power cooperation. This system continued in a less structured form, in the second period, 1822 to 1854. It was succeeded by an era of conflict and war from 1854 to 1870 until this was superseded by the Bismarckian period, 1870 to 1890, when Bismarck played balance of power politics through a flexible alliance system. The final period, 1890 to 1914, saw a growing rigidity in the alliance system leading to the polarisation of Europe and the outbreak of war between the great powers in 1914.

Like Nye, Craig and George (1990: 28) have suggested that the nineteenth century cannot be usefully analysed in terms of the operation of a single balance of power approach. Rather, it should be seen in terms of three variants tried at different points in the century. The first of these was the 'Vienna system' which emerged at the close of the Napoleonic Wars and which characterised European diplomacy for the subsequent 40 years. The second version was that devised and operated by the German Chancellor Otto von Bismarck in the 1870s and 1880s, and the third was that which characterised the period after Bismarck's dismissal in 1890. The best-known and certainly most effective of these three variants was the 'concert system' which emerged from the Congress of Vienna in 1815.

THE CONCERT SYSTEM

The Vienna settlement was a system-creating exercise similar to the peace settlements of Utrecht (1713) and Versailles (1919), though it had a more lasting success than either of the others. It was similar in that its creators were attempting to recast the European order to give it greater stability and make it more resistant to the danger of a state seeking to dominate the continent. There are clear parallels between the work of the diplomats at Vienna and those who ended the War of the Spanish Succession with the treaties of Utrecht, Radstadt and Baden in 1713–14, most notably in the effort to design a self-sustaining balance of power.

A second historical parallel is with the victorious allies of 1945 and their creation of the United Nations Organisation, an attempt to institutionalise the successful wartime alliance and carry forward into the peace the habit of cooperation between the great powers of the era. Similarly, in the aftermath of the defeat of Napoleon, the leaders of the Fourth Coalition, led by Castlereagh of Britain, and Metternich of Austria, were seeking to determine how far the successful wartime alliance could be 'transformed into some rudimentary international organisation to safeguard the peace and the equilibrium' (Bridge, 1979: 34).

Robert Jervis (1985–6: 58) has argued that the concert system has appeared three times in European history, 1815, 1919 and 1945, the two latter examples having only a very brief existence. The concert approach has always emerged after a major war fought to contain a hegemonic aspirant, because such a war 'undermines the assumptions of a balance of power system and alters the perceived payoffs in a way that facilitates cooperation' (1985–6: 60). It does this by developing unusually close wartime bonds between the allied states, by making them sensitive to the high costs of war and reluctant to engage in it lightly, by causing them to value the existence of the other allied states, and by increasing the openness of their relations with one another, all of which discourage rapid defection from the wartime coalition.

It is doubtful if it is reasonable to describe as a true 'concert' the extremely brief periods of great power cooperation after 1919 and 1945. A better example might be the integration of USSR/Russia into the existing Western security framework of cooperation on major security issues after 1990. This cooperation was evident over crises such as Iraq and Bosnia. However, this example lacks any of the preconditions identified by Jervis for the previous 'concerts', which suggests that the wartime bonding experience is not in fact essential, though a profound system change is.

Having defeated the French attempt to dominate Europe, at enormous cost, after nearly 20 years of warfare, Castlereagh and Metternich were determined that the new European order should be underpinned by a balance of power, though they had quite different ideas as to what constituted a 'balance' of power in that regard. The failure of many European states to recognise the danger posed by revolutionary and Napoleonic France, and to act to oppose it quickly enough, led them to believe that an equilibrium should be consciously created among the great powers, which would make it extremely difficult, if not impossible, for a future bid for hegemony to be successful. The French successes after 1792 led them to believe that the eighteenth-century balance of power mechanisms had proved inadequate for the task.

The result of this thinking was the process at Vienna whereby the negotiators deliberately redrew the borders of the European states in an effort to leave the great powers as evenly balanced as possible. These territorial alterations were also driven by a fear of a future resurgent and revanchist France. Thus, Russia's territory was expanded and her influence moved further west through the acquisition of considerable territory in Poland. Prussia was enlarged and placed as a check on the future expansion of France through the acquisition of a huge new province in the Rhineland. These Russian and Prussian gains were balanced by the transfer of Italian territory to Austria. Britain gained no territory on the European mainland, but was left secure in her overwhelming naval superiority. France was further constrained by the significant expansion of the Kingdom of Piedmont-Sardinia in the southeast and the creation of the new Kingdom of the Netherlands in the north.

Castlereagh had to defend these changes against criticism, for they had involved the annexation and extinction of a number of hitherto independent states such as Venice and Genoa in Italy and a considerable number of the small German principalities. In Britain at least, both critics and proponents of the Vienna settlement argued in terms of the balance of power. Castlereagh insisted that the creation and maintenance of a stable balance of power in Europe lay behind all the terms of the Vienna settlement. His critics argued that balance terminology was being used to support actions which were the antithesis of a true balance of power policy. Thus, the transfer of Genoa to Piedmont was denounced by Sir James Mackintosh in the House of Commons in March 1815 on the grounds that destroying the small states was sacrificing the ends to the means.

> In the new system small states are annihilated by a combination of the great. In the old, small states were secured by a mutual jealousy of the great.
>
> (Dankin, 1979: 32)

Mackintosh's argument misinterpreted the reality of the pre-1792 system, where in fact the balance of power system worked so as to preserve the larger states but demonstrably failed the smaller and weaker ones, as the partitions of Poland dramatically showed. What is illuminating, however, about the debate between Castlereagh and Mackintosh is that both based their arguments upon the requirements of balance of power theory.

One of the features of the concert system was that it was more explicitly a great power system than its eighteenth-century predecessor. The lesser states had few rights and were not treated as equal members of the system. The justification for this offered by von Gentz in 1818, that the five powers at the head of the federation were the only ones who could destroy the general system by changing their policies is a valid one. The 'concert' served as a mechanism for managing the rivalry between the great powers.

Unlike the statesmen of 1713-14, those of 1815 believed that a means needed to be found to enable rapid consultation and cooperation of states in the event of a future threat to the European balance of power. It was the absence of such a mechanism, they felt, which had been one of the major weaknesses of the eighteenth-century balance of power system. The method chosen was not to create an international organisation, but rather to make more or less permanent the wartime great power alliance and to hold periodic conferences at foreign minister level, in the words of the Quadruple Alliance (November 1815), 'for the purpose of consulting upon their interests, or for the consideration of measures which ... shall be considered the most salutary for the purpose and prosperity of Nations and the maintenance of the Peace of Europe' (Craig and George, 1990: 31). These conferences were to be more frequent than those which had followed the Utrecht settlement a century earlier. In all, the period 1822 to 1914 saw a total of 26 conferences in which all the great powers were represented. The permanence of the wartime alliance had been established by the Treaty of Chaumont, of March 1814, prior to the final defeat of Napoleon.

Henry Kissinger has argued (1955: 266) that there are in practice two potential forms of equilibrium. The first, analogous to the eighteenth-century system, acts as a deterrent to a state seeking hegemony. The second, a 'special equilibrium', is a 'condition of smooth cooperation'. For Kissinger, the concert system was an example of the second form of equilibrium.

Although it was not without its critics, by and large the concert system served Europe well over the subsequent four decades. The great powers themselves demonstrated a notable restraint in the exercise of their dominance, which was clearly instrumental in commending it to the less powerful states in the system. The most powerful of the second-rank states not surprisingly resented the existence of this 'senior management group' for the European state system, while the small states accepted the dominant position of the great powers and looked to them for protection. Many, indeed, found in a great power patron a guarantee both against external aggression and against internal revolution.

For their part, the great powers sought to operate the European system in a collegiate manner. On all major issues they consulted among themselves in search of a solution acceptable to all the great powers. Such consideration was not extended to the smaller powers, who on occasion were dragooned into line to accept the decisions of the major powers. An example of this was the military action taken against the Dutch in 1832 by Britain and France when Holland proved reluctant to accept the new border with Belgium decided by the London conference of that year.

Watson (1992: 240) emphasises the difference between this approach to the balance of power compared to that of the eighteenth century by calling it a 'diffused hegemony'. This raises difficulties with the theory. The balance of power system has, as its central purpose, the prevention of hegemony by one or more powers. Yet, according to Watson, the concert system, which is usually seen as a notable example of a successful balance of power system, was actually little more than thinly camouflaged hegemony. Moreover, since it included all the major powers and was diffuse, it did not trigger the formation of an antihegemonic coalition. This is a valid criticism. The concert was clearly a variant balance of power system, but it was one where the focus was upon maintaining a balance between the interests of such a small number of major states that the distinction from effective hegemony becomes badly blurred.

This approach served to develop a continental perspective among statesmen, one that promoted great power unity above unilateral action and sought European solutions to European problems. This applied particularly to any territorial changes (Elrod, 1976: 164). It serves therefore as a model for a balance of power system that can harmonise the actions of the great powers. However, for it to work effectively, not only must the major powers be acutely sensitive to each other's interests, but the smaller or weaker states in the system must be prepared to accept the right of the great power directorate to determine the outcome of all crucial security issues with broad ramifications.

The threat of actual use of force was not infrequently resorted to in this period. Though a major war was avoided and no great power wished to see such a war, nevertheless the powers did not shrink from the use of force when necessary. Though they sought to resolve difficulties through diplomacy whenever possible, the concert system ultimately rested on the sanction of the military instrument which was seen as a functional and entirely legitimate tool of foreign policy. None the less, the foreign policies of the great powers were characterised by caution and restraint, rather than by adventurism. Medlicott (1956: 18) argues that 'it was peace that maintained the Concert and not the Concert that maintained peace', but this gives insufficient credit to the degree to which the governments of the Concert positively contributed to the environment which prevented the inevitable tensions of the period from breaking out into great power war. Four decades would pass after Waterloo before one of the great powers provoked a diplomatic crisis so serious that it led to war between the great powers. For the most part the powers sought to defuse crises wherever possible and to contain them before they could escalate into more general conflicts.

The exception to this general rule was France, which used military force to seek unilateral advantages in Spain in 1823, Belgium in 1830 and Italy in 1848. However, France was the exception which proves the rule. She was the defeated power in 1815 and many, if not most, of the provisions of the Vienna settlement were designed with the containment and frustration of France as their objective. French statesmen could hardly be expected to look with favour upon such a diplomatic framework and France remained something of a 'revisionist' state throughout the period 1815 to 1854.

French statesmen and politicians of all factions were united in their opposition to the Vienna settlements. Their criticisms of the Second Peace of Paris and the Vienna settlement were implicitly criticisms of the entire international order constructed by the victorious allies of 1815. There was some justice to their complaints moreover, particularly when they noted that the great powers had benefited particularly from

> Europe's need to constrain France. Prussia had annexed the Rhineland, Austria had gained large territories in Italy, while long-standing French allies such as Saxony and Poland had been savagely dismembered by the Vienna Settlement. Britain's dominance at sea went unchallenged and nobody, the French could see, suggested that a balance of power should constrain British naval power. All in all the French had some grounds for believing that 'the new order in Europe was no more than an attempt by the allies to give legal title to their selfish aggrandisement'.
>
> (Bullen, 1979: 124)

Nor were the French alone in their criticism of certain aspects of the new European order. As early as 1818 Capodistraias, the Russian Foreign Minister, declared that the time had come to dispense with 'this kind of directory of four Powers who are arrogating to themselves the right to decide the affairs . . . of the rest of Europe without its participation' (Bridge, 1979: 37).

Despite being one of the victors in 1815 and a member of the great power Quadruple Alliance established on 20 November 1815, Russia felt that the Concert of Europe was designed to constrain Russia as much as France. Moreover, it believed, like France, that the balance of power established in 1815 was incomplete because while it constrained France and Russia on the European continent, it did nothing to limit British naval and colonial power throughout the rest of the globe.

Tsar Alexander I of Russia had held the most radical views of all the leaders regarding the system that should govern Europe once Napoleon had been defeated. He was alone in recognising that the nationalist forces released by the French Revolution could not be ignored or permanently suppressed. He proposed the recognition of the principle of national self-determination and a re-ordering of the European state system to reflect this. The new European order would be buttressed by a confederation which would prohibit the use of force amongst its members until peaceful methods had been exhausted. These ideas were based on the eighteenth-century proposals of St Pierre and Kant and would be echoed in the League of Nations Covenant in the twentieth century. They proved uncongenial to the leaders of the other great powers and were not pursued. They were prescient in that it was the force of national self-determination which would eventually undercut the 'balance of power' arrangements which the allies constructed at Vienna.

The 'Western' allies, however, felt that, considering France's actions in the period 1792–1815, she was being treated rather leniently, and deliberately so. They sought to 'chasten' and constrain France, but not to dismember or humiliate her. In this regard they could be said to have been obeying Kaplan's balance of power 'rule' to permit defeated or constrained essential national actors to re-enter the system as acceptable role partners. Britain and Austria insisted on placing France in diplomatic quarantine for two years after Waterloo as a precautionary measure, but it was always accepted that France would be brought back into the system once the threat from Napoleon was clearly past. By the middle of 1817 the allies agreed that an international congress should be held in 1818, which would arrange for the final withdrawal of the army of occupation from France and would also decide upon France's future role within the European concert.

The expansion of the Quadruple Alliance to embrace new members was a controversial issue. In the period 1815 to 1818, both Castlereagh and Metternich were firmly of the belief that the Quadruple Alliance would be weakened if it was broadened. However, in 1818 France was fully rehabilitated into the international system as a fully sovereign state and the alliance was expanded into a five-power 'concert'.

The phrase 'congress system', which is used to characterise the subsequent period of international relations, has been criticised as being misleading in that it implies a higher degree of international organisation than ever in fact existed. It was not a structured body such as the League of Nations or the United Nations, but rather a coordinating series of conferences. It anticipated the era of frequent 'summit conferences' after 1945, rather than the formal infrastructure of the UN.

The congresses of 1818 to 1822 can be seen as being a continuation of the periodic conferences between the wartime allies which characterised the final phase of the struggle against Napoleon Bonaparte. This 'system' if it can be called such, already contained the seeds of its own demise, because it was very much an expression of the personal diplomacy of Castlereagh, Metternich and Alexander I of Russia.

The allies themselves were divided by clear differences in outlook that became marked as the bond provided by common fear of, and hostility towards France, began to weaken after 1815. The more conservative states, particularly Austria and Russia, wished to turn the Quadruple Alliance into a grouping of states who would stand as a bulwark against the advance of democracy or liberalism and would act independently or together, to intervene and crush these forces wherever they appeared. As a comparatively liberal and increasingly democratic state, Britain was unable to align herself with the conservative allies in this endeavour. Britain therefore began to distance herself from the close alliance of the wartime era and in 1818 withdrew from the system of periodic ministerial consultations.

Nevertheless, despite these differences in outlook the system was notably effective in the period 1815 to 1854, and as Ragnhild Hatton remarked in another context, 'periods when progress was made in limiting wars and achieving a longish interval of peace by conscious rational efforts are worth examining in detail for lessons to be learnt' (1969: 26). The ideological differences between the conservative great powers Austria, Russia and Prussia and the 'liberal' states Britain and France, did not prevent them from achieving a degree of policy coordination which kept tensions at a low level and avoided war between the powers. Where major disputes occurred they often caused the powers to form temporary alliances which did not follow the pattern of ideological solidarity. The degree of ideological division in Europe after 1815 has in fact been exaggerated.

Crucially, the five concert powers were agreed upon the need to preserve the territorial *status quo* created in 1815 or at least, not to allow territorial changes that did not have the approval of the great powers. The Concert of Europe acted as a mechanism for transferring territory between the smaller or weaker states, but it was not able to achieve the same success when the territorial disputes were between two great powers. However, when such difficulties arose, the concert system did not collapse, it simply went into abeyance until a subsequent issue arose upon which the great powers were disposed to compromise.

Lord John Russell, on behalf of the British government, neatly encapsulated this outlook in 1852, on the eve of the system's collapse, declaring that,

> any territorial increase of one Power . . . which disturbs the general balance of power in Europe, . . . could not be a matter of indifference to this country, and would no doubt be the subject of a Conference, and might ultimately, if that balance was seriously threatened, lead to war.
>
> (Hinsley, 1963: 224)

The idea that territorial changes in Europe required the sanction of the great powers held sway from 1815 to 1853. However, the 15 years from the Crimean War to the Treaty of Frankfurt saw a period of revolution and popular nationalism and was once more characterised by war between the great powers. The Concert was to all intents and purposes abandoned. Territorial changes were now the result of war rather than great power agreement. However, the London Protocol of 1871 revived the principle that treaties 'could not be altered without the consent of all the signatory powers' (Bridge and Bullen, 1980: 4). For much of the period after 1815, therefore, treaties *did* remain sacrosanct and the balance of power system worked effectively.

The great powers in fact exercised a remarkable degree of self-restraint during the Concert period, forgoing gains they could have achieved in order to maintain the Concert. Such restraint was not characteristic of the preceding and subsequent centuries (Elrod, 1976: 168).

THE COLLAPSE OF THE CONCERT SYSTEM

In 1848 Europe was thrown into turmoil by a series of revolutions that swept the continent, undermining the stability that had been a feature for so long. Although the liberal revolutions were by no means successful everywhere, they did sweep away many of the attitudes and personalities that had dominated international relations since 1815. New political forces found expression in the policies of a new generation of young men in a hurry who were ambitious for their own countries and no longer willing to abide by the collaborative principles and practices invented and followed by the statesmen of Vienna.

(Craig and George, 1990: 35)

The new era would be dominated by aggressive statesmen like Bismarck of Prussia, Louis Napoleon of France and Schwartzenberg of Austria.

The critical event that released these energies and ended the Concert of Europe was the outbreak of the Crimean War in 1854. This war led to a fundamental change in the pattern of relations between the great powers. It brought to an end an era in which Britain and Russia had often combined effectively to stabilise the balance of power, as for example in 1848 when they had acted to prevent a general European war from breaking out. The Crimean War liberated France from the final constraints imposed by the post-1815 Concert, turned Russia into a revisionist power and left only Austria and Britain as defenders of the *status quo*.

By destroying the post-1815 great power consensus the Crimean War opened the floodgates to aggression and territorial revision in Europe. The collapse of the constraints exercised by the Concert is clearly shown by the predisposition of the great powers to war in the subsequent 15 years. Between 1854 and 1870 each of the great powers fought at least one, while Austria, Prussia and France were each involved in three. Britain, France, Piedmont-Sardinia and Russia fought the Crimean War. France and Piedmont-Sardinia were involved against Austria in the Italian War of 1859. Austria and Prussia fought Denmark in 1864. Austria fought Prussia in 1866 and France fought Prussia in 1870. The purpose of all these wars (with the exception of the Crimean War) was effectively to erode away the main features of the Vienna settlement. Each of the wars was followed by important territorial changes. These wars undermined the balance of power created at Vienna in 1815. The Vienna settlement was replaced by a new, less stable balance.

The nature of war itself appeared to be changing in this period. In the first half of the nineteenth century the conduct of war and preparations for it differed little from what would have been true a century earlier. There was no systematic effort to collect detailed information about the military resources of the other states in the system, nor was there detailed planning for future wars by a permanent general staff. The wars of the period 1815 to 1854, and even of the period 1854 to 1870, were initiated by political leaders with the opinions of the military carrying little weight.

This outlook changed after the spectacular Prussian successes against Austria in 1866 and France in 1870. More than anything else, Prussia seemed to have owed her victories to good organisation. She had efficiently mobilised enormous numbers of trained reservists and equipped them with the latest weapons. The impact of Prussia's example was such that the other great powers sought to model their armed forces and strategies upon the Prussian system in the hope of emulating Prussia's success. Conscription became the rule and general staffs were created.

The Franco-Prussian War was not followed by a period of peace and low tension. The wars of 1866 and 1870 had left Austria determined to make gains in the Balkans to offset what she had lost in Germany, while France was bitter about her humiliating defeat and the annexation of Alsace–Lorraine by Germany. France, indeed, was a deeply revisionist power after 1871, but whereas that was true also after 1815, after 1871 France had no reasonable prospect of revising the settlement. Germany's advantages in terms of population size and growth, economic strength and military power widened inexorably after 1878, while France was left diplomatically isolated. If 1871 was followed by a 'long peace' reminiscent of 1815–54, that peace was produced, 'not by the moral consensus of a conservative coalition, but simply by the brutal fact of German military superiority over France' (Bridge and Bullen, 1980: 7). There was nothing inevitable about French isolation. Germany had now replaced France as the most powerful European state, and had Austria gravitated towards a French alliance to 'contain' Germany, the system might have retained its flexibility. Instead, by allying with Germany, Austria helped create an even more powerful central European bloc and encouraged the slow, but remorseless division of Europe into two opposing camps.

The peace after 1871 was an unstable one, characterised by crises and recurrent international friction. The triumph of national self-determination in Italy and Germany by 1871 had erased most of the remaining small states from the map of Europe 'and thus the "buffers and shock absorbers" were gone leaving the great powers with common borders and directly clashing interests' (Craig and George, 1990: 36). The new era was to be one characterised by aggressive industrial and commercial rivalry, nationalism, imperialism and growing military influence in the formulation of foreign policy goals. It proved impossible to recreate anything similar to the great power consensus which had characterised the pre-1854 period. The sense of belonging to an advantageous system, of a great power society, which had existed after 1815, had now gone. This was important, because it meant that the new balance of power created by the wars of the 1860s and 1870s had no political directorate to maintain it in the way that the Concert had done for the Vienna settlement.

In its absence, Bismarck sought to sustain the new settlement through a system of secret alliances. Bismarck would justify this policy in retrospect by arguing that,

> one must not lose sight of the importance of being one of three on the European chess board. That is the invariable objective of all cabinets and of mine above all others. Nobody wishes to be in a minority. All politics reduce themselves to this formula: to try to be one of three as long as the world is governed by an unstable equilibrium of five great powers.
>
> (Craig and George, 1990: 38)

Bismarck was able to use Germany's power reputation to create a web of alliances with other states who had to accept Germany's terms for the alliance. The *Dreikaiserbund*, or league of three emperors linked Germany, Austria and Russia, while Italy was obliged to end her animosity to Austria before being admitted to the German alliance system. Though complex, the system at least reduced the chances of war between either Russia and Austria, or Italy and Austria. Bismarck's critics have argued that the complexity of this system was its weakness. It was maintained through continual diplomatic manoeuvre, secrecy and outright deception, and could not outlive the removal of Bismarck from office in 1890.

THE 'UNSTABLE EQUILIBRIUM' 1890–1914

At the beginning of the twentieth century the European balance of power assumed a new form, one which was characterised by bipolarity as the major European powers formed themselves into two hostile alliances. It was this inflexible variant of the politics of equilibrium that came to be seen as the normal manifestation of balance of power politics in the twentieth century.

After Bismarck was dismissed as chancellor in 1890, Germany abandoned its alliance with Russia. However, German policy-makers reacted with alarm when Russia responded by seeking an accommodation with France. German clumsiness over the next 20 years, particularly with regard to their aggressive colonial policy, left

Europe in a condition of instability. Both Britain and Russia, neither of whom were natural allies of France, were pushed toward an understanding with France by their common perception of Germany as an increasingly threatening state.

Germany, newly united after 1870, rapidly industrialising, with a population significantly larger than Britain or France's, would naturally have produced strains after 1870. Neither Britain nor France could welcome this new and dangerous rival. It was easy to perceive of Germany, not just as a rival but as an enemy. The result of British fears was the Entente Cordiale with France in 1904 and the Anglo-Russian agreement of 1907, which changed the nature of the European balance and produced a direct confrontation between the Triple Alliance and the Triple Entente.

Like the Bismarckian system which had preceded it, the post-1890 equilibrium lacked the kind of great power consensus which the Concert of Europe had produced. Unlike the previous system, however, and crucially, it was a bipolar system and far more unstable than its predecessor. There were no alliance ties which crossed the bipolar divide and no *status quo* state to give it leadership, as both the Vienna and Bismarck systems had had. Because of its bipolar character after 1907, the system encouraged a fear in both coalitions of losing allies to the opposite camp.

This was a significant and ominous development. A feature of the nineteenth-century balance of power system up to that point had been the fact that the great powers did not conceive of it as operating in 'zero-sum' terms, where one side could only benefit at the expense of the other. Warfare and political rivalry generally were to a significant extent 'limited', they did not embrace the objective of destruction of their rivals, only of outmanoeuvring them for marginal advantage. Where gains by one side were made, the overall impact was often ameliorated through the principle of great power compensation. This worked against the interests of the smaller states, however, who often became the victims as the great powers 'shared the spoils' from their diplomatic manoeuvres. As the nineteenth century progressed, and the myriad smaller states which had existed in 1815 were annexed, absorbed or united through national unification, the scope for reciprocal great power compensation diminished, and a zero-sum mentality did emerge after 1900.

However, although the era was characterised by war-scares and high levels of international tension, it is worth noting that in terms of great power wars, the period between 1871 and 1914 represents the second-longest period of peace in the history of the European state system, only surpassed by the 'long peace' after the Second World War. More than half of all the wars which did take place were the product of the demand for national self-determination by various nationalities (Holsti, 1991: 143).

Although the period 1815 to 1914 saw two of the three longest periods of peace in the history of the European state system (1815–53 and 1871–1914), the elimination of war was not seen as an objective within the nineteenth-century balance of power systems. War and the threat of military action were regarded as acceptable if the objectives were limited and did not threaten the stability of the balance of power system. It was therefore deemed legitimate to make war for limited gains which did not undermine one of the great powers or a key ally.

THE CONCEPT OF THE BALANCE OF POWER IN THE NINETEENTH CENTURY

According to Bridge and Bullen (1980: 15), 'the concept of the balance of power was hardly ever used except by British governments. The continental powers certainly did not consciously seek to uphold it.' This was not the case, but it is certainly true that European thinking about the balance of power differed significantly from British thinking on the subject. Continental statesmen and thinkers were in fact rather suspicious of the way in which Britain usually asserted the balance of power principle, since British governments tended to emphasise the need for equilibrium on the continent, while resisting suggestions for a naval balance of power. The British conception was clearly self-serving, therefore.

Kissinger argues that the differences between the British and the continental powers reflected a deeper division in perspective, with the European states having no loyalty to the balance principle which went beyond their historical self-image. 'To Castlereagh, the equilibrium was a mechanical expression of the balance of forces; to the Continental nations, a reconciliation of historical aspirations' (Kissinger, 1955: 267).

Britain and the German-speaking lands were the two areas which contributed to the development of the concept during the nineteenth century. Heern, the Göttingen historian, asserted that the balance of power was the mechanism which made the system of states possible (Holbraad, 1970: 82). In the decade or so after Waterloo German writers tended to link the balance of power system with the conservative principles advocated by the leading German states, Austria and Prussia.

The arguments of the conservatives, reflected in debates about the balance of power after 1815, proceeded from the assumption that the eighteenth century had been characterised by an effective and consistent balance of power system, which had prevented hegemony, reduced the incidence of war and moderated the process of change. Ranke, however, argued that this was an idealistic and inaccurate characterisation, and asserted that the eighteenth century had in reality been characterised by disorder and war.

Whereas conservatives saw the balance of power as a mechanism for maintaining the *status quo*, for Ranke it was the engine of development. He saw a state system where states were unique and individualistic, but were linked by geography, culture and continuous relations into a European state community. This is very much the 'Grotian' perception of international society, which had marked European thinking about international relations during the eighteenth century. Ranke's 'community', however, was characterised by continual struggle between the states. He went so far as to argue that war between states and their general struggle for power drove history forward and created national development as much as the civilising effects of cultural development did (Holbraad, 1970: 85). This was a quite different conception from the conservative German perspective. Clausewitz, for example, saw the purpose of the balance of power as being the maintenance of the *status quo*. Indeed, for Clausewitz, it was only this underlying desire for tranquillity and the *status quo* that made possible the existence of a European state system. Without it, the states would inevitably fuse into a single empire (Wright, 1975: 106).

Where German writers undoubtedly made a distinctive contribution to balance of power thinking, was in their willingness to discuss the concept in global terms, something their British counterparts were conspicuously unwilling to do. The second half of the nineteenth century was marked by dramatic European expansion into Africa and Asia. A purely Eurocentric balance of power approach would clearly miss the new realities of the age of European imperialism, where extra-European sources of power were a crucial component of the strength of the major European actors, in the case of Britain, overwhelmingly so. Only late in the century was Britain herself prepared to accept the logic of this. The British Prime Minister, Lord Salisbury justified the acquisition of Wei hai wei in China in 1898 in terms of the need to offset the Russian acquisition of Port Arthur which, he argued, had materially altered the balance of power (Clark, 1989: 137).

German advocacy of a global balance justified both her imperial ambitions outside Europe, and her efforts to assume a dominant role *in* Europe on the grounds that the existing imperial powers were thwarting her efforts to acquire territories and influence beyond Europe. German writers such as Friedrich von Bernhadi, argued that as long as Britain had a colonial and naval preponderance, while seeking to sustain an equilibrium on the European continent, then there was no true balance of power. If Britain maintained its opposition to balances outside Europe, then the balance inside Europe had to be overthrown by Germany to create a balance with Britain and the other non-European great powers (Russia and the United States) at the global level.

Nineteenth-century attacks on the balance of power to some extent echoed the criticisms of eighteenth-century writers, for example, in asserting that it was not a true deterrent to war and often indeed served as an excuse for war. However, the particular form which balance of power systems took during the nineteenth century, and the nature of the social transformations under way in the period, coloured the nature of much of the criticism of the balance of power. Fallati argued in 1844 that the system placed power higher than justice or right. Frobel denounced it for favouring the great powers at the expense of the secondary states, while for Oppenheim its weakness was that it placed the rights of states above those of peoples or nations.

In Britain, both support for and criticism of the balance of power system had a longer pedigree than in other European states. For the British, with 200 years of theorising and practice of the balance of power behind them, the *value* of the balance of power approach was deemed unquestionable. They tended to see its virtues as being self-evident. According to Palmerston, the balance of power idea 'is one which has been familiar to the minds of all mankind from the earliest ages in all parts of the globe' (Holbraad, 1970: 138). In believing this, like Hume in the eighteenth century, Palmerston was well wide of the truth, but the significant fact was that he *did* believe it to be true and that belief was shared by the overwhelming majority of the British foreign policy elite throughout the eighteenth and nineteenth centuries.

For Palmerston, the balance of power was the supreme principle of foreign policy. It was the watchword of individual states, 'it is the doctrine of self-defence, with the simple qualification that it is combined with sagacity and with forethought, and an endeavour to prevent imminent danger before it comes thundering at your doors' (ibid.). It was the keystone of international society for 'it means that it is to the interest of the community of nations that no one nation should acquire such a preponderance as to endanger the security of the rest' (ibid.: 139).

This did not mean that all British governments were equally supportive of the approach, indeed Canning in the 1820s was extremely sceptical of it. Nor did proponents necessarily agree on the ways in which it should be implemented. Palmerston and Castlereagh, for example, differed in their approach to the balance of power system and the Concert of Europe. Castlereagh tended to see the Concert of Europe as a standing organisation involving all of the great powers, whereas Palmerston saw it as 'a diplomatic instrument to be called into action when required' (ibid.: 140).

Indeed, the doctrine of the balance of power could even be put forward in defence of a policy of strict neutrality verging on isolationism. In 1874 Lord Derby, the British Foreign Secretary, argued that the mutual antipathy of France and Germany left Britain in a strong position to 'hold the balance'. But to achieve this advantage Britain 'must be friendly with all, exclusively allied with none, and show ourselves simply bent on the maintenance of treaties and the preservation of peace' (Howard, 1974: 101).

Robert Phillimore argued that the balance of power system was a recognised part of international law. He wrote that the maintenance of the balance of power

> does not require that all existing powers should retain exactly their present territorial positions, but rather that no single Power should be allowed to increase them in a manner which threatens the liberties of other States. The doctrine properly understood does not imply a pedantic adherence to the particular system of equilibrium maintained by existing arrangements, but to such an alteration of it as the right to self-defence, acting by way of prevention, would authorise other Powers in opposing.
>
> (Holbraad, 1970: 149–50)

The liberals of the nineteenth century produced some of the most ferocious denunciations of the balance of power principle ever made. For Cobden it was 'not a fallacy, a mistake, an imposture – it is an undescribed, indescribable, incomprehensible nothing; mere words, conveying to the mind not ideas, but sounds' (Anderson, 1993: 190). Much of this criticism was unfair. The balance of power as a system would be blamed by liberals for the outbreak of the First World War in 1914, but was given no credit for the long periods of peace which preceded it. This was ascribed to more general factors such as the growth of trade and social, scientific and aesthetic progress (Holsti, 1991: 165).

Similar criticisms came from Bright. He described the balance of power as 'a phrase to which it is difficult to attach any definite meaning' and 'a mischievous delusion' which was simply an excuse for intervention and war which had led to constant warfare over the preceding two centuries. He argued that it had done nothing to advance the cause of freedom in Europe: 'It was with the freedom of peoples rather than the independence of states that Bright was concerned' (Holbraad, 1970: 157). This was significant. The tone of much of the nineteenth-century criticism differed from that of the eighteenth because of the way in which the societies of Western Europe were changing. The forms of states were changing and being challenged by the idea of national self-determination, while other social forces such as nations and social classes were coming to be identified as crucial. In an era of such rapid change, the balance of power idea came to be seen by many as dated. Its form made it unsuited to cope with the new forces of nationalism. As Lord John Russell put it in 1864, the great powers 'had not the habit of consulting populations when questions affecting the balance of power had to be settled' (Taylor, 1954: 151).

For Holbraad, this produced a crucial question mark against the continuing validity of the balance concept. 'Opponents saw it as an obstacle to the rise of nations and the advance of democracy. The difference was between men guided by rules of prudence and men inspired by faith in progress' (Holbraad, 1970: 150).

There was a real sense in which confidence in the balance of power as a system declined as the century progressed. Henry Reeve in his article on the balance of power for the 1875 edition of the *Encyclopaedia Britannica,* noted that a sea-change in opinion had taken place since the publication of the previous edition. The balance of power theory had lost much of its former authority. However, despite his assertion that 'we do not retain the faith of our forefathers in the balance of power' (Wright, 1975: 122), Reeve still felt compelled to call for its modernisation and improvement, rather than its abandonment.

Nineteenth-century statesmen in fact used the term 'balance of power' in a variety of ways, not all of them consistent, and in addition used a wide variety of synonyms to convey their understanding of the general principles which they felt ought to underlie European international relations. Schroeder (1989: 137) identifies eleven main uses of the term. These can be compared with Wight's, described in Chapter 1. The main nineteenth-century uses were to describe:

1 An even or balanced distribution of power.
2 Any existing distribution of power.
3 Any existing general situation or status-quo, with no particular regard to power relations.
4 The European system or order, the general framework of European politics.
5 Some indeterminate meaning involving some combination of the above.
6 As a verb, to play the role of a balancer, which can mean
  (a) oscillating between two sides
  (b) being an arbiter between two sides, each of which roles may require either being within the balance or standing outside of it.
7 Stability, peace and repose.
8 A shifting condition in international affairs, tending toward resolution by conflict.
9 The rule of law and guaranteed rights.
10 The general struggle for power, influence and advantage – power politics according to the rule of *raison d'état*.
11 Hegemony.

Schroeder argues that two main themes emerge from this and that they are not fully reconcilable. The first is equilibrium as 'stability, peace, the rule of law, the mutual guarantee of right, under treaties, and the supervision of all major changes in the system by the great powers' (Schroeder, 1989: 137). This was the usage which was dominant between 1815 and 1854. The other theme was balance of power in the traditional restricted sense, 'an even distribution of power and the policy of checking and containing dangerous uses or accumulations of power by countervailing power' (ibid.). These two broad usages reflect the distinct 'Grotian' and 'Hobbesian' senses of the concept during its formative period at the end of the seventeenth century.

In fact, what the nineteenth century clearly demonstrated was that 'the balance of power' as a guiding principle or organising system was not a fixed reality, but an approach subject to the effects of the evolution of political thought and indeed, of broader cultural developments. In the early part of the century, the approach marked by the Concert represented a radical evolution of the system compared with its eighteenth-century predecessor. Indeed, it can be argued that the Concert represented the construction, not of a symmetrical balance of power in the eighteenth-century sense, but a hegemony made tolerable only because it was exercised by a whole category of states, rather than a single power or narrow alliance. It is clear that for Castlereagh, Metternich and Talleyrand the Concert was in reality not a balance, but a superiority, a preponderance of power in the hands of a small group of great powers opposed to the prospect of hegemony in the eighteenth-century sense. The Concert maintained the system of independent states, but very much on the terms acceptable to the 'first among equals' which the Concert represented. That Talleyrand, Castlereagh and their peers considered this a 'balance', indicates that their conception of what constituted a balance was markedly different from simply an equality of power among the key states in the system. A balance was insufficient, it must be an equilibrium where the powers opposed to hegemony in principle possessed a preponderance of power. This was the same interpretation as that which would be propounded by commentators such as Niebuhr and Lippmann during the cold war.

This elasticity was a result of the nature of the times. While European statesmen still appear to have believed that the balance of power was a crucial part of the European security system, there was an increasing diversity of opinion as to what form the system should take and a clear feeling that while it was central, it was no longer sufficient (Clark, 1989: 120). Increasingly in the second half of the century, the crucial core meaning of the power to be balanced came to mean military power. The subtleties of the broader connotation of the balance were being lost in an image which was increasingly bipolar and focused upon war-fighting capabilities.

Finally, there is the factor noted by both Holbraad and Schroeder, that there were fundamental differences of opinion about how the balance should actually be structured, for example between the German and British conceptions. 'What Germans meant by equilibrium then, was a complicated balancing of power, status and rights within Germany, contained and controlled within a German Confederation and guaranteed by a united Europe'. In contrast, the British image was of 'a united Germany, perhaps allied with Austria and Italy, watching and checking Russia and France, so that Britain would be arbiter of Europe and have a free hand for its extra-European concerns' (Clark, 1989: 140). Kissinger, for example (1955: 267–8), noted that the views of Castlereagh and Metternich concerning what constituted equilibrium were quite different. For Metternich the term embraced a Germany in which Prussian predominance was impossible, whereas for Castlereagh the avoidance of predominance applied only at the European level.

The problem created by the varied uses of the phrase balance of power in the nineteenth century, coupled with its clearly evolutionary character, is that it makes it difficult to decide at any particular moment what a statesman or government meant by the term and assess how influential that conception was in determining foreign policy actions or the ordering of the European state system in general. The varied interpretations do not detract from the fact that statesmen did believe in something called the 'balance of power' which ought to be sustained in order to maintain a stable, ordered and, as far as possible, peaceful environment for states to pursue their legitimate objectives within.

The nineteenth-century balance of power system, particularly in its first 'concert' variant, differed from its predecessor because of the way in which the framers of the Vienna settlements constructed new arrangements to implement a new set of norms. These norms were reflected in the assumptions about what constituted an acceptable international equilibrium that prevailed for the rest of the century. There was a much greater emphasis placed upon subjective rights seen in concern over spheres of influence, the right to an effective veto over changes in the territorial *status quo* not acceptable to all the great powers, and an obsession with status. 'Oversimplified, political equilibrium meant a balance of satisfactions, a balance of rights and obligations and a balance of performance and pay-offs, rather than a balance of power' (Schroeder, 1989: 143).

Schroeder argues that the methods used to maintain this European equilibrium show a divergence from traditional balance of power techniques. This is particularly notable with regard to the preference for imposing restraints on another great power by allying with it rather than by forming an alliance against it. This was an innovative approach, which conforms neither to traditional balance of power technique nor to the practice of bandwagoning. It involved a willingness to influence governments by appealing to them as friends, rather than threatening them as enemies and may be seen as a natural corollary to the group norms which the Concert of Powers had established (Schroeder, 1989: 145).

Such an approach relied upon a commitment to consensus. Between 1890 and 1914 this consensus ceased to prevail. The decisions by Britain and France in 1906 to settle the Moroccan dispute, and of Austria-Hungary in 1908 to annex Bosnia, both taken without consulting the other great powers (and in defiance of treaty obligations to do so), epitomised the breakdown of the Concert which had underpinned the system during its heyday. This breakdown removed one of the crucial restraints to great power war.

7 Competing perspectives

INTRODUCTION

The purpose of this book is to examine the concept called 'the balance of power' and so far we have looked at its many meanings, its historical origins and development, its manifestation as a foreign policy guide and as a description of a certain type of international system. We have also looked at its implementation over the past three centuries. All this has been necessary in order to illuminate an idea with such a rich and complex history as that of the balance of power.

However, focusing in this way, while necessary, is also rather misleading. By concentrating on this one concept, it is possible to give a misleading impression about its importance in various periods of history. The balance of power has been a powerful and influential idea in the history of the development of the international system, but it has not been the only one. Nor, in those periods when it has been seen as a critical foreign policy strategy, has it been the only strategy available to states. To gain a fuller picture of the concept, it is necessary to place it in the context of important competing ideas and strategies, both in order to define it more clearly and in order to assess its relative historical importance more accurately. Darkness cannot be defined without speaking of light, and the classical balance of power concept needs to be held up against its alternatives in order to be seen in perspective.

In this chapter we will look at three other ideas, 'correlation of forces', 'collective security' and 'bandwagoning', as well as an alternative conception of the balance of power itself. They throw light upon the balance of power as an idea, an organising principle of international security. The 'correlation of forces' concept is interesting because it appears at first to be so similar to balance of power thinking, yet its crucial differences bring out some of the hidden assumptions of balance of power. Collective security is examined because it is often seen as the polar opposite of balance of power and emerged in the twentieth century as a reaction to it. Yet it shares many features with balance thinking. In addition, since balance thinking argues both for the 'common sense' represented by balance policies and the almost *inevitable* nature of balance of power alignments, the third section looks at the argument that an alternative foreign policy exists for states which is equally, if not more common in history – the phenomenon of 'bandwagoning'. Finally, the idea of an 'associative' rather than an 'adversarial' balance of power is examined.

THE MARXIST-LENINIST CORRELATION OF FORCES CONCEPT

In the twentieth century the advent of communist states produced a new paradigm of balance of power thinking, the 'correlation of international forces'. The most detailed study of this concept is that by Lider (1986), upon which the following discussion relies heavily. The concept occupied a central place in discussions of international politics between East and West during the cold war era. The approach made three key assumptions:

1 International relations was seen as an extension of the domestic class struggle;
2 the correlations of internal and international forces produced a mutual impact;
3 The role of the working class occupied a special place in both kinds of interaction.

(Lider, 1986: 123)

Scholars in the Marxist-Leninist states insisted that the correlation of forces was a concept much broader and more subtle than the Western balance of power concept. 'It is a broad and complex class sociopolitical category. It should be viewed as a correlation of the class, social, economic, political, ideological, military, ethical and other forces in the two socio-economic systems of our times' (Lider, 1986: 124).

The correlation of international forces was regarded as an *objective* category, reflecting 'objectively existing conditions in the international sphere and objective historical tendencies' (ibid.: 127). Western balance concepts were criticised for either being too narrowly based by being restricted to military factors or, where they were more broadly defined, of offering no clear ranking of the importance of the various factors included. 'The Marxist-Leninist concept, on the other hand, consists in clearly defining all the basic potentials and presenting the sociopolitical and the structural-functional characteristics of the protagonist as the basis of the forces being compared' (ibid.).

The correlation of forces was defined by Tomashevsky as 'the totality of economic, political, legal, diplomatic and military contacts and interrelationships among peoples, among states and state systems [and] among the main social, economic and political forces and organisations functioning in the world' (Lynch, 1987: 91).

Marxist-Leninist specialists in international relations argued that the correlation of international forces in the cold war period was different from the traditional balance of power concept in a number of crucial ways:

1 The balance of power which was seen as representing a rivalry between several imperialist great powers, had been superseded by a bipolar correlation of forces with the latter reflecting the rivalry of world socialism and imperialism, forces defined in terms of class struggle.
2 The politics of 'spheres of influence' had been replaced by a process characterised by the struggle of the capitalist world to survive.
3 The domination of imperialism had been challenged by the growing impact of socialism on the international system.
4 Qualitative factors had come to outweigh quantitative factors. The class character of opposing forces was now more important than simply the traditional indices of state power.
5 The relative importance of certain power components had altered. Military factors had become less important, while economic and sociopolitical factors had grown in importance.
6 The nature of the protagonists had changed. Instead of simply consisting of states, they now included states, groups of states, international movements, classes, popular masses and parties.

The correlation of forces was described in terms of four alternative but complementary forms by Soviet writers (Lider, 1986: 146). It was seen as a correlation between two competing political systems, capitalism and socialism. Sometimes this was expressed as the balance between 'the forces of peace' and 'the forces of war'. Thirdly, it described the military correlation between the two superpowers.

Finally, this was often broadened to embrace the two alliance systems, NATO and the Warsaw Treaty Organisation.

Marxist-Leninist writings from the communist states sharply distinguished the concept of the correlation of world forces from Western theories of the 'global balance of power'. Raymond Garthoff (1951: 86–8) has pointed out that the Russian language itself lacks any term which conveys the same meaning as the English phrase 'balance of power', or indeed of the word 'power'. Russians do not use the Russian words which mean power in the sense of 'greatpowers', 'potency' or 'military forces', but rather the word for 'strength' or 'elemental force' in the sense of 'water-power' or 'force of gravity'. Balance is translated as 'equilibrium', and 'political balance' is defined as 'a comparative stability of the general relation of forces in the political struggle'. Margot Light (1988: 252) also notes this problem and the danger it created of the misunderstanding and misrepresentation of the views of both sides. There is thus a major gap in comprehension possible. Moreover, cultural differences contributed to the difference in perception. Alfred Vagts (1948: 85) suggested that the idea of the balance of power as something ethical, which states should seek to achieve, is peculiar to countries which experienced the Renaissance, and has therefore never been held in equivalent intellectual esteem in Russia.

Balance of power theory was criticised on a number of grounds. Balance of power theories overemphasise military power as the determinant of the total power of states, and ignore socio-economic and domestic political factors. They also disregarded the laws of social development. The balance of power theory was criticised as being based upon an obsolete view of the nature of the international system. In particular, it ignored the class struggle and placed an undue emphasis upon the foreign policies of the great powers. In looking at the great power competition, Western perspectives placed emphasis on particular models which distorted reality. Soviet theorists gave as an example of this the so-called 'strategic triangle' of China, the USA and USSR. Bipolar models were similarly seen as missing the central importance of class struggle.

Soviet writers also criticised the balance of power concept on the grounds that it accepted war as an effective instrument of policy. This was seen as legitimising war, a foolhardy attitude in the age of nuclear weapons. Marxist writers argued that the very difficulty of using military force in the nuclear age increased the importance of non-military elements such as ideological factors.

A further Marxist criticism of balance of power theories was that they found no place for the Third World. Significant actors such as national liberation movements were ignored since they were not states. Indeed, it was argued that balance thinking was used by Western imperialists to justify the suppression of national liberation movements. The existence of a so-called balance of power among the European great powers in nineteenth-century Europe had not prevented the emergence of empires and regional hegemonies outside Europe.

According to Garthoff (1966: 92–3), Soviet thinking on the balance of power encompassed four different meanings:

1 A general relation or distribution of power.
2 An equilibrium of two units. Such a balance was always seen as being a temporary phenomenon.
3 A situation involving a bipolar equilibrium with a detached 'balancer'. This does not take the classic western form of a balancer, but more an 'active neutrality', such as the Soviet Union argued it followed from 1939 to 1941.
4 A favourable imbalance, or preponderance of power.

As the cold war stabilised into the 'long peace', Marxist-Leninist thinkers softened their criticism of Western balance of power theories and accepted elements of it into their own thinking about international relations. Pozdnyakov, for example, drew a parallel between the Soviet belief in the global struggle between two competing value systems, capitalism and socialism, and the Western model of a 'bipolar' balance of power (Lynch, 1987: 95). This bipolar vision was not a new one. As early as 1919 Stalin had described the world as being split into two 'camps', those of imperialism and socialism (Garthoff, 1966: 70). The modified Marxist approach accepted the concept of the balance of power *as a system*. It was seen in terms of 'regularities characteristic of the mechanism of the functioning of the international system' (Lider, 1986: 203). A politico-military balance between states was held to preserve the system as a whole and its principal constituents. It was 'based on the interaction and balance of two contradictory elements: the changeability of particular elements (or states) and the relative stability of the ties between them in other words, of the structure of the entire system'. The international system was seen as a self-regulating mechanism characterised not by perfect balance, but by 'a tendency to establish such a balance which proceeds through an unlimited chain of non-balanced conditions' (ibid.). All these ideas were familiar ones in the traditional Western balance of power literature.

Marxism-Leninism accepted the idea of a bipolar balance of power, but did so by insisting that it was a transitory feature, characteristic of a particular epoch, but one which was less fundamental than the historical inevitability of progress towards socialism. In addition, while balance of power was accepted as a *system*, characterising certain objective conditions, balance of power *politics* was rejected as the policy of bourgeois states working to advance the cause of imperialism.

Despite this qualified acceptance, important differences continued to exist between the Soviet interpretation and the traditional Western view. There remained a fundamental difference between the concepts of balance of power and correlation of forces. The former described an approximate equality of power and was seen as being an approach limited to a particular historical epoch; the latter reflected 'an inherent qualitative superiority of one force – the socialist one – and at the very least a clear tendency of this side to grow ever stronger' (Lider, 1986: 205).

Western criticisms of the correlation of forces concept, mirrored in many respects Soviet criticisms of traditional balance of power theory. Western theorists, not surprisingly, did not accept the argument that the future would witness the inevitable triumph of socialism. In addition, they argued that the correlation of forces placed an undue emphasis on military strength and underplayed the importance of other key factors such as economic strength. Finally, despite the Marxist claims to the contrary, Western analysts held that the correlation was dependent upon a number of elements which were not capable of being accurately measured.

For example, Light (1988: 251) has pointed out that although Soviet scholars argued that the correlation of forces could be scientifically determined and calculated with precise accuracy, none actually provided detailed evidence to support the claim. Some Soviet scholars while asserting that power was measurable, defined it in such a way as to make this extremely difficult. Bolshakov and Vdovichenko, for example, defined power in terms of 'possibilities'. Power is seen as 'realised possibility' in a situation where 'the wider the margin of choice, the greater the power that is available to the actor' (Lynch, 1987: 90). Garthoff (1966: 84) argues that far from explaining how the correlation of forces might be accurately measured, Soviet ideology did not even *imply* what the criteria might be. It was also felt by Western critics to be deceptive to describe its character as being irreversible, when in fact the West had clearly been able to reverse certain Soviet gains, for example Afghanistan and Nicaragua, at various points during the cold war.

A further cluster of criticisms related to the instrumentality of the concept. It was held to justify Soviet hegemony in Eastern Europe, to justify the huge build-up of Soviet military power and to justify Soviet acts of aggression in terms of historical laws which obliged the Soviet Union to extend the influence of socialism. Moreover, it was used as a propaganda tool to win the support of Third World countries.

The differences between the two concepts can be seen in terms of four key elements. The first of these was the *protagonists,* In the Western concept these were great powers and blocs. In the Marxist approach they were socio-economic systems and international movements. Secondly, *the character of the correlation,* although in both approaches the military component continued to be the most important element, the Western approach tried to emphasise measurable power components, while the Marxist approach emphasised intangible elements. Thirdly, the *the view of the international system:* in the Western concept the balance of power was a feature of international politics and was made up of interacting states and alliances, whereas in the Marxist version the importance of *domestic* forces is stressed. Finally, in terms of the *the underlying philosophy of international development,* the Western concept can be held to be a rather static one, with its emphasis on the stabilising effect of the balance of power; the Marxist concept stressed the idea of progressive change in a particular historical direction.

Western balance concepts, dominated since 1945 by the Anglo-Saxon Hobbesian perspective, are based upon realist notions of the drive for power and a view of the international anarchy in which states must rely on self-help to pursue and defend their vital interests. This views international relations in terms of a *system* with a basic shape which gradually adjusts to changing conditions. In the Soviet view, international relations was a *process* in which changes fostered by progressive forces moved historically in a particular direction; though even here there were elements of convergence in Western and Soviet thinking, seen, for example, in Kokoshin's view that the structure of the international system defined its basic processes and phenomena (Lynch, 1987: 100), an essentially 'neo-realist' position in Western terms.

Thus, the correlation of forces idea throws useful light on the balance of power concept. It shares certain features with it, and those common features increased as the theory developed during the twentieth century. At the same time, the important differences are instructive, particularly the emphasis on class antagonism and non-state actors and the progressive view of history. The defeat of communism in the cold war ensured that this concept did not become the new paradigm for equilibrist thinking, but none the less, a more sophisticated balance of power model might usefully incorporate some of the insights contained in the correlation of forces concept.

COLLECTIVE SECURITY AND THE BALANCE OF POWER

Collective security is traditionally viewed as being the antithesis of balance of power politics. As an approach to the creation of national and international security, it emerged from the ashes of the First World War and was seen by many as the precursor of a new world order to replace the balance of power system which had allegedly failed in 1914. The American President Woodrow Wilson insisted that the Great War was a catastrophe which need not be repeated and argued that collective security was the way to prevent future wars, declaring that what the post-war world required was 'not a balance of power, but a community of power, not organised rivalries, but an organised common peace' (Miller, 1980: 45).

Certainly most 'realist' scholars after 1945 were clear in their belief that collective security and the balance of power were entirely dissimilar approaches to international security. Hans Morgenthau argued that whereas balance of power alliances are the product of rational decisions by statesmen on the basis of calculated national interest,

> the organising principle of collective security is the respect for the moral and legal obligation to consider an attack by any nation upon any member of the alliance as an attack upon all members of the alliance. Consequently, collective security is supposed to operate automatically; that is, aggression calls the counter-alliance into operation at once.
>
> (Morgenthau, 1959: 175)

However, there was another school of thought, which numbered many realists among its ranks, which argued that the two concepts in fact had a great deal in common, that the dividing line between the two approaches was a very thin one, if it existed at all. President Wilson assured Congress in February 1918 that 'the great game, now forever discredited, of the balance of power was abolished'. Yet

Martin Wight, a leading British realist after 1945, argued that Wilson had only been in a position to attempt such a reorganisation of international security because of the fact that the United States had itself become part of the balance of power system by entering the First World War in 1917. Indeed, Wight claimed that the supporters of the League of Nations in the interwar period saw collective security not as a way of abolishing the balance of power, but as a mechanism for improving, regulating and institutionalising it. It was simply 'a more scientific development of the doctrine of the balance of power as laid down by Pitt, Castlereagh and Palmerston', in other words, a refinement of the Concert of Powers (Wight, 1966: 173).

That collective security could be seen at one and the same time as both a refinement of the balance of power and as its antithesis is explained by two factors. The first point is that, like 'balance of power' itself, the term 'collective security' has, over time, come to be used to describe phenomena that are far removed from the original concept. In particular, it has often been used to describe partial alliances that would be better termed as examples of 'collective defence'. However, 'collective security' carries with it overtones of the civilised international community acting together in defence of higher ideals, and as such has a clear propaganda value. Not surprisingly, therefore, alliances have been happy to have the term applied to their enterprises in order to benefit from its positive connotations. However, by using the phrase 'collective security' to describe an alliance which is much closer to a traditional balance of power actor, the distinctions between the two approaches become blurred, as for example when describing NATO during the cold war as an example of collective security rather than collective defence.

The second reason why it was possible to argue that balance of power and collective security have much in common, is that the assertion had a great deal of truth. Though there are important differences between the two approaches, which will be looked at later, there are also very important similarities, so that it is not correct to view them as polar opposites. When viewed as points along a continuum from international anarchy to world government the differences are more obvious; when looked at in terms of underlying assumptions and even methods, they have much in common.

In their study of the balance of power, Niou, Ordeshook and Rose argue that the distinction between balance of power and collective security is 'meaningless', and that 'the idea of collective security is an essential part of the balance of power theory' (1989: 159). However, they achieve this by reformulating a definition of security which divests it of its specifically balance of power content, so that the exercise is rather tautological. The balance of power assumption that 'states act to prevent other states from gaining a preponderance of power', becomes the far less prescriptive, 'states formulate their strategic plans under the presumption that other states will act to avert their own elimination' (ibid.).

Though in reality the distinction between the two is not meaningless, there are important similarities, which were amplified by Claude (1962: 123–33). Both systems share the objective of managing power in international relations, but offer different solutions to the problem. Claude argues that while the balance of power approach focuses attention upon the potential of states, that is, upon their capacity for aggression assessed in terms of measurable indices of power, the collective security approach emphasises the question of political intent or purpose. The distinction is not absolute, since balance of power policies in practice also take into account the question of intent. Similarly, collective security regimes have to be concerned with the question of aggressive capacity, since the system can only work if no one state is more powerful than all the other states in the system. This requirement is shared with balance of power systems.

Claude argues that the two systems also share a belief in the general efficiency of deterrence, in that ordinarily, aspiring hegemons will be deterred by the knowledge that their defeat is inevitable if the system works as it is supposed to. In the case of collective security, deterrence is secured by the creation of a permanent blocking coalition, an overwhelmingly powerful alliance of states prepared to act against *any* aggressor. In the case of the balance of power, the relationship with a strategy of deterrence is more ambiguous. Unlike collective security, equality rather than preponderance should deter aggression. Again, in practice, the clear distinction becomes blurred. States can never reach a point of permanent equality, all seek a margin of disposable power in their own 'safe' hands. They seek preponderance rather than equality, but so long as they do so in competition, none is able to attain it. Thus, both systems seek to confront an aggressor with superior power as the preferred option, collective security simply makes this preference more explicit (Claude, 1962: 126).

Another feature common to both balance of power and collective security is a systemic security perspective. Both systems require states to take joint action against aggressors, even when their own territory or interests are not directly or immediately threatened.

> Self-defence becomes a matter of acting with others to forestall the development of a situation in the system at large which would presumably be disadvantageous to the interests of the state in the longer run, rather than confining response to an attack in the here and now.
>
> (Claude, 1962: 127)

Collective security imposes a stronger obligation in this regard, since it is grounded in a legal requirement, rather than merely a commonly perceived interest, but both seek to encourage states to identify their security with the security of other states in the system.

Claude also makes the important point that 'these two systems were designed to deal with essentially the same world; they rest upon broadly similar assumptions concerning the nature of the setting in which they are to operate' (ibid.: 129). For example, as already noted, both require an international system characterised by a diffusion of power among the constituent states. Neither balance of power nor collective security can operate successfully if one state in the system is more powerful than all the other states combined. Both systems depend upon an absence of ideological preference. It is crucial that the victim of aggression is supported, and the aggressor opposed, irrespective of the ideological make up of each party. Neither system will work if states prefer only to aid their 'natural' allies and oppose their 'natural' enemies. It is the fact of aggression which has to be opposed, the identity of the aggressor must be an irrelevance. Thus, Claude cites numerous historical quotations which could describe either the balance of power *or* collective security, for example Mowrer describing the balance in terms that sound like collective security – 'to the aggressive force of the strong individual or oligarchy, it opposes the united defensive force of an entire inter-national community' (ibid.: 132). As earlier chapters have noted, this way of looking at the balance of power as one of the unifying features of the international community has been one of the central ways of conceptualising the idea throughout its history.

Claude concludes by noting the number of scholars who have argued that collective security should be seen as a revised balance of power system, rather than as a completely different approach to the maintenance of international security. In Chapter 6, we noted Gulick's view that the nineteenth-century 'concert' system repre-sented the evolution of balance of power towards collective security, with the latter being a variant of the former (Gulick, 1955: 307–8). This was a view shared by the British historian and international relations theorist Martin Wight, who felt that the collective security approach represented the logical end-point of the gradual evolution of the balance of power system which had taken place in the eighteenth and nineteenth centuries. Collective security meant 'giving the system of the balance of power a legal framework, to make it more rational, more reliable, and therefore more effectively preventive' (Wight, 1973: 110). This view echoes Gulick's assertion that 'the collective security of 1919 or 1945 was merely an elaboration and refinement of the coalition equilibrium of 1815, just as the latter was an elaboration and refinement of the alliance balance' (Gulick, 1955: 307–8). Certainly, the 'Grotian' version of the purpose of a balance of power system brings it very close to the ideal represented by collective security.

THE DIFFERENCES BETWEEN BALANCE OF POWER AND COLLECTIVE SECURITY

For all the many similarities between the two approaches, there are crucial differences which justify classifying them as alternative approaches. There is, as Claude notes, a fundamental difference in the alliance systems which underpin the two approaches. Collective security involves a 'universal' alliance, whereas balance of power is characterised by competitive alliances. It unites rather than divides. For Claude,

> The balance of power system involves alliances which are essentially externally-oriented groupings, designed to organise cooperative action among their members for the purpose of dealing with conflict situations posed by states or groups of states on the outside. By contrast the collective security system looks *inward*, seeking to provide security for all its members against any of their number who might contemplate aggression. Balance of power postulates two or more worlds in jealous confrontation, while collective security postulates one world, organised for the cooperative maintenance of order within its bounds.
>
> (Claude, 1962: 145)

Where collective security differs fundamentally from balance of power is in the mechanism used to harness power. Both recognise the need to contain expansionist and aggressive powers, but where balance of power seeks to do this by manipulating rivalry, collective security seeks to emphasise the possibility of harmonising interests and developing cooperation. The former sees conflict as the norm, the latter treats it as exceptional. 'The former promises competitive security, while the latter promises cooperative security' (ibid.: 146).

Richard Betts argues that the key distinction between the two approaches is that a collective security system is much more dependent upon normative rules than is a balance of power system. It is based upon the norm that states 'must subordinate their own immediate interests to general or remote ones' (Betts, 1993: 269). In the collective security system, aggression should provoke an automatic response from all the other states in the system. The balance of power system is more voluntaristic. It is not aggression as such, but bids for hegemony which must be opposed. Individual states are left with far more latitude in deciding whether or not a particular state, or group of states, represents a genuine threat to the balance of power. If it does not, its aggression can safely go unchallenged if it does not threaten one's parochial national interests. Such aggression might even be welcomed if one's enemies are its victims. Whereas balance of power judges the fact of aggression purely in terms of its impact upon the distribution of power within the political system, collective security identifies aggression and war as inherently evil, to be opposed wherever it arises. The only exception is war in defence of the collective security system itself. Even the idealist Woodrow Wilson accepted that to maintain peace under a collective security system, the international community had to be willing to use military force against transgressors.

This, in turn, leads on to a final major difference between the two approaches. Collective security is not world government, but it certainly involves a far greater degree of political centralisation than does the balance of power system, which in its early eighteenth-century manifestation was almost a synonym for international anarchy, though this was far less true of the nineteenth-century 'concert' version.

Collective security is based upon the institutionalisation of commitment, of response made predictable by being based upon a legal obligation. A number of writers such as Gulick, Wight and Wright argued that collective security was a logical development from balance of power theory in the sense that the balance attempts to ensure that there will always emerge a preponderant coalition capable of defeating a drive for hegemony. Collective security institutionalises this coalition and makes it a permanent feature of the political landscape. It is possible, from this perspective, to view the history of the international system since 1700 as representing a halting, but definite process of steadily greater institutionalisation of the balance of power system, culminating in the emergence of collective security after the First World War.

COLLECTIVE SECURITY IN PRACTICE

Palmer and Perkins argue that the three outstanding historical examples of collective security systems have been the Concert of Europe, the League of Nations and the United Nations. Although they credit the Concert with surviving until after 1878, they conclude that 'instead of superseding the balance of power, it had been dependent upon a balance which for a time had made great power cooperation both desirable and possible' (Palmer and Perkins, 1954: 328). In fact, as noted in the previous chapter, it is going too far to describe the Concert of Europe, even in the era of the Congress System, as 'collective security'. While it did represent a significant modification of the classical eighteenth-century balance of power system, it was nevertheless a variant of the balance.

The League of Nations has a far stronger claim as an example of an attempt to institutionalise and implement collective security in practice. The statesmen who drafted the Covenant of the League of Nations clearly saw the organisation as embodying the principle of collective security. In the first flush of post-war enthusiasm for building a new world order in 1919, governments were remarkably idealistic in their hopes for the League. Their outlook was founded upon their views as to what constituted the 'lessons' of the First World War and the crisis of July–August 1914.

However, the institution they created proved unable to turn the ideal of collective security into reality. There were many reasons why this proved to be the case. Some were the result of the nature of the Covenant itself, others were the product of the reality of the foreign policies pursued by the member states during the League's existence.

As an instrument for institutionalising collective security the League was deficient in a number of respects (Claude, 1962; Hinsley, 1963). The key Covenant Articles in this respect were Article 10, where member states agreed to preserve the independence and territorial integrity of other member states against external aggression, and Article 16, which mandated automatic economic sanctions against states which went to war in defiance of Articles 12 to 15 (which established procedures designed to make possible the pacific settlement of disputes, though they allowed for the use of war if their procedures were tried in good faith and failed). Article 10 was interpreted by member states as meaning that it was up to them to decide what action they should take and that they were by no means obliged to go to war in defence of the attacked state. Though its implementation was called for on a number of occasions, Article 10 was never applied.

A similar emasculation occurred with Article 16. This article declared that if a League member went to war in defiance of its obligations under the Covenant 'it shall *ipso facto* be deemed to have committed an act of war against all other members of the league which hereby undertake immediately to subject it to the severance of all trade and financial relations', and further that it would in such an event be the duty of the Council of the League

> to recommend to the several Governments concerned what effective military, naval or air force the members of the League shall severally contribute to the armed forces to be used to protect the covenants.

Again, the member states quickly moved to dilute this commitment. As early as 1921 the League Assembly decided that it was up to member states, not the League, to decide whether a breach of Articles 12 to 15 had occurred and that no automatic obligation to go to war followed. Article 16 was only implemented once, against Italy after her invasion of Abyssinia in 1935. The League's member states did not impose full immediate sanctions and their token efforts failed to impress Italy and led to a breakdown in confidence in the League and in collective security.

In practice, the League's member states proved reluctant to accept the obligations imposed upon them by the principle of collective security. The European core members of the League were unwilling (and perhaps even unable given their economic weakness) to oppose Japanese aggression against China in 1931. In the 1935 crisis a notable feature was the prevalence of balance of power thinking over a commitment to collective security. Britain refused to impose full-scope sanctions against Italy, because she felt that this would drive Italy into an alliance with Germany.

The League had in any case been crippled from the outset by the fact that a number of major powers remained outside its membership. The United States, Germany and the Soviet Union were not members. Germany was not allowed to join until 1926, the Soviet

Union did not join until 1934 and the United States never joined. The American absence in particular was crucial. The collective security concept implied a universal membership, yet the absence of some of the world's most powerful states, and in particular the United States, robbed it of the overwhelming power it required. The states who were thereby forced to take on the mantle of leadership, Britain and France, had neither the resources nor the desire to fill the gap left by the United States. As the League's authority collapsed in the 1930s it appeared a victory for the balance of power concept. D'Abernon argued that 'the balance of power is a condition for an effective League of Nations' (Palmer and Perkins, 1954: 329).

For Martin Wight, the failure of the League experiment in the 1930s was of critical historical importance. He argues that by 1919 the development of the international system had reached a point where it would either evolve into a genuine collective security system or it would fall back into a more primitive bipolar balance of power system (Wight, 1993: 110). Certainly, the Second World War marked both the final collapse of the League experiment and the emergence of the United States and the Soviet Union as the two 'superpowers' who played a dominant role in the international system for the next 45 years. However, the League's failure led to the creation of a significantly modified successor, the United Nations Organisation, born from the successful wartime alliance and the hope that great power cooperation would mark the period after 1945, as it had after 1815.

The United Nations was in many ways a strengthened version of the League, and the areas where it differed from the League represented in large part concessions to realism, concessions which tended to reduce its ability to act as an instrument of collective security. Those who supported both the United Nations and the concept of collective security reacted to this by broadening the definition of collective security so that UN activities in the security field could be subsumed under the collective security heading. Ernst Haas, for example, argued that UN collective security activities derived from two concepts current within the organisation in the 1950s. One was 'permissive enforcement', based on the anti-communist policies of the United States and its allies. The second was 'balancing', which reflected the efforts of groups of states within the UN to prevent it becoming the tool of one particular group of states, so that UN policy reflected shifting majorities issue by issue (Haas, 1955: 42). According to Haas, collective security ideas, as manifested in the

UN system, 'are derived from the operations of the United Nations and as such reflect the ends of national policy, the conflicts of policy, and the manner in which clashes are reconciled within the institutional structures of United Nations procedures and forces' (ibid.: 43). Haas justified this reinterpretation simply in terms of the failure of the original concept of collective security. 'Collective security based either on universal moral obligations or on a concert of the powerful, while perhaps clearer in its ideological and normative assumptions than the alternatives here proposed, has not in fact flourished' (ibid.: 60).

In Haas' formulation, collective security itself is to a large extent dependent upon a process of balancing, in this case, of groups within the UN. By this, he means a process by which *ad hoc* majorities emerge on specific issues within the UN so that the great powers, and particularly the United States, do not always get their way, and when they do, it is with the resultant policy modified to reflect to some extent the preferences of other states. Haas himself noted that these 'balancing operations are closer to traditional diplomacy, though within the procedural framework of the United Nations, than to the processes assumed by the Wilsonians' (1955: 61-2).

As the article by Haas demonstrates, in the period after 1945 the phrase 'collective security' began to lose its distinctive meaning and came to be applied to arrangements that would be better described as 'collective defence' or 'collective action'. Describing regional security organisations such as NATO as examples of collective security is highly misleading. NATO was simply a traditional defensive alliance whose members were bound together by a pledge of common defence against a perceived threat, in this case that of the Soviet Union and its European allies. There was no sense in which NATO was designed to deter the use of the military instrument *as such*. It remained indifferent to the use of force by its members both inside and outside the areas covered by the NATO treaty. NATO, in fact, far from being an example of collective security, was a classic example of realist balance of power politics.

Similarly, United Nations peacekeeping operations since 1945 are examples of the international community taking collective action in the security field, but bear no resemblance to collective security as such. There is no sense in which such operations reflect an obligation of all states to oppose aggression by any state at any time. The closest it has come to such an approach has been the Korean operation of 1950-3 and the Iraq-Kuwait War of 1990-1, the latter far more so than the former. Unless collective security means an automatic response based upon legal obligation, irrespective of each states direct concern in the area at issue, then the concept has no distinctive meaning.

BALANCING AND BANDWAGONING

The central argument of proponents of the balance of power theory, particularly those concerned with the tendency for balances to materialise at the systemic level, is that balance of power policies are essentially automatic given the nature of the international anarchy. The 'realist' school of international relations in particular has argued, on the basis of what appears to be ample historical evidence, that since 1700 balance of power politics has been a regular and predictable aspect of international relations.

However, this interpretation of diplomatic history is not without its critics. In particular, Schroeder (1991) has taken issue with it on almost every point. According to Schroeder, the pattern of recurrent balance of power policies identified in the historical record is largely an illusion and, in the periods which have been most strongly identified with balance of power politics, other foreign policy strategies were usually preferred to the option of balancing. These views are an extraordinary deviation from the traditional interpretation and deserve to be discussed in some detail.

Schroeder (1991: 5) presents a radically different interpretation of the historical record. For example, Gulick, in his classic study of the balance of power takes the Revolutionary and Napoleonic Wars as his case study, seeing the successive anti-French coalitions as an attempt by the other major powers in Europe to restore political equilibrium to a Europe thrown out of balance by the emergence of the French Empire under Napoleon Bonaparte. Schroeder, however, argues that that First Coalition (1792–97), far from being created to constrain a dominant France, was in fact formed at a time when France was weak, and states joined the coalition precisely because it seemed stronger than France and likely to prevail. When France's power became more evident as the decade progressed, this did not cause new states to flock to the coalition, but rather, led existing allies to desert (Prussia, Tuscany) and in some cases to join the French side, as Spain did. The Second Coalition (1799–1801) saw a similar pattern. From 1799 to 1813, although France had clearly emerged as the dominant continental power, the majority of states chose to ally with France rather than oppose it, a phenomenon known as 'bandwagoning'.

Every major power in Europe except Great Britain (Prussia, Austria, Russia, Spain) became France's active ally for a considerable period during the Napoleonic Wars; many smaller states joined his system, some willingly, others under duress. Wars continued to break out not because European states continually insisted upon trying to balance against the hegemonic power, but because Napoleon's insatiable ambition and lawless conduct frustrated their efforts to hide or bandwagon.

(Schroeder, 1991: 5)

Europe began to swing against Napoleon only after his disastrous invasion of Russia in 1812 and particularly after his defeat at Leipzig in 1813.

Schroeder identifies a similar pattern in the Second World War (1939–45). Prior to its outbreak states in Central and Eastern Europe chose to bandwagon or lie low, but not to firmly oppose Germany. Belgium, Holland, Denmark and Norway all chose neutrality, and even Britain and France moved to oppose Germany only in 1939 when it became clear that Hitler's demands, like Napoleon's, were insatiable. By concluding the Molotov–Ribbentrop pact in 1939 the Soviet Union 'bandwagoned' while Vichy France, Hungary and Romania similarly backed rather than resisted expansionist Germany during the Second World War. Neutral states such as Spain and Sweden leaned towards Germany. Only when Germany was clearly on the road to defeat did Sweden, for example, move to support Germany's opponents.

In between these two clear examples, Schroeder cites the examples of the Crimean War and the First World War. It should be noted that the Crimean War is not usually thought of as a balance of power conflict even by proponents of the concept. However, Schroeder's point concerning these two conflicts is that it is difficult to say clearly whether balancing or bandwagoning was going on. Although the winning side chose to talk in balance of power terms, the reality was that the winners *always* represented a dominant coalition. Russia was not generally seen as a military threat by most European states in the 1850s, and in the 1914–18 conflict most states joined the Allies – the larger of the two coalitions (Schroeder, 1991: 5–6).

More generally, Schroeder argues that the past 300 years has not been characterised by a series of systems in which individual states instinctively pursue balance of power policies when threatened by an expansionist power. States always have alternative options available when pursuing their foreign policy goals. There are various strategies a state might pursue during a dangerous period in international politics. A high-profile strategy of using one's own power to oppose an expansionist state is by no means the automatic response of states. Schroeder identifies a number of alternative strategies which historically states adopted instead of balancing techniques.

One such strategy was 'hiding'. This involved efforts to avoid having to become a direct participant in the crisis on one side or the other. In its most extreme form this would involve adopting an ostrich attitude, paying no attention to the threat or denying its existence. Other techniques were

> declaring neutrality in a general crisis, possibly approaching other states on one or both sides of a quarrel to get them to guarantee it; trying to withdraw into isolation; assuming a purely defensive position in the hope that the storm would blow over; or, usually as a later or last resort, seeking protection from some other power or powers in exchange for diplomatic services, friendship or non-military support without joining that power or powers as an ally or committing itself to any use of force on its part.
>
> (Schroeder, 1991: 3–4)

A second, rarer, strategy was what Schroeder calls 'transcending', which he defines as

> an effort to surmount international anarchy and go beyond the normal limits of conflictual politics by striving for an international consensus or formal agreement on norms, rules and procedures to solve the problem, end the threat and prevent its recurrence.
>
> (Schroeder, 1991: 4)

Schroeder's third strategy is that known as 'bandwagoning', defined as 'joining the stronger side for the sake of protection, even if this meant insecurity *vis-à-vis* the protecting power and a certain sacrifice of independence' (ibid.).

To exemplify these strategies in practice, Schroeder cites the European crisis of 1785, the Bavarian succession crisis when the Austrian Emperor attempted to exchange his territories in the Austrian Netherlands (modern Belgium and Luxembourg) for Bavaria. The German states saw this as a real threat to their security, but their responses differed widely. Some chose to hide, that is, to ignore the issue or remain neutral, despite their recognition that the crisis had grave implications for their own future independence. Some, most notably Prussia, moved to balance the threat from Austria. Some initially adopted neutrality and then bandwagoned by supporting

Prussia once it had become clear that Austria was likely to back down. A number of the smaller states attempted to 'transcend' the issue by forming an alliance of small states whose objective was to reform the institutions of the Holy Roman Empire to guarantee the existing territorial arrangements and create mechanisms for the arbitration of subsequent disputes.

It has been argued that in situations of conflict between the great powers, small or weak states will prefer to remain neutral or band-wagon rather than balance (Baker-Fox, 1957: 186–97, Rothstein, 1968: 11, Walt, 1987: 29). This clearly runs counter to the expectations of a balance of power system. Walt argues that weak states do this because they believe that their strength is too limited to influence the outcome and that they would suffer heavily in the conflict. It is therefore imperative for them to be on the winning side at all times, irrespective of whether or not the winning side threatens the balance of power (Walt, 1987: 29–30). However, Walt also argues that weak states can be expected to pursue balance of power strategies when they are threatened by states with similar capabilities to their own. According to Labs (1992: 385), 'most literature on weak state behaviour in international relations theory accepts that weak states tend to bandwagon with a threatening Great Power'.

Labs himself does not subscribe to this view and cites a number of examples of states resisting a great power. Some of these examples are dubious, however. Belgium in 1914 or Finland in 1939, where a small state chose to fight a great power without a guaranteed promise of military support from allies, are hardly examples of 'balancing'. There was no sense in which these actions were conscious attempts to create or restore a balance of power. Labs goes on to accept that in other cases, Czechoslovakia in 1938, for example, small states did effectively bandwagon. The question this provokes therefore, is under what circumstances do small states prefer to bandwagon rather than balance?

As noted in Chapter 4, Walt argues that a state's threat assessment is effected not only by a simple calculation of relative military strength, but includes geographic proximity, offensive capability and aggressive intentions as well. Thus, while states will tend to balance, the choice of who to balance against, may well not be simply the strongest military power or combination. Looked at in these terms it is possible to see for example, the alliance patterns of the First World War as reflecting balancing rather than bandwagoning. The later-joining allies were responding not just to the military balance, but also to the relative sense of aggressive intention, which inclined them to oppose the Central Powers. However, this still cannot account for all the anomalies. For example, as Schroeder (1991: 4) points out, when Japan and China joined the Allied Powers in the First World War, they were simply bandwagoning – Japan in order to seize German possessions and China in order to gain the protection represented by alliance with Britain and France.

Balancing behaviour can also be affected by a phenomenon which Barry Posen calls 'buckpassing' (Posen, 1984: 63). In a multipolar balance of power system, while the need to oppose expansionist states may be evident, it may not be so evident as to which state or states should accept the responsibility for doing so. Each major power may decide to allow this responsibility to fall elsewhere, and if they all do this then the threat would not be countered. To accept the responsibility would be to assume burdens and costs while providing free benefits for the other great powers in the system. Only those states so geographically close to the threat as to be unable to avoid responding may take action, and these may be insufficiently powerful in themselves to achieve success. Posen argues that 'buckpassing' contributed to the British and French failure to deter Germany in the 1930s.

Like Schroeder, Labs argues that states (in his case weak states) have a number of policy options available to them during great power crises, not all of which involve following the 'rules' of the balance of power (Labs, 1992: 389–90). In his typology the options are: non-alignment, bandwagon, balance and not fight, ally with other weak states, balance and fight, fight alone. Only two of the options fall into the balance of power category. The order in which the options are listed reflects the order of preference of states, at least in the view of most scholars. Significantly, even a limited commitment to balance emerges as only the third choice.

Labs himself does not find this argument convincing and challenges the evidence from the diplomatic history of the 1930s, on which it is based. The critical factor, in his view, is the presence or not of a promise by a great power to come to the support of the weak state, should it follow balancing 'rules' and oppose the aggressor. 'Weak states need the hope that the aggressor will ultimately be defeated to balance against it. That the weak state might suffer considerable destruction in the meantime rarely affects this inclination to balance' (Labs, 1992: 393). Labs modifies the order of preference as: non-alignment, balance with a protecting great power without fighting, balance with a protecting great power and fight, seek an alliance of weak states, fight alone, bandwagon.

In this significant re-ordering, the two balance of power strategies have advanced to second and third preference, while the strategy most antithetical to balance of power politics, bandwagoning, is relegated to least attractive option. Labs supports his argument with a detailed case study of the international politics of German unification between 1860 and 1866.

What is clear from these arguments is that the adoption of balance of power policies is by no means an automatic response by states. International relations theorists have tended to identify broad patterns of behaviour as evidence for the existence of balance of power systems. There is clearly a need for more detailed research in this regard. More exhaustive historical studies of particular eras might well reveal that the balance of power concept served an ideological function in justifying policy, rather than a prescriptive purpose in mandating it. Much might depend on what exactly statesmen conceived of when they spoke of the 'balance of power' or 'international equilibrium'.

THE 'ASSOCIATIVE' BALANCE OF POWER

In Chapter 1 it was suggested that the intellectual tradition in which balance of power thinking has historically been embedded is that of power politics, or 'realism'. This is certainly the prism through which it is usually analysed. However, this traditional interpretation is not without its critics. In particular, Richard Little and Paul Schroeder have proposed that the historical record provides clear evidence that the 'power-politics' interpretation of the balance of power is not the only one.

Schroeder's arguments have already been looked at in the context of the nineteenth-century balance of power system. His critique rests upon a distinction between 'balance of power' and 'political equilibrium' and the argument that the nineteenth-century system 'depended mainly not on balancing power against other power but on balancing other vital factors in international politics, and that pure balance of power politics destroys political equilibrium rather than sustains it' (Schroeder, 1989: 135).

Little's critique identifies two competing traditions within balance of power thought and argues that, since the emergence of international relations as an academic discipline in the twentieth century, there has been a consistent and misleading tendency to identify and discuss only one of the conceptions. Little calls these two conceptions the 'adversarial' and 'associative' balance of power traditions.

The former 'depicts political actors in competitive and self-interested terms', while the latter 'assumes that in a balance of power political actors can be cooperative and pursue policies which embrace the interests of others' (Little, 1989: 88).

The adversarial balance concept is rooted in realist assumptions about the nature of international relations. It embodies a coercive conception of power and an image of international politics which reflects the implications of the 'security dilemma', with states seeking to expand by force and fearing the similar tendencies in their neighbours. The emphasis is on the accumulation and use of military force, an atmosphere of tension and uncertainty and a constant struggle to survive and expand. It is the 'Hobbesian', Anglo-Saxon version of balance of power theory noted in earlier chapters.

Little contrasts this with the 'associative' balance of power. This conception, it is argued, originally emerged in the domestic state context and is founded upon a 'communal' or cooperative conception of power. In this perspective to have power is to be 'empowered by a certain number of people to act in their name' (Arendt, 1970: 44). Little points out that neither classical nor modern thinkers have emphasised this conception of power in respect to international relations. Yet statesmen who have conceived of the balance of power as a system have frequently employed a conception of the international equilibrium which implies an associative rather than an adversarial balance of power. Little cites as historical examples the policies of Metternich and Castlereagh in the first half of the nineteenth century. In this conception, a balance of power does not arise as an incidental by-product of the selfish power-seeking policies of individual states. Rather, it is the result of a deliberately fostered equilibrium, based upon a just settlement which recognises and attempts to harmonise the interest of all states, so that they have an interest in supporting and defending the new *status quo*. Thus, for the Austrian statesman Metternich, 'The establishment of international relations on the basis of reciprocity under the guarantee of respect for acquired rights ... constitutes in our time the essence of politics' (Little, 1989: 95), and it was this that produced an equitable and effective balance of power. This is a conception which is much closer to the European interpretation that emerged at the end of the seventeenth century as one of the responses to the 'general crisis' of that century and which has been referred to as the 'Grotian' conception in this study, because it accords with Grotius' ideas regarding the nature of international society. Thus, to produce a stable balance, it is necessary not only to oppose the hegemonic drives of expansionist states and pursue settlements that do not create future threats, but to do so in ways that create or maintain an overall acceptance of the *status quo*. These are demanding requirements which will not always be easy to reconcile. However, if successfully pursued, they allow for the international system to be conceived of as an international society, rather than as an international anarchy.

CONCLUSIONS

According to Stubbs (1886: 225), balance of power is 'the principle which gives unity to the political plot of European history'. However, in seeing the balance of power idea in this way it is important to bear in mind three things. Firstly, that the balance of power has not been the only organising principle in international relations and its currency should not delude us into thinking that it has been. Secondly, even in periods when balance of power policies have been generally recommended or approved of, not all states have chosen to allow them to determine their foreign policies. Thirdly, even when the 'balance' has been the publicly proclaimed objective of statesmen, caution is required since the phrase can cover so many different meanings. It is going too far to argue that 'where balance of power is not a meaningless mantra, it is used as a substitute for something else' (Gellman, 1989: 178), but none the less it is important to identify the particular sense in which a balance of power is being sought and to recognise that even with that caveat 'it follows that balance of power doctrine can account for only part of the world's political behaviour' (Sterling, 1972: 70).

8 The balance of power in the nuclear era

INTRODUCTION

There was a school of thought in the 1950s which argued that the traditional mechanisms of the balance of power had been rendered obsolete by the advent of nuclear technology, and that nuclear deterrence represented a new and quite different method for regulating the international anarchy. Burns (1957: 494–529) can be taken as exemplifying this approach. Against this were the views of those such as Snyder, who argued that 'the balance of power theory is still generally valid and still a useful model of at least certain aspects of contemporary world politics. The new military technology has not terminated but only modified the balance of power process' (Snyder, 1965: 186). According to Snyder, what occurred after 1945 was the superimposition of a new system of equilibrium, whose use of phraseology like 'the balance of terror' reflected a continuing preoccupation with balance, upon the pre-nuclear balance of power system. 'The two systems operate according to different tendencies and principles and can be separated analytically, but in practice they are inextricably mixed in a new balance of power in which elements of the old coexist with the new' (ibid.).

It is often asserted that the First World War closed the age of the balance of power, that the twentieth century has been guided by other techniques for managing the international system, such as collective security and the nuclear balance of terror. But this is not entirely true. The international system between 1945 and 1990 was marked by the pursuit and maintenance of equilibrium between the superpowers and their respective blocs. It was clearly not the classical system in which the balancing of power was crucial to the maintenance of the system and the avoidance of instability, but though it differed from the balance of power system in important respects, it also shared some features with its predecessor. Michael Mandelbaum has suggested that,

> if the balance of power is defined by the condition of the international system rather than its composition – in behavioural rather than formal terms – then the system since 1945 has been as 'balanced' as it was before and after Napoleon. Out of the same fundamental condition, anarchy, came the same general result – equilibrium, defined as the absence of preponderance.
>
> (Mandelbaum, 1981: 54)

NUCLEAR DETERRENCE

A month before the American nuclear attacks on Japan in 1945, the first test of a nuclear weapon took place. As he watched the test, the weapon's chief designer J. Robert Oppenheimer recalled some lines from the Hindu religious epic *The Bhagavad Gita*, 'Now I am become death, destroyer of worlds, waiting the hour that ripens to their doom'. A few months later Bernard Brodie published *The Absolute Weapon,* in which he argued that such was the awesome destructive power of nuclear weapons that they would be a tremendous inhibitor of aggression and that in the future, the primary task of the world's armed forces would not be to win wars, but to avert them (1946: 76).

Certainly, the advent of nuclear weapons seemed to presage a world very different from the old, the true dawning of a new age in international politics. President Truman declared that nuclear weapons represented 'a new force too revolutionary to consider in the framework of old ideas' (Mandelbaum, 1981: 1). There was a general expectation that nuclear weapons would render earlier practices, such as the balance of power, clearly obsolete.

However, the subsequent course of political history showed that these expectations were unwarranted. In crucial ways the development of nuclear weapons did not change the nature of international relations. Most notably of all, the international anarchy persisted. Despite the incredible dangers represented by nuclear weapons, the international system did not develop into a form of world government in order to control the weaponry. Nor indeed was interstate war abolished, as some had thought it might be, though there was no war between the great powers. However, Kenneth Waltz has argued that nuclear weapons did effectively abolish direct war between the United States and the Soviet Union, and that only the international opposition to the further spread of nuclear weapons has prevented the 'nuclear peace' from embracing a steadily larger number of states (Waltz, 1981: *passim*). Indeed, one critic of Waltz's views has argued that implicit in Waltz's argument is the idea that nuclear weapons *do* have the capacity to abolish the condition of international anarchy, that 'nuclear capability orders the state system in much the same way that Hobbes' Sovereign does civil society; peace is guaranteed for all actors, borders between the actors are preserved, and the actors face law-like certainty (Deudney, 1993: 15).

Certainly, the existence of nuclear weapons strongly influenced the ways in which the great powers behaved towards each other in this period. The danger of nuclear war encouraged the two super-powers in particular to treat each other with tremendous circumspection, treading with great care when their interests came into conflict. It encouraged both sides to explore possibilities of moderating their competition through the mechanism of arms control, and it encouraged the development of a balance of power system based upon the doctrine of deterrence; one in which the great powers paradoxically amassed huge amounts of military power in the hope that they would never have to use it.

The idea of deterrence is not novel to the nuclear era, nor to international relations. It is simply the attempt to influence behaviour by making a contingent threat to inflict a punishment greater than any reward the opponent might gain from carrying out its original intention. Deterrence does not have to depend on military force – it might involve sanctions of some other kind, but the greater the threatened punishment, the more impressive the threat, and the threat to use nuclear weapons represents an ultimate sanction that no state could afford to ignore.

Unlike the use of military force in the pre-nuclear balance of power system, nuclear deterrence does not work through physically obstructing a particular course of action, but instead makes the action appear an unattractive option to choose in the first place, because the costs would outweigh the gains.

Although the concept of deterrence is a simple one, it proved an extremely complicated one to implement. For nuclear deterrence to operate effectively, a number of elements need to be successfully implemented. The first of these relates to communication. Communication is central in the sense that deterrence is based on a believable contingent threat. It is crucial, therefore, that the adversary knows precisely what actions are forbidden. Similarly, the adversary must be aware of precisely what will happen if it ignores the threat.

Secondly, in order to deter, a state must possess the capability to implement its threat. In the early 1950s there was a tendency to believe that all that was required in this respect was the possession of a number of nuclear weapons. It was assumed that no state would be foolish enough to challenge a state that possessed such weapons. During the 1950s, however, this simple notion began to be challenged in a number of ways, particularly once the Soviet Union had become the second nuclear-armed state.

The idea that a few nuclear weapons were all that were required was vulnerable on a number of grounds. In 1945 the United States had possessed complete air superiority over Japan and could attack its targets at will. In the 1950s, however, US planners had to consider that the USSR would attempt to intercept and destroy American nuclear bombers and, therefore, for its threat to be credible the US needed to possess large numbers of nuclear weapons, carried to their targets by delivery vehicles that would be very difficult, and preferably impossible, to intercept. Missiles would be superior to manned bombers in that respect.

In the late 1950s attention was drawn to the vulnerability of these systems. In theory, the possession of a number of nuclear weapons which could reach their targets after launch provided deterrence. However, most of the weapons were vulnerable to a surprise attack. For example, in the late 1950s a sudden, unexpected Soviet attack on the USA might have caught all the American bombers on the ground, and the few long-range missiles, which could be fired only after long preparation, would be unable to launch. In this case, all the American weapons would be destroyed and would be unable to punish the Soviets for their attack. Analysts such as Albert Wohlstetter (1959: 211–35) argued that in such a situation the weapons could not deter such an attack. Therefore, what mattered was not the absolute number of nuclear weapons a state possessed, but the rather the proportion of that force which could survive a sudden 'first strike'. It was this 'second-strike capability' which would actually be the deterrent, since the other side only needed to fear what would survive to be launched in retaliation. Thus, the USA acquired additional weapons (to allow for losses) and deployed a significant proportion on invulnerable submarines. A proportion of the bomber fleet was kept ready for immediate take-off and the planes dispersed to a much larger number of airfields, and the older missiles were gradually replaced with quick-response missiles housed in protected underground silos. All this made the 'second-strike capability' almost invulnerable.

Although it was possible that the other side might achieve a technological breakthrough which threatened this second-strike capability, by basing one's deterrent on a 'triad' of three different technologies – manned bombers, land-based missiles and submarine-based missiles – the risk represented by this danger could be reduced almost to zero. It was very unlikely that all three types of technology would be threatened by novel developments at the same time.

One further refinement was added to the deterrent calculation in the mid-1960s. Deterrence was based on the idea that a state would be deterred from action by the threat that if it did so it would have to pay too high a price, it would suffer 'unacceptable damage'.

But this raised the question of what exactly constituted 'unacceptable' damage. Unacceptable to whom? Would a level of death and destruction that would have deterred the USA do the same for the USSR? Deterrence is primarily a psychological phenomenon. What matters is not how you would react, but how the person you are trying to deter would react in the same circumstances. The USA, therefore, had to try to estimate, through Russian eyes, what would seem 'unacceptable' when viewed from the perspective of the Soviet leadership in Moscow.

Having decided upon a satisfactory level of assumed destruction, one final complication remained. The logic of the 'triad' of delivery systems was that the other side might at some point in the future achieve a technological breakthrough that would undermine the effectiveness of one element of the triad. For example, new anti-aircraft missiles or fighters might mean that the bombers could not get through. It might take several years to overcome this and restore the effectiveness of the manned bomber element of the triad. It was almost certain that this kind of threat would face one leg of the triad at some point. However, the two other systems could bear the burden of deterring the enemy while this problem was overcome. It was even possible, though much less likely, that two legs of the triad might be threatened simultaneously. In this case, the remaining leg would have to deter the adversary unaided by the other two.

However, given that there was an identified minimum level of assured destruction required to deter, and given that it was theoretically possible that for a period a single leg of the triad might have to carry the burden on its own, then that leg would on its own have to be able to inflict the necessary 'unacceptable' levels of destruction on the enemy, and do so even after absorbing the enemy's first strike. This requirement pushed the total number of weapons required up to very high levels, and those high levels were bound to seem disproportionately menacing to the other side.

Even more difficult to achieve for deterrence to work was the question of credibility. For deterrence to be effective, the adversary must not only calculate that in the event of the aggression the costs *could* outweigh the gains, it must be convinced that they *would* do so. In other words, it must be convinced that the threat would be implemented, almost automatically.

This situation is not intrinsically easy to achieve. For one thing, the threat is almost unbelievable. Except in the direst circumstances, perhaps a direct nuclear attack on one's own homeland, the risks involved in retaliating are enormous. For example, the USA gave a nuclear guarantee to its European NATO allies, that it would use nuclear weapons against Soviet conventional forces if necessary. But to do so would almost certainly have triggered Soviet retaliation, eventually leading to an all-out nuclear exchange in which the United States would be totally annihilated. It is not easy to convince the adversary that in certain circumstances you would initiate a course of action that would lead to the death of your entire population. Nor, since nuclear deterrence must always work, can you prove your sincerity by occasionally fighting a small nuclear war. You can demonstrate resolve by fighting conventional wars, but that would still not be proof that you would cross the nuclear threshold if necessary, since the implications are so enormously different in each case.

The policy of deterrence was criticised for a number of reasons. It was argued that it was a dangerous development that under deterrence policy was 'based on the idea of preventing war by the threat of punishment, rather than the time-honoured principle of avoiding war through negotiation and diplomacy' (McGuire, 1986: 24).

In addition, critics such as McGuire argued that the doctrine of deterrence led to a particularly dangerous mind-set among the strategic planners. The need to ensure a second-strike capability under all circumstances led to the adoption of the most extreme form of worst-case analysis. At the same time, the advantages of actually striking first were so great that each side had to work hard to reassure the other side that it was not attempting to acquire a first-strike capability. This latter requirement forced both sides to attempt to display self-restraint when it came to weapon deployments, but this proved extremely difficult to achieve, because it could only be achieved by denying oneself the means to limit damage if deterrence failed and nuclear war broke out (for example by pursuing strategic defences, and counterforce weapons).

DIFFERENCES BETWEEN BALANCE OF POWER AND BALANCE OF TERROR

Snyder argues that to compare and integrate the two systems, a number of fundamental questions have to be posed. What is the nature of the 'power' which each system is attempting to balance and what is the nature of 'equilibrium' in each case? (Snyder, 1965: 188). In traditional balance of power theory, the emphasis was upon the physical capability to take or hold territory. An equilibrium existed when each side possessed military capabilities which were approximately equal. But as Hedley Bull (1977: 122) pointed out, this kind of relationship was not necessary in a nuclear balance. In the latter case, all that was required was a devastating retaliatory capability, an assured 'second strike'. It did not have to represent equality. The levels of death and destruction were so great that even quite large differences between the two sides were of no practical military significance.

In any case, nuclear weapons cannot take or hold territory. Physical conquest still requires the use of conventional forces. However, nuclear weapons can make a major contribution to the first goal in the Napoleonic sense – by eliminating the armed forces of the enemy, his territory and population are then at your mercy. The implication of this is that in the case of the balance of terror, it is essentially political power which is being balanced, not crude military capacity.

Another important difference distinguishes the eighteenth-century balance of power from the two centuries which followed. In the eighteenth century equilibrium was produced through the interaction of European foreign policies without a high degree of coordination. In contrast, the nineteenth and twentieth centuries have seen a significant degree of coordinated balancing policies between the major powers, even when, as after 1945, they have been clear antagonists, in fact 'since the Napoleonic Wars there has been a conscious management of military might to forestall disequilibrium' (Mandelbaum, 1981: 54).

Both Snyder and Bull argue that a further difference between the balance of power and the balance of terror is that the latter involves rather more subjective judgement than the former. Equilibrium is seen as being as much determined 'within the minds' of the opponents 'as upon an objective comparison of military capabilities' (Snyder, 1965: 189). For example, deterrence thinking relies heavily upon rational cost-benefit calculations and these are subjective judgements. The equilibrium that is being sought is one based upon the ability to inflict 'unacceptable' levels of destruction upon the other side. But it is difficult to estimate objectively what constitutes 'unacceptable' damage in the eyes of the other side, particularly since this may change in response to changes in the nature of the issues at stake.

The participants in the deterrent balance face the problem of ethnocentrism. On key questions, it might be clear to them how they would react in a given situation, but they might be unsure how the other side would react when faced with the same situation. For example, in assessing what constitutes 'unacceptable' levels of destruction, the criteria will be levels which 'we' would find unacceptable. For the other side, however, this same point might be higher or lower and it is virtually impossible to be certain when making the calculation.

Thus, there is scope for misjudgement about the state of the balance (though this was true also in the balance of power). There may be an equilibrium and yet one side may fear that the other side has a full first-strike capability. However, for deterrence to occur, it is not necessary to establish absolute certainty in the mind of the enemy that retaliation will follow. Given the nature of that retaliation, a high probability that it will be initiated should be enough to deter.

Despite these subjective factors, a nuclear balance of terror still requires the ability to estimate relative military strengths, as was clearly demonstrated during the strategic arms race between the United States and Soviet Union. The nature of that equilibrium is different, however, since it does not rely on numeral parity, though for political reasons such a parity may still be sought. As long as the weaker side can absorb a first strike and still inflict 'unacceptable' damage in retaliation, then strict numerical equivalence, 'optical parity' as it has been called, is unimportant.

A further distinction between the two approaches concerns the relative importance of deterrence and defence. In the traditional balance of power, the same forces and capabilities performed both functions, though deterrence was essentially a secondary by-product of the ability to successfully defend. Unlike the classical balance of power approach, deterrence operates primarily in terms of perceptions, and particularly, intentions. In the balance of power system, defensive war was the main balancing mechanism and war was seen as entirely appropriate if the balance *per se* failed to act as a deterrent.

With the balance of terror, however, the calculations are quite different. Here, deterrence is everything, and is achieved through the threat of unendurable punishment. If the threat ever has to be implemented, the result is an all-out nuclear war, with catastrophic consequences for both sides. Both sides have a powerful incentive to avoid action which requires the deterrent threats ever to be implemented. If nuclear weapons are ever used, then deterrence will have failed. Whereas war in the balance of power system was a legitimate and appropriate part of the balancing process, in nuclear deterrence it signifies the catastrophic failure of that process.

According to Herz (1960: 36) a further critical difference between the two approaches is the role played by war. In the earlier system, war or the threat of war was a central, functional tool used by states to defend their status and interests. In the nuclear era, in contrast, although the military power at the disposal of the nuclear states is infinitely greater, it is far less functional in that it cannot be used against the major adversary without triggering a retaliatory strike which would mean national annihilation. Thus, 'nuclear war defeats its own purpose by exposing to annihilation that which it was the function of previous wars to protect : the national substance' (ibid.).

Herz argues that the pre-nuclear balance of power system was simple by comparison, because the role of war and weapons was simple. War in the classical system was limited in terms of means, techniques and objectives. 'War served to maintain a system of independent nation-states' (Snyder, 1960: 38). It did not guarantee the continuing existence of every specific state, as the partitions of Poland showed, but it did maintain the system of sovereign states.

Mandelbaum argues that *attitudes* towards war are a major distinguishing feature between the classical balance of power and the post-1945 system. War was certainly a normal and acceptable instrument of policy in the eighteenth century. However, as early as the nineteenth century this was ceasing to be the case. Although war has been no less frequent, the major powers have become less eager to embrace it as a tool of foreign policy and have sought to consciously limit it where they could. Indeed, the avoidance of war has itself become an objective of twentieth-century balance of power politics, in a way that was certainly never true of the eighteenth-century system, at least in the sense of avoidance of a general war involving all the major states. 'In the eighteenth century the favoured instrument of the balance of power was war, in the nineteenth and twentieth centuries it has been diplomacy' (Mandelbaum, 1981: 55).

This change in attitude had a similar origin in both cases – a military revolution that made general war, and therefore the traditional working of the balance of power system, too costly to continue. War did not cease to be a usable tool of policy for defending the balance, but it had come to be one that involved an enormous cost.

In both 1815 and 1945 the victorious wartime coalition initially attempted to construct a collective security framework to manage the post-war world, but in both cases this eventually crumbled, to be replaced by a system based upon balance of power logic. Neither the Quadruple Alliance after 1815, nor the United Nations after 1945 was able to sustain the wartime harmony of interests indefinitely, though the former was far more successful than the latter. Both failed because the great powers after each major conflict were ideologically divided. They were therefore unable to agree upon and implement a post-war world order that reflected an ideological consensus between them.

In neither case did the system move all the way back to a 'pure' decentralised balance of power, though neither did it move forward to collective security. It was 'a modified, managed balance, with a measure of co-operation among the leading states and some rules to govern their interaction that went beyond the avoidance of hegemony' (Mandelbaum, 1981: 65).

In important ways, however, both the post-1815 systems were very different from the eighteenth-century system. Both were characterised by a significant degree of cooperation between the major states in the system and the need for this cooperation was recognised by the actors themselves. In addition, in the post-1815 systems there was a general recognition that, not only should the military strength of the major powers be in equilibrium, but also that the foreign policies of the great powers should be characterised by self-conscious restraint.

In the nineteenth century, the cooperation was an outgrowth of the workings of the wartime coalition against Napoleon. In the post-1945 system it was a necessity brought about by the mutual possession of nuclear weapons. The managed balance of power system after 1945 was therefore a 'nuclear system'.

A further, and more controversial, difference between the balance of power system and the balance of terror is suggested by McGuire's critique of deterrence. The eighteenth-century 'classical' balance operated in an age largely unaffected by ideology and nationalism. Defeated states were quickly re-integrated into the system. Warfare itself was limited, and to a great extent its effects were limited to the warring armies. Compared to the preceding century and the Napoleonic period, the eighteenth century was characterised by limited war fought with limited means for limited objectives.

The nuclear balance of terror inhabits a very different moral and political context. Nuclear deterrence requires supposedly civilised states to credibly threaten an act of unspeakably vile barbarism, to unleash the worst crime in human history. During the cold war, for example, Britain and the United States held the people of Eastern Europe hostage. Had deterrence failed, Britain and America would have burned, exploded and irradiated to death hundreds of millions of people in Eastern Europe and Central Asia. The slaughter would have extended to the old, the very young, the sick or mentally retarded in hospital, with no distinction between soldier and civilian, government and governed, indeed, in countries where the people had no genuine opportunity to influence their government. It would have been a genocidal attack upon the innocent and helpless.

To pose the 'second strike' in these terms, unclouded by jargon or anodyne language, demonstrates how difficult such an action is to contemplate. Not surprisingly, strategists preferred to speak of 'counter-value targeting' and 'collateral damage' to describe genocide. In order to make such a horrible threat acceptable, it was necessary for Western public opinion to believe that the peoples of Eastern Europe could deserve such a terrible fate. They therefore had to be constantly reminded of the reality of the Soviet military threat to the West and assured of the essentially evil nature of communists and their people. Such a perspective, however, was not conducive to the negotiation of rules of restrained conduct between the two sides which the deterrent structure required if stability was to be maintained. It was present in high places as late as the early 1980s, as President Reagan's 'Evil Empire' speech demonstrated.

Thus, according to McGuire, there was a mismatch between two objectives in this period – deterring the other side and avoiding nuclear war. The 'threat' from the other side tended to be simply taken for granted rather than constantly questioned. If an enemy course of action was conceivable, it was assumed that they would do it. Nuclear deterrence became a cult, with its own arcane mysteries and rituals. Periodic attempts to improve the political relationship before the mid-1980s tended to founder in the face of the conflicting reality of massive nuclear 'overkill' and continuing rapid weapons development and deployment.

INTERACTIONS IN THE 'MIXED' BALANCE OF POWER

In the period after 1945 the nuclear and conventional balances were not self-contained mechanisms, rather they interacted with each other in a number of important ways. To this extent therefore, the balancing process during the NATO–Warsaw Pact era involved a combination of the two. According to Snyder (1965: 192), an overall balance within the system existed when either of two conditions were met. These were either that the two balances, nuclear and conventional, were separately in equilibrium, or that the two were not in balance, but the advantage in each was held by a different side, so that its preponderance in one area compensated for its inferiority in another. The system was unbalanced if disequlibrium was present in both sub-balances, or if one was balanced while the other was not.

These processes could be seen at work in the post-1945 competition between the United States and the Soviet Union. For most of the period the USSR and its Warsaw Pact (WTO) allies were seen as holding a definite superiority in the conventional balance of forces in Europe. Just how significant this advantage was, was always difficult to estimate accurately, because the Warsaw Pact advantage was essentially numerical and NATO commanders always believed that this was offset to a large degree by the superiority of NATO equipment, training and motivation in defence. This led to rising NATO concern during the 1970s, as qualitative improvements in Warsaw Pact weaponry narrowed NATO's edge in this area and increased the perceived WTO conventional preponderance.

NATO strategy attempted to offset the WTO conventional superiority with a preponderance in nuclear weapons. The nature of the nuclear weapons NATO used for this purpose evolved over time, and eventually became part of a complex multi-layered nuclear capability. Initially, the nuclear component was represented by American strategic nuclear weapons. During the 1950s the United States possessed a clear strategic nuclear superiority over the Soviet Union. The USSR did not have ICBMs or long-range bombers capable of delivering a major nuclear assault on the United States. The USA, which had hundreds of long-range bombers able to operate from airfields in Western Europe, could threaten the USSR with nuclear devastation in the event of war. 'Massive (nuclear) retaliation' would thus be the NATO response to any Soviet invasion of Western Europe.

However, as the 1950s progressed, the Soviet Union gradually began to deploy long-range nuclear forces of its own. By the end of the decade the reliability of the US nuclear guarantee to Europe was brought into question. It no longer seemed credible that the USA would invite its own nuclear destruction by using its strategic nuclear forces to counter a Soviet conventional attack on Europe. The credibility of the deterrent had declined, because the ability of the USSR to retaliate with a 'second strike' made the NATO allies doubt whether America would risk using its nuclear weapons. The advent of strategic parity was beneficial to the stability of the super-power balance in the bilateral relationship, but seemed to undermine the concept of 'extended deterrence', that is, America's willingness to risk everything on behalf of its allies.

NATO was therefore faced with the problem of how to restore deterrence in Europe. One possibility was for NATO to increase its own conventional force level to match those of the WTO. This option was ruled out, however, both because it would have been extremely expensive and because the European allies feared that if a conventional balance was achieved it might make the idea of fighting a European conventional war thinkable.

If a conventional balance was unattainable, and perhaps ultimately undesirable, the alternative, clearly, was increased reliance on nuclear weapons. It was argued that the WTO armies could be attacked and destroyed using 'tactical' or 'battlefield' nuclear weapons with comparatively low yields. This being the case, the WTO would have no incentive to attack and deterrence would be restored. It was felt that nuclear weapons were in any case a more effective deterrent psychologically than were conventional weapons, because the threat posed was so much greater.

The European doubts were not assuaged, however. The European NATO allies felt that 'an attempt to deter conventional aggression in Europe with a nuclear arsenal controlled by a non-European power that is itself subject to nuclear retaliation' was hardly 'an example of political and military rationality' (Freedman, 1981–2: 50).

The United States attempted to overcome these doubts with the doctrine of 'flexible response', adopted by NATO in 1967. Under flexible response NATO would enhance its military capabilities at all levels, so that at whatever level a WTO threat emerged, it could be matched in kind. However, to achieve this would require just the kind of massive, sustained increases in defence spending which the European NATO allies had been resisting since the early 1950s. They therefore failed to make the effort required to match the WTO conventional forces.

Even if the money had been available, Europe would not have implemented the strategy fully. European leaders feared that by acquiring the capacity to fight a credible conventional war in Europe, NATO might encourage the USSR to believe that it could launch a conventional attack on Western Europe without having to fear a nuclear response. Flexible response seemed to some Europeans to reduce rather than increase the likelihood that America would fulfil its nuclear guarantee. The doctrine held that if the deterrent failed at any level, NATO would escalate to the next level and ultimately would be willing to use strategic nuclear weapons. Yet if this was the case, Europeans argued, why bother with the intermediate steps? The ultimate guarantee remained the American willingness to use nuclear weapons even if that risked retaliation against the United States itself. Thus, NATO doctrine continued to be what one critic described as 'an inadequate conventional defence backed by an incredible nuclear guarantee' (Freedman, 1981–2: 55).

Although NATO's nuclear doctrine contained obvious inconsistencies, European leaders appeared to welcome the ambiguity of the European nuclear equation. Some of their decisions acted to increase this ambiguity, for example, the procurement of large numbers of weapons which were 'dual-capable', that is, capable of carrying either nuclear or conventional warheads, such as 155mm artillery and F-111 fighter-bombers. Such systems were cheaper to procure than two-weapon systems (one for each task), but had the effect of blurring the distinction between conventional and nuclear weapons and bringing forward the moment in a conflict when NATO would have to go nuclear.

Until the mid-1970s the system remained in overall balance because it reflected Snyder's second version. Imbalances existed at both the strategic nuclear and conventional level, but these favoured different sides. NATO reassured itself by creating linkages between the two levels. The conventional imbalance was tolerable because NATO could, if necessary escalate any conflict to the battlefield and 'theatre' nuclear levels where it retained an advantage and, if this failed, could escalate to the strategic nuclear level where it was unambiguously superior. The steady build-up of Soviet nuclear weaponry after 1960 gradually undermined this position, however. NATO's superiority at the battlefield nuclear level and theatre levels disappeared as the WTO deployed similar or greater numbers of equivalent systems. As long as the United States possessed superiority at the strategic level this was tolerable, but by the end of 1972, this strategic nuclear balance had been frozen and codified in the first Strategic Arms Limitation Treaty, SALT I.

NATO now perceived itself to be in a situation where there was an imbalance favouring the WTO at the conventional level, and balances or marginal WTO advantages at all the higher levels. In Snyder's conception this was not a situation of equilibrium and it triggered a major effort by the NATO states at all levels to attempt to close the gap at the conventional level and to re-establish a margin favouring NATO at the higher levels. This was reflected in the Long-Term Defence Programme to boost conventional forces, the 1979 'twin-track' modernisation decision for new theatre nuclear weapons, and US efforts to boost warhead numbers, deploy more capable first-strike systems such as the MX missile, and ultimately to deploy strategic defences via the SDI programme. The need to fund these efforts severely weakened the American economy generating a ballooning budget deficit, but the economic pressures induced by attempting to match the American programme by the USSR ultimately led to the collapse of communism in Eastern Europe and of the Soviet Union itself.

The evolution of NATO doctrine and weapon procurement patterns demonstrates the inescapable linkages between nuclear and conventional forces which existed for NATO and the WTO. NATO's conventional inferiority did not matter so long as NATO forces were powerful enough to require a massive WTO assault to overcome. This would be sufficient to exceed the American political 'threshold of nuclear response' and trigger a chain of events that would lead to catastrophe for the Soviet Union and its allies. The primary function of the tactical and theatre nuclear weapons was to form a 'bridge' between the conventional and strategic balances.

The balance of power system, as earlier chapters have emphasised, is very much characterised by the operation of military alliances. During the superpower confrontation, the USA and USSR also dominated important alliance systems, and the way in which nuclear deterrence is affected by alliance commitments was critical, arguably far more so than in the traditional balance of power.

This produced a further complicating element in the nuclear balance of power. Credible threats are even more difficult to achieve when the threat is being made on behalf of an ally rather than oneself. It is inherently difficult to believe that one country will die for another, yet this is what extended deterrence against another nuclear armed state involves. Thus, for example, the USA was essentially declaring that, in the event of a Soviet invasion of Western Europe, it would use nuclear weapons, including attacks on Soviet cities, to hold the Soviet offensive, and would do so in the knowledge that this would almost certainly trigger Soviet nuclear attacks on the United States itself.

According to Snyder, the assessment of intentions in the nuclear era is not only more important than in the pre-nuclear era, but is important in a different way. Under the traditional balance of power system the intentions which were important related to the political decision of whether or not to intervene, and which side to intervene on behalf of. In the bipolar military balance which was characteristic of the cold war era, the uncertainty about which states might be allies in wartime was virtually eliminated (though not entirely, for example, France in NATO, Romania in WTO), but a new type of uncertainty arose regarding which weapons the opponent was likely to use and the degree of destruction he would find acceptable in pursuit of his objectives. The threat to escalate to higher levels of violence therefore superseded the 'threat' to recruit additional states to the *status quo* coalition.

THE QUESTION OF STABILITY

Various distinctions can be made between 'equilibrium' and 'stability' in both the conventional balance of power and the nuclear balance and between different forms of stability. Equilibrium in both balances can have varying degrees of stability, and it is even possible to have disequilibrium with relatively high stability. It is possible to distinguish between crisis stability and general stability, and the latter can be present even when the former is not. That is to say, both sides may wish to avoid war and may pursue general foreign policy strategies designed to sustain peace, yet this peace might not survive the particular strains of an acute crisis.

In the classical balance of power theory, stability tended to be defined in terms of the overall equilibrium in the system. Disturbances caused by a bid for hegemony would trigger countervailing forces which would tend to bring the system back towards equilibrium. Snyder (1965: 197) identifies three key features of this mechanism:

1   The tendency or lack of tendency towards an arms race;
2   tendencies either to stimulate or inhibit war;
3   tendency of the process to preserve the major actors.

What was significant about these elements was that warfare was not seen as being evidence of instability, but rather was a crucial tool for maintaining stability.

In contrast, as Hedley Bull (1977: 123–4) points out, the dimension of stability which is deemed of greatest importance in the nuclear balance of terror concerns the ability to preserve peace, which is accorded a higher priority than the preservation of the component states of the system in a political sense.

The yardstick by which this war-propensity was measured was the 'first-strike capability' of each side. When neither side had a first-strike capability and both had an assured second-strike capability, the equilibrium was deemed to be highly stable. The closer one or both sides came to an effective first-strike capability, or the further either fell from an assured second-strike capability, then the less stable the situation was deemed. Thus, deployment of an effective first-strike weapon, or deployment of effective strategic defences by one side, were seen as highly destabilising developments. Even the reasonable prospect that such systems were being developed introduced significant instability into the relationship, given that perceptions play such a critical role in nuclear deterrence.

As was the case with the traditional balance of power, there are differences of opinion regarding the relationship between the stability of the central strategic nuclear balance and the lower levels of the balance. On the one hand, it could be argued that the more stable is the central strategic nuclear balance, the less stable are likely to be the balances at the lower levels. This is because if both sides have a secure second-strike capability and need not fear the outbreak of strategic nuclear war, then they would feel less inhibited about initiating conventional war and perhaps even tactical nuclear warfare. However, the opposite case can also be made. Conventional and tactical nuclear warfare may be made less likely by the existence of strategic stability because of the greater likelihood of a gradual escalation towards a strategic nuclear war that neither side could win.

Another stability hypothesis noted by Snyder (1965: 199) suggests almost the opposite of the previous one. This contends that stability at the conventional level tends to increase stability at the strategic level. The logic here is that when both sides can defend themselves at the conventional level, then there is no pressure to escalate to the strategic level, and conventional aggression itself may well be deterred. Against this, it was sometimes argued during the cold war that the NATO allies, in seeking to bolster their conventional capabilities, were indicating an unwillingness to use nuclear weapons, an impression which might be seen as threatening deterrence.

A further difference between the nuclear and pre-nuclear balances of power is that in the nuclear era a bipolar balance is generally seen as being the most stable and a multipolar one as being least stable, whereas in the traditional balance of power the opposite was felt to be true. In the traditional system, bipolarity was felt to be unstable, because it lacked either a choice of alliance partners or an unattached 'balancer'. A multitude of power centres was deemed to be more stable because there were a variety of potential alliance partners and given this, a potential aggressor would face great uncertainty about the number and identity of states likely to oppose any bid for hegemony. However, a bipolar balance of terror is deemed stable because there are only two decision-making centres which could initiate a nuclear war, and this in itself is likely to encourage caution in any situations which involve the danger of nuclear war.

The comparatively rigid nature of the bipolar nuclear balance means that it can also be seen as potentially unstable, at least in theory. In the absence of other potential allies or a 'balancer' third force, it is hard to maintain the equilibrium through the classical method of rearranging allies. Thus, even minor changes can create an imbalance and given that war cannot be used to restore such an imbalance (because nuclear war would lead to Armageddon), the imbalance might become permanent and produce a hegemony (Herz, 1960: 39).

In the nuclear era an expansion of the group of great powers is not viewed favourably, that is, nuclear proliferation is very definitely (Waltz excepted) seen as a highly destabilising development. There are a number of reasons for this. These include a simple numerical view that the more nuclear weapon states there are, the higher the statistical possibility of a nuclear war breaking out. There is also the view that the more states that go nuclear, the greater the probability that one of the later entrants lacks the moderation characteristic of its predecessors.

Herz was distinctive in arguing that nuclear weapons had an effect which rendered virtually meaningless all the pre-nuclear instruments of balance of power foreign policy. He argued that the advent of nuclear weapons had led to the phenomenon of the 'penetrated state', a situation where the great powers had absolutely no means of protecting their territories or populations in wartime against nuclear attack. In this situation, the traditional indices of military power, such as bases, political satellites, allies and security zones, lost any value they might previously have had. The logic of this pointed towards only one ultimate solution – world control by one single power. This was so because, in a situation of mutual nuclear deterrence, neither superpower could ever feel truly secure and only the elimination of the rival could end this feeling of absolute insecurity. But the reality of nuclear deterrence, with its contingent threat of mutual and assured destruction, ruled even this possibility out.

This situation would not be improved by an increase in the number of nuclear weapon states. Though this would recreate a superficial resemblance to the classical balance of power, it would, in the nuclear age, make it far more difficult to carry out the accurate assessments of capability and credibility so crucial to the effective working of the nuclear deterrence system, as well as dramatically complicating the problems involved in terms of clear communication of threats between all parties. The problems of having to deter several states, requiring major vertical proliferation and a risk of a nuclear attack whose initiator might not even be clearly identifiable, would significantly increase the risks of disaster.

In such an environment, it would be naive to assume that a nuclear war could be avoided indefinitely. At some point, either through miscalculation or rational choice, a crisis was likely to end with the nuclear threat being implemented.

Such an outcome could arise from a number of potential causes, including miscalculation through technical error, misunderstanding through a failure to communicate the threat clearly, technical developments making a first strike possible or simply the dangers inherent in the process of nuclear proliferation.

The dangers of a breakdown in deterrence triggered by technical breakdown or miscalculation produced a need to continually refine the deterrent balance to try to maintain and if possible increase its stability. Far more so than in the eighteenth- and nineteenth-century systems, the nuclear balance required continuous monitoring if stability was to be maintained. Herz suggested a number of ways in which stability might be increased.

In order to minimise the risk of accidental nuclear war, Herz proposed a clearly defined *casus belli nuclearis*, that is, the conditions under which a state should each make a declaration that they would not be the first to use nuclear weapons. However, it is doubtful if a statement of this kind would actually be of much value, given that in a crisis states might not abide by it, and their adversaries would not expect them to abide by it. During the cold war the Soviet Union regularly called for NATO and WTO to make a mutual declaration of this kind, but NATO consistently rejected the suggestion on the ground that it would achieve nothing of real value. In any case, it hardly made sense in a situation where NATO felt that it needed nuclear weapons to redress a perceived conventional disadvantage.

Of Herz's other two suggestions, one is a traditional balance of power technique, the other a distinctive feature of the nuclear age. The first involves an acceptance of the *status quo* and the recognition of spheres of power and influence for both sides. Again, in the context of the ideological outlook of the cold war, this requires a significant move towards the more pragmatic attitudes characteristic of the classical balance of power era.

> A delimitation of spheres, a drawing of lines of *de facto* control, which, far from implying moral sanction or political approval, would merely be expressive of the prevailing power status, seems to be the first prerequisite of the 'holding operation' or stopgap policy here suggested.
>
> (Herz, 1960: 45)

The final proposal for stabilising the nuclear balance of terror involved attempting to bring to an end the process of nuclear proliferation and ending the further testing of nuclear weapons. Both these proposals were to feature on the arms control agenda after 1960 and, in fact, arms control represented a novel element, and a crucially important one, in stabilising the nuclear balance of power. The central role played by arms control in this respect was another way in which the balance of terror differed from the classical balance of power.

ARMS CONTROL

The arms control approach emerged in the late 1950s. It was a technique designed to increase the stability of the strategic balance of power between NATO and WTO. The clearest definition of what arms control is was that of Schelling and Halperin:

> We mean to include all the forms of military co-operation between potential enemies in the interest of reducing the likelihood of war,

its scope and violence if it occurs and the political and economic costs of being prepared for it. The essential feature of arms control is the recognition of the common interest, of the possibility of reciprocation and co-operation even between potential enemies with respect to their military establishments.

(Schelling and Halperin, 1961: 2)

Whereas proponents of disarmament were philosophically opposed to the possession of weaponry and the use of military power, the arms control community promoted a conception in which a balance of military power was sustained by using arms control to complement unilateral force improvements as a means to achieve security (Lefever 1962: 122). The advocates of arms control believed that weapons were a symptom rather than a cause of distrust between states and their possession simply reflected the naturally differing interests of states whose promotion or protection would periodically necessitate the use of the military instrument. Arms controllers therefore sought the creation and maintenance of a stable balance of power, acceptable to both sides, in which neither was tempted to attack by the weakness of the other.

The balance of power in terms of military capabilities was seen as being stabilising, and an

unconstrained arms race was identified as being more likely to undermine the balance of power and national security than to guarantee it. Thus while the relationship between the superpowers was characterised by a large degree of conflict, it also contained significant incentives to cooperate.

(Sheehan, 1983: 190)

Arms control therefore sought to discriminate between 'those kinds and quantities of forces and weapons that promote the stability of the balance of power, and those which do not; to tolerate or even promote the former and to restrict the latter' (Bull 1961: 61).

Arms control was based upon the idea that security is a shared value, something that states in rivalry can pursue together; that it is not something they can only acquire at each other's expense. It recognised that while 'arms racing' would continue to be a significant feature of the competition between the major alliance systems, because of the shared danger of nuclear holocaust, a degree of control, which could only be exercised through explicit diplomacy, was clearly necessary.

Although novel in a historical sense, arms control as an approach can be seen as falling clearly within the realist and power balancing perspectives on international relations. As Schelling and Halperin put it,

> Arms Control is essentially a means of supplementing unilateral military strategy by some kind of collaboration with the countries that are potential enemies. The aims of arms control and the aims of a national military strategy should be substantially the same.
>
> (Schelling and Halperin, 1961: 142)

Throughout the period of the cold war arms control remained true to its origins as a fundamentally conservative undertaking. It was concerned with managing the deterrent balance, not with challenging it or ending it. It was rooted in acceptance of the continuing validity of the balance of power concept and sought to provide means of making the balance work to preserve peace among the great powers. In this latter regard it moved beyond traditional balance of power thinking, but it did so because of the new situation created by the possession of massive nuclear firepower on both sides.

9 The future of the balance of power concept

NEO-REALISM AND THE END OF THE COLD WAR

For three centuries the balance of power idea played a central role in the workings of the European great power state system. In that period the meaning of the concept, and the way in which it was operationalised, changed significantly. During the twentieth century in particular, the rising costs associated with the use of the military instrument meant that balance of power politics fell into intellectual disfavour. They were redeemed to a large extent during the cold war, both because the rigid, at times almost Manichean, opposition between the two global political and military alliance systems lent itself to a simple conceptualisation of the international system in bipolar realist balance of power terms and because the advent of nuclear weapons produced a new version of balance of power thinking in the form of nuclear deterrence theory.

The waning of the cold war during the second half of the 1980s might have been expected to lead to an accompanying decline in the attention paid to balance of power theory. In fact, this was not the case. On the contrary, the concept advanced to the centre of the debate about the theory and practice of international relations. There were a number of interrelated reasons why this was so.

At the level of international relations theory, the decade saw a continuing debate sparked by the publication of Kenneth Waltz's 1979 book, *Theory of International Politics*. Waltz's book advanced a simple and elegant theoretical explanation for the continuities in the underlying structure of international relations which balance of power theory purports to explain. Indeed, Waltz made balance of power explicitly the fundamental organising principle of international politics, declaring that 'if there is any distinctively political theory of international politics, balance-of-power theory is it' (Waltz, 1979: 117). Waltz's book advanced a systemic theory of international politics which explained its workings in terms of its structure. The theory itself can be criticised on a number of grounds and in its pursuit of clarity and parsimony is rather simplistic. Nevertheless, it was extremely important, both in terms of the fact that it reinvigorated 'realist' political theory, particularly in the United States, and because it helped to generate a vigorous debate on international relations theory in general. Before going on to look at the place of balance of power theory within general international relations theory subsequent to the debates of the 1980s, it is worth looking at the role played by balance of power theory within Waltz's structural theory of international politics or 'neo-realist' theory.

Waltz describes earlier structural approaches to explanation in international politics as being 'reductionist'. By this, he means that they attempt to understand large systems by breaking them down into their component parts and then explaining the ways in which the various components interact with each other. As an approach to the study of the international system this has the obvious difficulty that there are simply too many possible variables to take into consideration. This makes it highly unlikely that the interactions of the variables will be accurately comprehended (Waltz, 1979: 39). Since the study of a system involves the analysis of the units comprising the system and the structural effects of the system itself, Waltz chooses to avoid the problems associated with the number of potential variables at the unit level by focusing instead on the structural level effects. 'Definitions of structures must omit the attributes and the relations of the units' (ibid.: 40).

Waltz's theory of the balance of power emerges from the structural constraints he identifies. He argues that in a system characterised by self-help, the units are compelled to be functionally alike, that is, alike in the tasks that they pursue. They differ in their capabilities, but as certain states pursue successful foreign policy strategies, the other states that comprise the system 'will emulate them or fall by the wayside' (Waltz, 1979: 118). As others emulate the successful states, so power balancing ensues. The power of Waltz's explanation comes from his insistence that these processes are inevitable and unavoidable because of the nature of the system. Only two requirements are necessary to produce balance of power politics, and such politics will prevail whenever these requirements are met – that the international order be anarchic and that it be populated by units wishing to survive.

Concentrating on this level has two important effects upon Waltz's analysis. In the first place, recurrent patterns in the history of the international system become evident. From the era of classical Greece onwards, the nature of states has steadily altered, but crucially, the patterns of the relationships *between* states is seen to have remained essentially unaltered. This perspective can be seen as reinforcing a 'classical realist' view, that earlier historical periods have lessons for the present because, despite enormous changes in many factors over time, 'human nature' and the realities of politics remain largely the same throughout the ages. Though, as was noted in Chapters 1 and 2, a major weakness of this kind of realist methodology is the ahistorical manner in which certain time periods and areas of the world are identified as exemplars, but all else is ignored. One could, for example, point out that if balance of power thinking is indeed ubiquitous, why is it not identified in periods prior to classical Greece? Why does it disappear from view for two millennia afterwards, and why are the examples produced by the realists' piratical raids on the historical literature, confined to Europe?

Waltz adds a second crucial assumption to this traditional view, however, one which clearly distinguishes him from classical realists such as Hans Morgenthau. For Waltz, the recurring patterns that he identifies demonstrate that it is the structure of the system, and not the political skills of statesmen or women, that accounts for the historical survival of balance of power politics and anarchic international systems. A balance of power will therefore emerge whether or not any particular state or group of states desires one. States may seek power domination, but the system as a whole opposes it consistently.

This theory can be criticised on a number of grounds. In the first place, in seeking simplicity or 'parsimony', Waltz simply ignores or underplays anything that doesn't fit neatly into his theory. He does this by simply relegating it to the unit level of analysis. In Keohane and Nye's words, the unit level simply becomes 'the dumping ground for all unexplained variance' in the theory (1987: 746).

A second criticism already noted, is that it is ahistorical. A realist analysis of international relations should, almost by definition, be grounded in historical example and precedent. Yet the simple neo-realist explanation of international relations flies in the face of the historical record. It is not reasonable to suggest that examples as historically remote from the present as classical Greece are evidence of 'recurring' balance of power patterns and then to ignore contrary historical examples such as the long period of hegemonic dominance in Europe enjoyed by the Roman Empire.

A further criticism relates to the question of change in international relations. The theory does not allow for the possibility of structural change. Indeed, the 'deep structure' identified is so deep that it is difficult to see what in fact *would* constitute 'change' in Waltz's terms. Yet, an analysis that would not see the alterations in the international system since the collapse of the state communist regimes in Europe post-1989 as constituting real change in the system, seems to have limited utility. Indeed, in the sense that realism is premised upon an engagement between theory and practice, it is not really even 'realist'. Nevertheless, the energy and clarity with which Waltz expressed his ideas ensured that 'neo-realism', with its emphasis upon structural explanation of international relations, became a leading paradigm in the study of international politics during the 1980s and 1990s, most notably in the United States.

During the 1990s balance of power theory once again became the centre of a controversy over the operative features of the international system. The emergence of a 'new world order' could be seen as marking the demise of balance of power thinking or as initiating an era in which it would re-emerge in a traditional multipolar form. Critics argued that the end of the cold war meant that balance thinking was a thing of the past. At the level of state behaviour, it was argued that the concept could no longer serve a useful purpose as a guide to foreign policy-makers, on the grounds that the post-cold war international order was one characterised by new possibilities for international cooperation and consensus, in which the adversarial attitudes of the balance of power mindset were no longer appropriate. Not surprisingly, given the essential bipolarity of the cold war era, the balance of power 'image' that dominated such arguments was the Anglo-Saxon 'Hobbesian' version, rather than the classical European 'Grotian' alternative.

At the level of theorising about international relations, a significant minority of international relations scholars emerged who questioned the philosophical foundations on which the study of international relations had traditionally been based. Central to their critique was an assault on the intellectual tradition of 'realism'. It was argued that realism was a school of thought in the academic study of international relations which, for various reasons, had come to dominate the way in which the subject was thought about and taught from the late 1930s to the 1980s. Most significantly from the perspective of this study, critical theorists argued that the realist international relations scholars had 'privileged' a particular interpretation of history in order to confirm the validity of their view of international politics. The origins of this critique lay in the critics' view of the meaning of reality itself. It was argued that realist writers started with a predisposition to see international politics in terms of conflict and to view the state as the essential actor in the drama in a normative as well as a purely descriptive sense. Viewing history in terms of power struggles between states led them to sift through the historical record and discover evidence, such as the existence of recurrent balances of power, which confirmed the correctness of their original disposition. The implication of this is that the 'history' of international relations discussed by realists is in fact a caricature, where certain themes have been identified and emphasised, but contrary evidence has been ignored in order to produce a version of history which tells a particular story. In support of this 'self-fulfilling hindsight', it is argued, historical thinkers were selectively adopted and their ideas 'decontextualised' in order to make them fit the realist world-view (Booth, 1995: 333). At the same time alternative historical narratives remained unspoken.

The idea of the study of international relations being a contested area in which the selection of 'facts' is a judgmental exercise is not in itself a novel view, Schwarzenberger (1969) made the same point in *Power Politics* in 1941. However, the significance of arguments such as Booth's is that they call into question the historical narrative upon which most international relations texts, including this one, have been based over the past three-quarters of a century. The essential argument, that 'facts' and interpretations of history are, to a considerable degree, contestable, is not at issue here. What is at issue is the question of whether or not the particular version of historical international relations in which the balance of power concept plays a central role is a valid and useful conceptualisation. In this author's view, that conception is a valid one. For all its inconsistencies and ambiguities, the balance of power concept has been intellectually and politically significant in the development of the current international system and, precisely because of that, it remains significant, and worthy of study.

The latter point is important because, in the period following the end of the cold war, realist scholars argued that the demise of the Warsaw Treaty Organisation and the Soviet Union would not see the end of balance of power politics in the northern hemisphere, but on the contrary, would see it rapidly re-emerging in a multipolar form. Opinion was divided on the question of whether the new balance of power, when it emerged, would be essentially stable and characterised by cooperative relations between the great powers or whether it would see growing instability, tension and, eventually, war between the great powers. The two positions can be seen exemplified in the arguments of Meirsheimer on the one hand, and Kegley and Raymond on the other.

Meirsheimer's arguments are premised on a neo-realist interpretation of the nature of the international system and a perception, which he shares with Kenneth Waltz, that bipolar balance of power systems are inherently more stable and less productive of war than are multipolar systems. Stability is, in fact, defined in terms of absence of war in the system. A bipolar system is seen as being particularly stable because such a system is characterised by high levels of certainty and predictability. As the number of key actors increases then, by the same token, certainty and predictability decrease. In a bipolar system the enemy is easy to recognise, the issues are clearer, alliance patterns are simpler, there is only one other culture and political system that has to be monitored and understood, interdependence is low. In a multipolar system, in contrast, the number of potential adversaries is greater, alliance patterns are more fluid, interdependence is greater, the problems caused by ethnocentric perceptions are more marked, spheres of influence are vaguer and therefore less likely to be respected. These perceptions are largely the result of a concentration on the US–Soviet example of bipolar stability. Earlier historical examples, such as the Habsburg–Valois rivalry in sixteenth-century Europe do not exhibit this degree of stability. None the less, Meirsheimer's assessment of the implication of emerging multipolarity is an ominous one: 'the prospects for major crisis and war in Europe are likely to increase markedly' (Meirsheimer, 1990: 6).

For Meirsheimer, the 'long peace' that characterised international relations in Europe between 1945 and 1990 was a function of the particular balance of power system variant that formed the setting for great-power rivalry during the period. The three key features which distinguished this period of history from the violent era which preceded it were the fact that the system was essentially bipolar, the approximate equality of military power between the two main military alliances and the possession of nuclear weapons by both sides. In advocating this thesis in fairly robust terms, Meirsheimer also dismisses alternative explanations for the long peace, such as the influence of the international economic order and the idea that democracies are intrinsically less warlike than other states, as well as the argument that war itself is becoming increasingly obsolescent. Despite the advent of nuclear weapons, Meirsheimer sees the emerging balance of power system in remarkably traditional terms, even to the point of advocating (in a period before the collapse of communism in the Soviet Union), that 'Soviet power could play a key role in balancing against Germany and in maintaining order in Eastern Europe' (1990: 55).

The alternative realist view propounded by Kegley and Raymond is the result of a number of different assumptions which underpin their analysis. Prominent among these are their more nuanced views about multipolarity, the meaning of 'stability' and the relationship between systemic polarity and the amount of warfare characteristic of the system. As they point out, defining stability simply in terms of the avoidance of great power war 'fails to capture the turbulence and recurrent threats to global peace that were a salient characteristic of the bipolar cold war system' (Kegley and Raymond, 1992: 576).

In addition, Kegley and Raymond point out that, by taking a longer historical perspective than simply the post-1945 era, it becomes apparent that 'the distribution of power within the state system historically has *not* been related to the onset of war' (1992: 579; emphasis in original). This conclusion is based upon the evidence from a number of studies (Bueno de Mesquita, 1981; Ostrom and Aldrich, 1978; Levy, 1985), all of which indicate that there exists no inevitable correlation between the distribution of power and the probability of war.

Finally, and crucially, Kegley and Raymond make the point that a simplistic comparison between bipolar and multipolar systems overlooks the obvious point that there are many possible types of multipolar system and the vices and virtues of each may differ in significant ways. Different combinations of features in each system may lead to different consequences. Because they identify historical systems that have been characterised by periods of great-power cooperation and relative harmony and discern the potential elements of such a great-power 'concert' in the post-cold war situation, Kegley and Raymond are more sanguine about the prospects for peace in the new era (1992: 583; 1994: 234–5).

REALIST VERSUS NEO-GROTIAN APPROACHES TO THE BALANCE OF POWER

In the international relations literature scholars tend to be either for or against the balance of power. The fault-line which divides them is the degree to which they subscribe to the 'realist' world-view. Realist theoreticians of international politics tend to give the balance of power a central role in their explanations of the way in which the system operates and, indeed, of how it has historically operated over the centuries. In contrast, opponents of the realist perspective tend to downplay or dismiss the balance of power along with all other aspects of the realist explanation.

This is unfortunate, because the balance of power is not synonymous with realism, a fact largely obscured by the appropriation of the concept by realists since the middle decades of the twentieth century. Balance of power can be explained equally well, if not better, within a neo-Grotian framework. Virtually the only leading theorist of international relations to suggest this in recent decades was Hedley Bull. Bull saw the balance of power as playing a central part in his explanation of the existence and operation of the 'international society'. According to Bull, seventeenth-century thinkers such as Grotius and Pufendorf saw the balance of power as a

> product of policies consciously directed towards it, and in so far as they have asserted that states are obliged to act so as to maintain it, they must be taken also to embody the idea of international society and of rules binding upon its members.
>
> (Butterfield and Wight, 1966: 39)

Similarly, Martin Wight, while not accepting the Grotian perspective, argued that balances of power can be explained and justified within the parameters of the Grotian approach (1991: 164–8).

The balance of power as an approach can be identified in an emergent form in the Italian city-state system of the fifteenth century, but it was the way that system was reflected upon by subsequent Italian historians that produced a model for seventeenth-century statesmen to follow. In the eighteenth-century system, the balance concept was not just a mechanical action–reaction sequence triggering recurrent alliance formation. It was also in a real sense the 'constitution' of the international system, one of the foundations of an emerging international society that provided a sense of unity to fragmented Christendom. But it was a unity based upon and underpinning a system of independent sovereign states. Napoleon's efforts to provide genuine political unity for Europe under French hegemony were unacceptable to the new order of states. Yet as soon as Napoleon had been defeated by an alliance self-consciously pursuing the recreation of a balance of power system, the post-war equilibrium which the allies built was premised on the idea of a 'concert' of powers. The Concert was a clear demonstration of the continuing hold on the European imagination of the 'Grotian' perspective of an international 'equilibrium', not a crude military balance, but an approximate parity of capabilities between the leading states such that none could dominate the others, thereby enabling the 'social' aspects of the international system to operate, such as international law, mediation, a balance of interests and dignities, and the pursuit of limited foreign policy objectives. This interpretation remained dominant among the continental powers until the second half of the century.

This broader conception of the role played by the balance of power faded for most of the twentieth century, pushed to one side by the emphasis placed upon the pursuit of military parity, in an era when political reconciliation between the major powers was not sought with any energy. This was most marked during the Manichean nuclear confrontation between the two superpowers at the height of the cold war. Yet the very dangers of that confrontation led to the pursuit of arms control, the recognition that the two sides had common interests as well as major points of contention. In the final years of the period of US–Soviet rivalry, with the Gorbachev–Shevadnadze foreign policy dominating the political agenda, the balance of power began to evolve into something recognisably similar to the post-1815 'concert'. A more subtle version of international great power equilibrium was reappearing, taking the balance of power idea back to its late seventeenth-century roots.

RECOVERING THE CONCEPT

Critics of the balance of power concept do not pull their punches. Organski (1958: 298) declared firmly that 'we must reject the theory of the balance of power. Its concepts are fuzzy, it is logically unsound and contradicts itself, it is not consistent with the events that have occurred, and it does not explain them'. Yet despite criticisms such as these, the concept continues to hold a central place in thinking about international politics and a survey of the diplomatic records shows that it has done so for three centuries. For Inis Claude (1989: 84) 'the naturalness of the balance of power system is limited and may be shrinking, but it remains significant enough to give balance of power easy superiority over its competitors'.

Balance of power remains in vogue for many reasons. It is an idea with an appealing elegance and simplicity. It suggests a symmetry and rhythm to events which is reassuring when faced with a subject as complex and kaleidoscopic as international relations. It was this aspect which caused it to be embraced so enthusiastically by the eighteenth century of the 'Enlightenment.' It is echoed in the 'rules' for balance of power systems published by Kaplan in the 1960s.

Yet the concept remains elusive. The central idea is simple and transparent, that states act in alliance to prevent the rise to hegemonic dominance of a powerful state or group. How far this simple idea can be traced back in history is debatable, but the eighteenth-century rationalists who detected its operation by leaders in classical Greece were mistaken. For a true balance of power system to arise certain key elements need to be present, and these elements are not discernible prior to the emergence of the European state system after the Peace of Westphalia in 1648. The European version of the balance of power concept has always involved more than just the minimalist commitment to oppose hegemony, however. During the eighteenth and nineteenth centuries the concept had a positive normative connotation as well. It stood for a commitment to the idea of the states of Europe forming a society, however rudimentary. As the complex interdependence of the states comprising the international system has developed during the twentieth century, this element in original balance thinking has lost its centrality, other aspects of international relations superseding its role in that respect.

A feature of historical surveys of the balance of power idea is the chronicling of the evolution of the principle from its Renaissance origins in Italy to its zenith in the nineteenth century. Yet, at this point its evolution is deemed to have stopped, having achieved its final form. There is no logical reason why it should be seen in this way. There is no 'end of history' and the balance of power idea is one that has been adapted and modified by successive generations, most obviously in the appearance of the nineteenth-century congress system and the twentieth-century nuclear balance of terror. Changes in the theory and practice of the balance of power have reflected changes in the social and philosophical environment of the states which comprised the international system. Seen in this light, the idea of collective security as a further refinement of balance of power theory is not so surprising, nor is the notion that the concept may serve an evolving international system in adapted form in the future, perhaps embracing more of the 'associative' balance of power tradition identified by Richard Little, which draws upon the underemphasised 'Grotian' or international societal side of the balance of power idea.

This aspect is one which it is important to recover. As the post-cold war debates about the future of European security have shown, it has proved difficult for the NATO states to find a way to integrate Russia into the post-Soviet European security architecture in a way that satisfies the concerns of all the states in the system for equal security. The balance of power concept was one of the ways in which Europe redefined itself after the great schisms of the sixteenth century. Post-cold war Europe is still searching for a similar integrating form. It need not, indeed, should not, be the balance of power idea in the form in which the twentieth century has invariably conceptualised it. A more positive approach would be to look more deeply at the problem for which the balance of power idea was a partial solution in the early period of the modern state system in order to develop solutions to the security issues of the post-cold war era.

The balance of power idea was a way of reconciling two apparently opposite requirements – on the one hand, the desire to recognise and sustain an international system based upon a number of competing state sovereignties and, on the other, the wish to preserve the ideal of the political community of Christendom, in the sense of a Europe united by many common features and conceiving of itself as forming a society.

Any attempt to achieve a similar reconciliation in the late twentieth century has to recognise that it is a very different world, one in which the idea of the sovereign state no longer holds unchallenged sway as the vehicle for individual or group interests. Moreover, it is one in which the meaning of 'security' can no longer be limited to considerations of military issues, but must embrace a host of other threats, such as those posed by economic and environmental problems. It is necessary to look at the idea of security in a more critical manner in order to develop structures for dealing with these broader 'security' issues in ways that recognise their frequent interaction for many states and recognise too that some are more central than others for certain states.

Thinking of the 'Russian' or East European 'security' problem purely in military terms does a disservice to clear thinking. Europe's security problems, even seen in the narrow sense of military security, are more likely to be resolved within a framework that emphasises non-military issues and Russia's place within a family of European states evolving in novel constitutional directions.

Examination of the balance of power in operation is instructive. The broad generalisations often made about the working of the balance in history do not always stand up to the detailed scrutiny of historians. Other interpretations of events are possible and counterbalancing strategies such as bandwagoning have often held their attractions, particularly for the smaller or weaker states, for whom the operation of the balance of power system offers fewer guarantees. Historically, the balance of power has worked so as to preserve major powers, it has not provided security for all states. Nor has it acted as a deterrent to war, though in truth it was never designed to do so. War has been a fundamental mechanism for defending an existing equilibrium, which is why the nuclear deterrent balance represents such a dramatically novel manifestation of the balance principle, since in the era of mutually assured destruction, war could not effectively be used to defend or redress the balance. At least nuclear war or direct conventional war between the nuclear powers could not be used in the traditional manner.

Because of its 'holistic' mind-set and its encouragement of system-wide watchfulness, the balance of power idea was both a creation of an emerging international system and an important catalyst for encouraging leaders to think in terms of an international system. It thus played an important part in the development of thinking about international relations. In practice, historical systems such as that of eighteenth-century Europe were by no means as coherent as was suggested either at the time or subsequently. But they represented an enormous advance over what had gone before. They demonstrated clearly that the system is one of *balancing* rather than balance, of counterpoise rather than equipoise, as Friedrich von Gentz put it.

The nineteenth century offered a more structured balance of power system, but at the same time demonstrated that conceptualising the balance principle is significantly influenced by national concerns and perspectives. The differences between the British and German views of what should constitute the balance of power showed that history and geography could not help but shape views on the subject. In the assault on balance of power politics by the proponents of nationalism, it was made clear that as an organising principle the balance of power idea was and is, not a fixed reality but an approach subject to the influences of social change and the evolution of political thought. Changes such as those of the nineteenth century must give us caution. The balance of power has a long history, but it has also been given many different meanings and a student of the subject must be on guard against the beguiling assumption that the same phenomenon is being described or observed in each case. It is also important to be aware of the ever-present lure of alternative foreign policy strategies.

The balance of power approach has existed for as long as the modern international state system itself. It has been subject to continuous criticism but, to date, no permanantly satisfactory alternative to it has emerged. Having said this, however, it is also important to highlight the fact that while for three centuries states have felt it to be necessary, they have also thought simple balances of military power to be insufficient. The eighteenth century was acutely aware of this deficiency and attempted to repair this through the mechanism of the 'concert'. Nineteenth-century Europeans, as Schroeder has shown, looked beyond a simple balance of military power to a more complex and sophisticated balance of satisfactions and rights. In the post-1945 nuclear balance of terror it came to be accepted that a stable balance could only be secured if the dangerous confrontation between the superpowers was ameliorated through arms control negotiations and a dialogue between the two dominant powers in the system. The balance of power idea is seen as a crucial basis for maintaining national security, but it has to be supplemented by other diplomatic techniques if stability is to be maintained without a costly resort to constant warfare. It is this feature which means that in practice the balance approach shares certain features with other security approaches which similarly seek to maintain order in the system of sovereign states.

If the balance of power idea is to exercise a positive role in post-cold war Europe it must be in its 'Grotian' form. The sophistication of the mid-nineteenth-century notion of equilibrium needs to be combined with late-twentieth-century ideas on collective security, common security and arms control to produce an 'equilibrium' based upon the right of states and individuals to equal security. The Hobbesian balance of power image is not about to disappear, as the mentality of the adversaries in areas as distant as former Yugoslavia and Korea demonstrates. But for international society, it is the Grotian image which offers by far the greatest possibility for achieving a future in which the incidence of war and the threat of war are significantly diminished and a more mature version of 'anarchy' prevails which supports the continuing development of the societal elements of the international system.

Bibliography and further reading

Albrecht-Carrie, R. (ed.) (1968) *The Concert of Europe 1815–1914* (Harpers, New York).

Alcock, N. and Newcombe, A. (1970) 'The Perception of National Power', *Journal of Conflict Resolution*, Vol. 14, pp. 335–43.

Alexandroff, A., Rosecrance, R. and Stein, A. (1977) 'History, Quantitative Analysis and the Balance of Power', *Journal of Conflict Resolution*, Vol. 33, pp. 35–56.

Anderson, M. S. (1970) 'Eighteenth Century Theories of the Balance of Power' in R. Hatton and M. S. Anderson (eds), *Studies in Diplomatic History* (Archon, London).

Anderson, M. S. (1976) *Europe in the Eighteenth Century 1713–83* 2nd edn (London).

Anderson, M. S. (1993) *The Rise of Modern Diplomacy 1450–1919* (Longman, London).

Anon. (1694) *Reflections on the Conditions of Peace Offered By France* (London).

Anon. (1720) *Two Essays on the Balance of Europe* (London).

Anon. (1731) *A Defence of the Measures of the Present Administration* (London).

Anon. (1741) *Europe's Catechism* (London).

Anon. (1750) *The Present State of Europe* (London).

Anon. (1753) *Occasional Reflections on the Importance of the War in America, and the Reasonableness of Supporting the King of Prussia* (London).

Anon. (1796) *Review of the Events and Treaties which Established the Balance of Power in Europe* (London).

Arendt, H. (1970) *On Violence* (London).

Aron, R. (1966) *Peace and War* (Weidenfeld & Nicolson, London).

Aspaturian, V. (1980) 'Soviet Global Power and the Correlation of Forces', *Problems of Communism*, Vol. 29 (May–June), pp. 1–18.

Baker-Fox, A. (1957) *The Power of Small States* (University of Chicago Press, Chicago).

Baldwin, D. A. (1979) 'Power Analysis and World Politics', *World Politics*, Vol. 31, No.1, pp. 161–94.

Barker, Thomas M. (ed.) (1972) *Frederick the Great and the Making of Prussia* (Krieger, New York).

Barnett, A. (1970) 'The New Multipolar Balance in East Asia: Implications for United States Policy', *Annals of the American Academy of Political and Social Science*, 390 (July), pp. 73–86.

Beer, F. (1970) *Alliances: Latent War Communities in the Contemporary World* (Holt, Rinehart & Winston, New York).

Bethel, S. (1668) *The World's Mistake in Oliver Cromwell* (London), in *State Tracts* (London, 1689).

Bethel, S. (1671) *The Present State of England Stated* (London).

Beloff, M. (1967) *The Balance of Power* (Montreal).

Black, J. (1983) 'The Theory of the Balance of Power in the First Half of the Eighteenth Century: A Note on Sources', *Review of International Studies*, Vol. 9, pp. 55–61.

Blainey, G. (1973) *The Causes of War* (Sun Books, Melbourne).

Botero, G. (1956) *Reason of State* (Venice), trans. P. and D. Waley (London).

Brams, S. (1969) 'The Structure of Influence Relationships in the International System', in J. N. Rosenau (ed.) *International Politics and Foreign Policy* (Free Press, New York).

Bridge, F. and Bullen, R. (1980) *The Great Powers and the European States System 1815–1914* (London).

Bridge, R. (1979) 'Allied Diplomacy in Peacetime: The Failure of the Congress System, 1815–23', in A. Sked (ed.) *Europe's Balance of Power, 1815–48* (Macmillan, London), pp. 34–53.

Brodie, B. (1946) *The Absolute Weapon* (New York).

Brougham, Lord (1872) *Works, Vol. VIII, Dissertations – Historical and Political* (Edinburgh).

Brzezinski, Z. (1972) 'The Balance of Power Delusion', *Foreign Policy*, Vol. 7 (Summer), pp. 54–9.

Bueno de Mesquita, B. (1978) 'Systemic Polarisation and the Occurrence and Duration of War', *Journal of Conflict Resolution*, Vol. 22, pp. 241–67.

Bueno de Mesquita, B. (1981) 'Risk, Power Distributions and the Likelihood of War', *International Studies Quarterly*, Vol. 25, pp. 541–68.

Bueno de Mesquita, B. and Lalman, D. (1978) 'Empirical Support for Systemic and Dyadic Explanations of International Conflict', *World Politics*, Vol. 41, pp. 1–20.

Buerig, E. (1955) *Woodrow Wilson and the Balance of Power* (Indiana University Press, Bloomington).

Bull, H. (1961) *The Control of the Arms Race* (Weidenfeld & Nicolson, London).

Bull, H. (1966) 'Society and Anarchy in International Relations', in H. Butterfield and M. Wight (eds), *Diplomatic Investigations* (London).

Bull, H. (1971) 'The New Balance of Power in Asia and the Pacific', *Foreign Affairs*, Vol. 49, No. 4, pp. 669–81.

Bull, H. (1977) *The Anarchical Society* (Macmillan, London).

Bullen, R. (1979) 'France and Europe, 1815–48: The Problem of Defeat and Recovery', in A. Sked (ed.) *Europe's Balance of Power, 1815–48* (Macmillan, London), pp. 122–45.

Burn, A. R. (1968) *The Warring States of Greece* (Thames & Hudson, London).

Burns A. L. (1957) 'From Balance to Deterrence: A Theoretical Analysis', *World Politics*, Vol. 9, No. 4, pp. 494–529.

Burr, R. N. (1955) 'The Balance of Power in Nineteenth-century South

America: An Explanatory Essay', *The Hispanic American Historical Review*, Vol. 35 (February), pp. 37–60.

Burr, R. N. (1965) 'By Reason or Force: Chile and the Balancing of Power in South America, 1830–1905', University of California, Berkeley, Publications in History, Vol. 77 (October).

Burrows, M. (1877) 'The Balance of Power', *Quarterly Review*, Vol. 143 (London), pp. 526–50.

Butterfield, H. (1953) *Christianity, Diplomacy and War* (London).

Butterfield, H. (1966) 'The Balance of Power', in H. Butterfield and M. Wight *Diplomatic Investigations* (London).

Butterfield, H. and Wight, M. (1966) *Diplomatic Investigations* (Allen & Unwin, London).

Campbell, J. (1750) *The Present State of Europe* (London).

Carr, E. H. (1946) *The Twenty Year Crisis 1919–39* (London, Macmillan, 2nd edn).

Chandler (1742) *Chandlers History and Proceedings of the House of Commons from the Restoration to the Present Time* (London).

Chatterjee, P. (1972) 'The Classical Balance of Power Theory', *Journal of Peace Research*, Vol. 8, pp. 50–61.

Chevallez, G. (1964) *The Congress of Vienna and Europe* (Pergamon, Oxford).

Chi, H. (1968) 'The Chinese Warlord System as an International System', in M. A. Kaplan (ed.), *New Approaches to International Relations* (St Martins Press, New York).

Churchill, W. (1960) *The Gathering Storm* (London).

Churchman, C. (1968) *The Systems Approach* (Delacorte Press, New York).

Clark, I. (1989) *The Hierarchy of States: Reform and Resistance in the International Order* (Cambridge University Press, Cambridge).

Claude, I. (1962) *Power and International Relations* (Random House, New York).

Claude, I. (1989) 'The Balance of Power Revisited', *Review of International Studies*, Vol. 15, No. 2 (April).

Cobbett, W. (1806–20) *Parliamentary History of England* 36 Vols (London).

Cobden, R. (1867) *Political Writings* Vol. I (London).

Craig, G. (1960) 'The Great Powers and the Balance of Power 1830–1870', in *New Cambridge Modern History*, Vol. X (Cambridge University Press, Cambridge).

Craig, G. (1960) 'The System of Alliances and the Balance of Power', in *New Cambridge Modern History*, Vol. X (Cambridge University Press, Cambridge).

Craig, G. and George, A. (1990) *Force and Statecraft*, 2nd edn (Oxford University Press, Oxford).

Crowe, Sir Eyre (1928) 'Memorandum on the Present State of British Relations with France and Germany' in G. P. Gooch and H. Temperley (eds) *British Documents on the Origins of the War 1898–1914* (London, HMSO).

Dankin, D. (1979) 'The Congress of Vienna, 1814–15 and its Antecedents', in A. Sked (ed.) *Europe's Balance of Power, 1815–48* (Macmillan, London), pp. 14–33.

Davenant, C. (1701) *Essay upon the Balance of Power* (London).

Davis, H. R. and Good, R. C. (eds) (1960) *Reinhold Niebuhr on Politics* (New York).

Deane, M. J. (1976) 'The Soviet Assessment of the "Correlation of World Forces": Implications for American Foreign Policy', *Orbis*, Vol. 20, pp. 625–36.

Deane, M. J. (1978) 'Soviet Perceptions of the Military Factor in the Correlation of World Forces', in D. C. Donald (ed.) *International Perceptions of the Superpowers' Military Balance*

Defoe, D. (1711) *The Balance of Europe* (London).

Dehio, L. (1963) *The Precarious Balance* (Chatto & Windus, London).

Derry, J. (1976) *Castlereagh* (Allen Lane, London).

Deudney, D. (1993) 'Dividing Realism: Structural Realism versus Security Materialism on Nuclear Security and Proliferation', *Security Studies*, Vol. 2 Nos 3/4 (Spring/Summer).

Deutsch, K. and Singer, J.D. (1964) 'Multipolar Power Systems and International Stability', *World Politics*, Vol. 16, pp. 390–406.

Donald, D. C. (ed.) (1978) *International Perceptions of the Superpowers' Military Balance* (Praeger, New York).

Donnadieu, L. (1900) *Essai sur la théorie de l'equilibre* (Paris).

Dorn, W. L. (1940) *Competition for Empire 1740–63* (New York).

Dupuis, C. (1909) *Le principe d'équilibre et le concert européen* (Paris).

Elder, R. E. (1950) 'Factors Affecting Stability of the Balance of Power', *Western Political Quarterly*, Vol. 3, No. 2, pp. 155–60.

Elrod, R. B. (1976) 'The Concert of Europe: A Fresh Look at an International System', *World Politics*, Vol. 28, pp. 159–74.

Farrell. J. C. and Smith, A. P. (eds) (1967) *Theory and Reality in World Politics* (Columbia University Press, New York).

Fay, S. (1930) 'Balance of Power', *International Encyclopedia of the Social Sciences*, Vol. II (Macmillan, New York), pp. 395–9.

Fay, S. (1937) 'Concert of Power', *International Encyclopedia of the Social Sciences*, Vol. II (Macmillan, New York).

Fedder, E. (1968) 'The Concept of Alliance', *International Sudies Quarterly*, Vol. 12, pp. 65–86.

Ferris, W. H. (1973) *The Power Capabilities of Nation States* (Lexington Books, London).

Fleiss, P. J. (1966) *Thucydides and the Politics of Bipolarity* (Louisiana State University Press, Baton Rouge).

Forsyth, M. G., Keens-Soper, H. M. A. and Savigear, P. (1970) *The Theory of International Relations* (Allen & Unwin, London).

Fox, W. T. R. (ed.) (1959) *Theoretical Aspects of International Relations* (University of Notre Dame Press, Notre Dame).

Franke, W. (1968) 'The Italian City-State System as an International System', in M. Kaplan (ed.) *New Approaches to International Relations* (St Martins Press, New York), pp. 430–58.

Freedman, L. (1981–2) 'NATO Myths', *Foreign Policy*, No. 45 (Winter), pp. 48–68.

Friedman, J., Bladen, C. and Rosen, S. (eds) (1970) *Alliances in International Politics* (Boston).

Galtung, J. (1964) 'Balance of Power and the Problem of Perception: A Logical Analysis', *Inquiry*, Vol. 7, No. 3, pp. 277–94.

Gareau, F. H. (ed.) (1962) *The Balance of Power and Nuclear Deterrence* (Boston).

Garnham, D. (1976) 'Power Parity and Lethal International Violence', *Journal of Conflict Resolution,* Vol. 20, pp. 379–94.

Garthoff, R. (1951) 'The Concept of the Balance of Power in Soviet Policy Making', *World Politics,* Vol. 4, No. 1, pp. 85–111.

Garthoff, R. (1966) *Soviet Military Policy: A Historical Analysis* (Faber, London).

Geller, D. S. (1988) 'Power System Membership and Patterns of War', *International Political Science Review,* Vol. 9, pp. 365–79.

Geller, D. S. (1992a) 'Capability Concentration, Power Transition and War', *International Interactions,* Vol. 17, pp. 269–84.

Geller, D. S. (1992b) 'Power Transition and Conflict Initiation', *Conflict Management and Peace Science,* Vol. 12, No. 1, pp. 1–16.

Gellman, P. (1989) 'The Elusive Explanation: Balance of Power "Theory" and the Origins of World War I', *Review of International Studies,* Vol. 15, No. 2, pp. 155–82.

von Gentz, F. (1806) *Fragments upon the Balance of Power in Europe* (London).

Gibbs, G. C. (1969) 'The Revolution in Foreign Policy', in G. Holmes (ed.), *Britain After the Glorious Revolution 1689 – 1714* (London).

Gilbert, F. (1951) 'The "New Diplomacy" of the Eighteenth Century', *World Politics,* Vol. 4, pp. 1–38.

Gilmore, M. P. (1952) *The World of Humanism* (New York), pp. 139–45.

Gilpin, R. (1981) *War and Change in World Politics* (Cambridge University Press, Cambridge).

Gochman, C. S. (1990) 'Capability-Driven Disputes', in C. S. Gochman and A. N. Sabrosky (eds), *Prisoners of War? Nation-States in the Modern Era* (Lexington Books, Lexington, Mass.), pp. 141–59.

Gray, Richard B. (ed.) (1969) *International Security Systems* (Itasca, Ill.).

Graymer, L. (ed.) (1971) *Systems and Actors in International Politics* (Chandler, San Francisco).

Greene, F. (1964) *Dynamics of International Relations* (New York).

Greenstein, F. and Polsby, N. (eds) (1959) *International Politics* (Reading, Mass.).

Gross, F. (1948) 'The Peace of Westphalia, 1648–1948', *American Journal of International Law,* Vol. 42, pp. 20–41.

Gulick, E. V. (1943) *The Balance of Power* (Pacifist Research Bureau, Philadelphia).

Gulick, E. V. (1955) *Europe's Classical Balance of Power* (Ithaca, New York and London).

Gulick, E. V. (1960) 'Our Balance of Power System in Perspective', *Journal of International Affairs,* Vol. 14, No. 1, pp. 9–20.

Gulick, E. V. (1965) 'The Final Coalition and the Congress of Vienna, 1813–15' in *The New Cambridge Modern History,* Vol. IX (Cambridge), pp. 639–67.

Haas, E. (1953a) 'The Balance of Power: Prescription, Concept or Propaganda', *World Politics,* Vol. 5, No. 4, pp. 442–77.

Haas, E. (1953b) 'The Balance of Power as a Guide to Policy Making', *Journal of Politics,* Vol. 15, No. 3, pp. 370–98.

Haas, E. (1955) 'Types of Collective Security', *American Political Science Review*, Vol. 49, pp. 41–62.

Haas, M. (ed.) (1974) *International Systems* (Chandler, New York).

Hafner, D. L. (1980) 'Castlereagh, the Balance of Power and Non-Intervention', *Australian Journal of Politics and History*, Vol. 26, pp. 71–84.

Haines, R. (1971a) 'The Balance of Power System in Europe', in L. Graymer (ed.), *Systems and Actors in International Politics* (Chandler, San Francisco), pp. 9–32.

Haines, R. (1971b) 'A Century of System Change', in L. Graymer (ed.) *Systems and Actors in International Politics* (Chandler, San Francisco), pp. 33–66.

Halecki, O. (1950) *The Limits and Divisions of European History* (London and New York).

Halifax, Marquess of (1969) *The Character of a Trimmer* (London, 1685), in J. Kenyon (ed.), *Halifax: Complete Works* (Penguin, Harmondsworth).

Handel, M. (1981) *Weak States in the International System* (Frank Cass, London).

Hart, J. (1974) 'Symmetry and Polarization in the European International System 1870–1879: A Methodological Study', *Journal of Peace Research*, Vol. 11, pp. 229–44.

Hart, J. (1976) 'Three Approaches to the Measurement of Power in International Relations', *International Organisation*, Vol. 30, pp. 289–305.

Hartmann, F. (1952) 'Alliances and the Balance of Power' in F. Hartmann (ed.) *Readings in International Relations* (New York).

Hartmann, F. (1973) *The Relations of Nations*, 4th edn (New York).

Hassall, A. (1919) *The Balance of Power 1715–1789* (4th edn, London).

Hatton, R. (1969) *War and Peace 1680–1720* (Weidenfeld & Nicolson, London).

Hatton, R. and Anderson, M. S. (eds) (1970) *Studies in Diplomatic History* (London).

Hawksworth, H. and Kogan, M. (eds) (1992) *Encyclopaedia of Government and Politics* (Routledge, London).

Healey, B. and Stein, A. (1973) 'The Balance of Power in International History', *Journal of Conflict Resolution*, Vol. 17, No. 1, pp. 33–61.

Herz, J. (1959) *International Politics in the Atomic Age* (Columbia University Press, New York).

Herz, J. (1960) 'Balance Systems and Balance Policies in a Nuclear and Bipolar age', *Journal of International Affairs*, Vol. 19, No. 1, pp. 35–48.

Hinsley, F. H. (1963) *Power and the Pursuit of Peace* (Cambridge University Press, Cambridge).

Hinsley, F. H. (1966) 'The Concert of Europe', in Laurence W. Martin (ed.) *Diplomacy in Modern European History* (Macmillan, London), pp. 43–57.

Hinsley, F. H. (1971) 'The Development of the European States System Since the Eighteenth Century', in G. Quester (ed.), *Power, Action and Interaction: Readings on International Politics* (Little Brown, Boston), pp. 284–94.

Hoadly, B. (1727) *An Enquiry into the Reasons of the Conduct of Great Britain* (London).

Hoffman, S. (1968) 'Balance of Power', *International Encyclopedia of the Social Sciences*, Vol. I (Free Press, New York), pp. 506–10.

Hoffman, S. (1972) 'Weighing the Balance of Power', *Foreign Affairs*, Vol. 50, No. 4, pp. 618–43.

Holbraad, C. (1970) *The Concert of Europe* (London).

Holsti, O. (1976) 'Alliance and Coalition Diplomacy', in J. N. Rosenau, K. W. Thompson and G. Boyd (eds) *World Politics: An Introduction* (Free Press, New York), pp. 337–72.

Holsti, O. (1991) *Peace and War: Armed Conflicts and International Order, 1648–1989* (Cambridge University Press, Cambridge).

Hopf, T. (1991) 'Polarity, the Offense–Defense Balance, and War', *American Political Science Review*, Vol. 85, pp. 475–93.

Hopkins, R. and Mansbach R. (1973) *Structure and Process in International Politics* (Harper & Row, New York).

Howard, C. (1974) *Britain and the Casus Belli: 1822–1902* (Athlone Press, University of London).

Houweling, H. and Siccama, J. G. (1988) 'Power Transitions as a Cause of War', *Journal of Conflict Resolution*, Vol. 32, pp. 87–102.

Hsi-Sheng, C. (1968) 'The Chinese Warlord System as an International System', in M. Kaplan (ed.), *New Approaches to International Relations* (St. Martins Press, New York), pp. 405–25.

Huth, P., Bennett, D. S. and Gelpi, C. (1992) 'System Uncertainty, Risk Propensity and International Conflict among the Great Powers', *Journal of Conflict Resolution*, Vol. 36, pp. 478–517.

James, A. (1964) 'Power Politics', *Political Studies*, Vol. 12, No 3, pp. 307–26.

James, A. (ed.) (1973) *The Bases of International Order* (Oxford University Press, Oxford).

Jervis, R. (1976) *Perception and Misperception in International Politics* (Princeton University Press, Princeton, N.J.).

Jervis, R. (1979) 'Systems Theories and Diplomatic History', in P.G. Lauren (ed.), *Diplomacy: New Approaches in History, Theory and Policy* (New York).

Jervis, R. (1985–6) 'From Balance to Concert: A Study of International Security Cooperation', *World Politics*, Vol. 38, pp. 58–79.

Johnson, H. C. and Niemeyer, G. (1954) 'Collective Security: the Validity of an Ideal', *International Organisation*, Vol. 8, pp. 19–35.

Justi, J. H. von (1758) *Die Chimäre des Gleichgewichts von Europa* (Altona).

Kaeber, E. (1907) *Die Idee des europäischen Gleichgewichts in der publizistschen Literatur vom 16 bis zur Mitte des 18 Jahrhunderts* (Berlin).

Kagan, D. (1969) *The Outbreak of the Peloponnesian War* (Cornell University Press, Ithaca, New York).

Kahle, L. M. (1744) *La Balance de L'Europe considérée comme la règle de la paix et de la guerre* (Berlin).

Kaplan H. (1972) 'Prince Henry and the Balance of Power', in Thomas M. Barker (ed.), *Frederick the Great and the Making of Prussia* (New York).

Kaplan, M. (1957) *System and Process in International Politics* (John Wiley, New York).

Kaplan, M. (1960) 'Theoretical Inquiry and the Balance of Power', *Yearbook of World Affairs*, Vol. 14, pp. 19–39.

Kaplan, M. (ed.) (1968) *New Approaches to International Relations* (St Martins Press, New York).

Kaplan, M. (1969) 'Balance of Power, Bipolarity and Other Models of International Systems', in Richard B. Gray (ed.), *International Security Systems* (Itasca, Ill.).

Kaplan, M., Burns, A. L. and Quandt, R. E. (1960) 'Theoretical Analysis of the Balance of Power', *Behavioural Science*, Vol. 5, No. 3, pp. 240–52.

Kaufman, R. G. (1992) 'To Balance or To Bandwagon? Alignment Decisions in 1930's Europe', *Security Studies*, Vol. 1, No. 3, pp. 417–47.

Kaye, F. B. (1924) *Bernard Mandeville, The Fable of the Bees* (Oxford).

Kegley, C. and Raymond, G. (1992) 'Must we Fear a Post Cold War Multipolar System?', *Journal of Conflict Resolution*, Vol. 36, pp. 573–85.

Kegley, C. and Raymond, G. (1994) *A Multipolar Peace: Great Power Politics in the Twentieth Century* (St Martin's Press, New York).

Kelly, E. W. and Leiserson, N. (eds) (1970) *The Study of Coalition Behaviour* (Holt, Rinehart & Winston, New York).

Keohane, R. and Nye, J. (1987) 'Power and Interdependence Revisited', *International Organisation*, Vol. 41, pp. 725–53.

Kim, W. (1989) 'Power, Alliance and Major Wars 1816 – 1975', *Journal of Conflict Resolution*, Vol. 33, pp. 255–73.

Kim, W. (1992) 'Power Transitions and Great Power War from Westphalia to Waterloo', *World Politics*, Vol. 45, pp. 153–72.

Kim, W. and Morrow, J. D. (1992) 'When Do Power Shifts Lead to War?', *American Journal of Political Science*, Vol. 36, pp. 896–922.

Kissinger, H. A. (1955) 'The Congress of Vienna: A Reappraisal', *World Politics*, Vol. 8, pp. 264–80.

Kissinger, H. A. (1957) *A World Restored* (Boston).

Kissinger, H. A. (1979) *White House Years* (Little Brown, Boston).

Knorr, K. and Rosenau, J. (1970) *Contending Approaches to International Politics* (Princeton University Press, Princeton, N.J.).

Koenigsberger, H. G. (1987) *Early Modern Europe 1500 – 1789* (Longman, London).

Kovacs, A. F. (1957) 'The Balance of Power', *Thought Patterns*, No. 5, pp. 1–19.

Kovacs, A. F. (no date) 'The Development of the Principle of the Balance of Power from the Treaty of Westphalia to the Congress of Vienna', unpublished Ph.D., University of Chicago Library.

Kugler, J. and Arbetman, M. (1989) 'Choosing among Measures of Power: A Review of the Empirical Record', in Stoll, R. J and Ward, M. D. (eds), *Power in World Politics* (Lynne Rienner, Boulder, Colo.), pp. 49–77.

Labs, E. (1992) 'Do Weak States Bandwagon?', *Security Studies*, Vol. 1, No. 3, pp. 383–416.

Langer, W. L. (1950) *European Alliances and Alignments,* new edn (New York).

Lasswell, H. (1965) *World Politics and Personal Insecurity* (Collier-Macmillan, London).

Latham, Earl (ed.) (1958) *The Philosophy and Politics of Woodrow Wilson* (Chicago).

Laue, T. von (1950) *Leopold Ranke: The Formative Years* (Princeton University Press, Princeton, N.J.).

Lauren, P. G. (ed.) (1979) *Diplomacy: New Approaches in History, Theory and Policy* (New York).

Lawson, F. H. (1976) 'Alliance Behaviour in Nineteenth-Century Europe', *American Political Science Review*, Vol. 70, pp. 932–4.

Lebow, R. N. (1987) 'Conventional versus Nuclear Deterrence: Are the Lessons Transferrable?', *Journal of Social Issues*, Vol. 43, pp. 5–72.

Lefever, E. W. (ed.) (1962) *Arms and Arms Control* (New York).

Lerche, C. (1956) *Principles of International Politics* (New York).

Levy, J. S. (1983) *War in the Modern Great Power System 1495–1975* (University of Kentucky Press, Lexington, Ky).

Levy, J. S. (1985) 'The Polarity of the System and International Stability: An Empirical Analysis', in A. N. Sabrosky (ed.), *Polarity and War* (Westview, Boulder, Colo.), pp. 41–66.

Levy, J. S. (1987) 'Declining Power and the Preventative Motivation for War', *World Politics*, Vol. 40, pp. 82–107.

Lider, J. (1980) 'The Correlation of World Forces: The Soviet Concept', *Journal of Peace Research*, Vol. 27, pp. 151–71.

Lider, J. (1986) *Correlation of Forces* (Gower, Aldershot).

Light, M. (1988) *'The Soviet Theory of International Relations* (Wheatsheaf, Brighton).

Link, Arthur S. (ed.) (1982) *Woodrow Wilson and a Revolutionary World 1913–1921* (University of North Carolina Press, Chapel Hill, N.C).

Lippmann, W. (1943) *US Foreign Policy: Shield of the Republic* (Boston).

Liska, G. (1957) *International Equilibrium* (Cambridge, Mass.).

Liska, G. (1977) *Quest for Equilibrium* (Baltimore).

Little, R. (1978) 'A Systems Approach', in T. Taylor (ed.), *Approaches and Theories in International Relations* (Longman, London), pp. 182–204.

Little, R. (1989) 'Deconstructing the Balance of Power: Two Traditions of Thought', *Review of International Studies*, Vol. 15, pp. 87–100.

Lynch, A. (1987) *The Soviet Study of International Relations* (Cambridge University Press, Cambridge).

McGowan, P. and Rood, R. (1975) 'Alliance Behaviour in Balance of Power Systems: Applying a Poisson Model to Nineteenth Century Europe', *American Political Science Review*, Vol. 69, pp. 859–70.

McGowan, P. and Rood, R. (1976) 'Alliance Behaviour in Nineteenth-century Europe', *American Political Science Review*, Vol. 70, pp. 934–6.

McGuire, M. (1986) 'The Insidious Dogma of Deterrence', *Bulletin of the Atomic Scientists* (December), pp. 24–9.

McKay, D. and Scott, H. M. (1983) *The Rise of the Great Powers 1648–1815* (Longman, London).

Mandelbaum, M. (1981)*The Nuclear Revolution: International Politics before and after Hiroshima* (Cambridge University Press, Cambridge).

Mandelbaum, M. (1988) *The Fate of Nations: The Search for National Security in the Nineteenth and Twentieth Centuries* (Cambridge University Press, Cambridge).

Manning, C. A. (1962) *The Nature of International Society* (Bell, London).

Mansergh, N. (1949) *The Coming of the First World War: A Study in the European Balance 1887–1914* (Longman Green, London).

Marriott, J. (1936) *Castlereagh* (Methuen, London).

Martin, R. (1971) 'The Concept of Power: A Critical Defence', *British Journal of Sociology*, Vol. 22, No. 3, pp. 240–56.

Maurice, J. F. (1888) *The Balance of Military Power in Europe* (London).

Maurseth, P. (1964) 'Balance of Power Thinking from the Renaissance to the French Revolution', *Journal of Peace Research*, Vol. 1, No. 2, pp. 120–36.

Medlicott, W, N. (1956) *Bismarck, Gladstone and the Concert of Europe* (London).

Meirsheimer, J. (1990) 'Back to the Future: Instability in Europe after the Cold War', *International Security*, Vol. 15, pp. 5–56.

Midlarsky, M. (1974) 'Power Uncertainty and the Onset of International Violence', *Journal of Conflict Resolution*, Vol. 18, No. 3, pp. 395–431.

Midlarsky, M. (1975) *On War: Political Violence in the International System* (Free Press, New York).

Midlarsky, M. (1981) 'Equilibria in the Nineteenth Century Balance of Power System', *American Journal of Political Science*, Vol. 25, pp. 270–96.

Midlarsky, M. (1983) 'The Balance of Power as a Just Historical System', *Polity*, Vol. 16, pp. 181–200.

Midlarsky, M. (1989) 'Interpretations of the Balance of Power: "Justice", Polarisation and the Approach to Systemic War'. Paper delivered at the annual convention of the International Studies Association, London 29 March–1 April.

Miller, A. J. (1977) 'Patterns of Cleavage: The Balance of Power Reprieved', *Millennium*, Vol. 6, pp. 11–27.

Mills, C. Wright (1959) *The Causes of World War Three* (Secker & Warburg, London).

Morgan, P. (1977) *Deterrence: A Conceptual Analysis* (Beverly Hills, Ca.).

Morgenthau, H. (1978) *Politics Among Nations*, 5th edn (Knopf, New York).

Morgenthau, H. and Thompson, K. (eds) (1950) *Principles and Problems of International Politics* (New York).

Morris, R. B. (ed.) (1939) *The Era of American Revolution: Studies Inscribed to Evarts Boutelle Greene* (New York).

Moul, W. (1985) 'Balances of Power and European Great Power War, 1815–1939: A Suggestion and Some Evidence', *Canadian Journal of Political Science*, Vol. 43, pp. 481–528.

Moul, W. (1989) 'Measuring the "Balances of Power": A Look at Some Numbers', *Review of International Studies*, Vol. 15, pp. 101–21.

Mowat, R. B. (1930) *The Concert of Europe* (Macmillan, London).

Murry, W. (1984) *The Change in the European Balance of Power 1938–39: The Path to Ruin* (Princeton University Press, Princeton).

Naidu, M. V. (1974) *Alliances and Balance of Power* (London).

Napier, M. (1854) 'The Balance of Power', *Encyclopaedia Britannica*, 8th edn (London).

Nathan, J. A. (1980) 'The Heyday of the Balance of Power: Frederick the Great and the Decline of the Old Regime', *Naval War College Review*, Vol. 33, pp. 53–67.

Nelson, E. W. (1943) 'The Origins of Modern Balance of Power Politics', *Medievalia et Humanistica*, Vol. 1, pp. 124–42.

Newman, W. (1968) *The Balance of Power in the Interwar Years* (New York).

Nicholas, H. G. (1982) 'Woodrow Wilson and Collective Security', in Arthur S. Link (ed.) *Woodrow Wilson and a Revolutionary World 1913–1921* (University of North Carolina Press, Chapel Hill, N.C.), pp. 174–89.

Nicolson, H. (1945) *The Congress of Vienna* (London).

Niou, E. M. S. and Ordeshook, P. C. (1986) 'A Theory of the Balance of Power in International Systems', *Journal of Conflict Resolution*, Vol. 30, No. 4, pp. 685–715.

Niou E. M. S. and Ordeshook, P. C. (1988) 'An Experimental Test of a Theory of the Balance of Power', *Simulation and Games*, Vol. 19, No. 4, pp. 415–39.

Niou, E. M. S., Ordeshook, P. C. (1990) 'Stability in Anarchic International Systems', *American Political Science Review*, Vol. 84, pp. 1207–34.

Niou, E. M. S., and Ordeshook, P. C. and Rose, G. (1989) *The Balance of Power: Stability in International Systems* (Cambridge University Press, Cambridge).

Nye, J. S. (1993) *Understanding International Conflict: An Introduction to Theory and History* (HarperCollins, New York).

Nys, E. (1893) 'La Théorie de l'équilibre Européen', *Revue de droit international et de législation comparée*, Vol. 25, pp. 34–57.

Oliver, J. K. (1982) 'The Balance of Power Heritage of "Interdependence" and "Traditionalism"', *International Studies Quarterly*, Vol. 26, pp. 373–96.

Oppenheim, L. (1905) *International Law*, Vol. I (London).

Oren, N. (1984) 'An Image: Israel as the Holder of the Regional Balance', in N. Oren (ed.), *Images and Reality in International Politics* (New York and Jerusalem), pp. 248–57.

Oren, N. (ed.) (1984) *Images and Reality in International Politics* (HarperCollins, New York).

Organski, A. F. K. (1968) *World Politics*, 2nd edn (Knopf, New York).

Organski, A. F. K. and Kugler, J. (1980) *The War Ledger* (University of Chicago Press, Chicago).

Osgood, R. E. (1958) 'Woodrow Wilson, Collective Security and the Lessons of History', in Earl Latham (ed.), *The Philosophy and Politics of Woodrow Wilson* (Chicago).

Osgood, R. E. and Tucker, R. W. (1967) *Force, Order and Justice* (Baltimore).

Ostrom, C. and Aldrich, J. (1978) 'The Relationship between Size and Stability in the Major Power International System', *American Journal of Political Science*, Vol. 22, pp. 743–71.

Overbury, Sir T. (1903) 'Observations on the State of France in 1609 under Henry IV', in C. H. Firth (ed.), *Stuart Tracts 1603–1693* (London).

Padelford, N. J. and Lincoln, G. A. (1967) *The Dynamics of International Politics* 2nd edn (New York).

Palmer, N. D. and Perkins, H. C. (1954) *International Relations* (London).

Parkinson, F. (1977) *The Philosophy of International Relations* (Sage, Beverly Hills and London).

Pelz, S. (1991) 'Changing International Systems, the World Balance of Power and the United States 1776–1976', *Diplomatic History*, Vol. 15, pp. 47–81.

Penrose, E. F. (1964) 'Political Development and the Intra-Regional Balance of Power', *Journal of Development Studies*, Vol. 1, No. 1, pp. 47–70.

Penrose, E. F. (1965) *The Revolution in International Relations: A Study in the Changing Nature and Balance of Power* (Frank Cass, London).

Perry, M. (1993) *An Intellectual History of Modern Europe* (Houghton Mifflin, Boston).

Phillips, W. (1907) 'The Congresses 1815–22', in A.W. Ward (ed.), The *Cambridge Modern History*, 14 Vols (Cambridge), Vol. X, pp. 1–39.

Pillinini, G. (1970) *Il Sistema degli Stati Italiani 1454–1494* (Venice).

Pollard, A. F. (1923) 'The Balance of Power', *Journal of British Institute of International Affairs,* Vol. 2, pp. 51–64.

Poole, DeWitt Clinton (1947) 'The Balance of Power', *Life,* Vol. 23, No. 12 (22 Sept), pp. 77–92.

Posen, B. (1984) *The Sources of Military Doctrine: France, Britain and Germany Between the World Wars* (Cornell University Press, Ithaca, N.Y.).

Purnell, R. (1978) 'Theoretical Approaches to International Relations: The Contribution of the Graeco-Roman World', in Trevor Taylor (ed.), *Approaches and Theory in International Relations* (Longman, London), pp. 19–31.

Quester, G. (1977) *Offence and Defence in the International System* (New York).

Rabb, T. K. (1975) *The Struggle for Stability in Early Modern Europe* (Oxford University Press, Oxford).

Read, C. (1925) *Mr Secretary Walsingham and the Policy of Queen Elizabeth,* 3 Vols (Oxford) Vol. I.

Reinken, D. L. (1968) 'Computer Explorations of the "Balance of Power"', in M. Kaplan (ed.) *New Approaches to International Relations* (St Martins Press, New York).

Reynolds, P. A. (1971) *An Introduction to International Relations* (London, Longman).

Reynolds, P. A. (1975) 'The Balance of Power: New Wine in an Old Bottle', *Political Studies,* Vol. 23, pp. 352–64.

Rice, E. F. and Grafton, A. (1994) *The Foundations of Early Modern Europe, 1450–1559,* 2nd edn (W.V. Norton, New York).

Riker, W. H. (1962) *The Theory of Political Coalitions* (Yale University Press, New Haven, Conn.).

Roberts, P. (1947) *The Quest for Security 1715–40* (New York).

Romani, R. (ed.) (1972) *The International Political System* (Wiley, New York).

Rood, R. (1973) 'Agreement in the International System: A Comparison of some Theoretical Aspects of Alliance Structures in a Balance of Power International System with the European State System of 1814–1914', Ph.D dissertation, Syracuse University.

Rosecrance, R. (1963) *Action and Reaction in World Politics* (Little Brown & Co., Boston).

Rosecrance, R. (1971) 'Diplomacy in the Eighteenth Century', in B. Sanders and A. Durbin (eds) *Contemporary International Politics: Introductory Readings* (New York), pp. 192–7.

Rosecrance, R. (1973) *International Relations: Peace or War?* (McGraw-Hill, New York).

Rosecrance, R., Alexandroff, A., Healey, B. and Stein, A. (1974) *Power, Balance of Power and Status in Nineteenth Century International Relations* (Sage, Beverly Hills and London).

Rosen, S. and Jones, W. (1974) *The Logic of International Relations* (Winthrop, Cambridge, Mass.).

Rosenau, J. N. (ed.) (1969) *International Politics and Foreign Policy* (Free Press, New York).

Rothstein, R. L. (1968) *Alliances and Small Powers* (Columbia University Press, New York).

Rummel, R. (1972) *The Dimensions of Nations* (Sage, London).

Russett, B. (1968) 'Components of an Operational Theory of International Alliance Formation', *Journal of Conflict Resolution*, Vol. 12, pp. 285–301.

Russett, B. (1969) 'The Young Science of International Politics', *World Politics*, Vol. 22, pp. 87–94.

Russett, B. (ed.) (1972) *Peace, War and Numbers* (Sage, Beverly Hills).

Sabrowsky, A. N. (ed.) (1985) *Polarity and War* (Westview, Boulder, Colo.).

Sanders, B. and Durbin, A. (eds) (1971) *Contemporary International Politics: Introductory Readings* (New York).

Savelle, M. (1939) 'The American Balance of Power and European Diplomacy', in R. B. Morris (ed.), *The Era of the American Revolution: Studies Inscribed to Evarts Boutelle Greene* (New York).

Savigear, P. (1978) 'European Political Philosophy and the Theory of International Relations', in T. Taylor (ed.), *Approaches and Theory in International Relations* (Longman, London), pp. 32–53.

Schelling, T. C. and Halperin, M. (1961) *Strategy and Arms Control* (Twentieth Century Fund, New York).

Schenk, H. G. (1947) *The Aftermath of the Napoleonic Wars* (Oxford University Press, Oxford).

Schroeder, P. (1972) *Austria, Great Britain and the Crimean War: The Destruction of the European Concert* (Cornell University Press, Ithaca, N.Y.).

Schroeder, P. (1977a) 'Quantitative Studies in the Balance of Power: An Historian's Reaction', *Journal of Conflict Resolution*, Vol. 21, No. 1, pp. 1–22.

Schroeder, P. W. (1977b) 'Quantitative Studies in the Balance of Power: An Historian's Reaction and a Final Rejoinder', *Journal of Conflict Resolution* Vol. 21, No. 1, pp. 3–22, 57–74.

Schroeder, P. (1989) 'The Nineteenth-century System: Balance of Power or Political Equilibrium?', *Review of International Studies*, Vol. 15, pp. 135–53.

Schroeder, P. (1991) 'The Neo-Realist Theory of International Politics: An Historian's View', occasional paper, Program in Arms Control, Disarmament and International Security, University of Illinois at Urbana-Champaign.

Schuman, F. (1969) *International Politics*, 7th edn (McGraw-Hill, New York).

Schwarzenberger, G. (1964) *Power Politics*, 3rd edn (London).

Schwarzenberger, G. (1965) 'From Bipolarity to Multipolarity?', *Yearbook of World Affairs 1965* (Stevens & Sons, London), pp. 179–85.

Scott, A. M. (1956) 'Challenge and Response: A Tool for the Analysis of International Affairs', *Review of Politics*, Vol. 18, pp. 207–26.

Seabury, P. (ed.) (1965) *Balance of Power* (Chandler, San Francisco).

Sheehan, M. (1983) *The Arms Race* (Martin Robertson, Oxford).

Sheehan, M. (1988) 'British Thinking on the Balance of Power 1660–1714', *History*, Vol. 73 (February), pp. 24–37.

Sheehan, M. (1989) 'The Place of the Balancer in Balance of Power Theory', *Review of International Studies*, Vol. 15, pp. 123–34.

Sheehan, M. (1992) 'Arms Control and Disarmament', in M. Hawksworth and M. Kogan (eds), *Encyclopaedia of Government and Politics,* 2 vols (Routledge, London), Vol 2, pp. 1266–85.

Simowitz, R. (1977) 'The Logical Consistency, Soundness and Applicability of the Balance of Power Theory When the Initial Power Distribution is Equal', *Papers of the Peace Science Society (International)* Vol. 27.

Simowitz, R. (1982) *The Logical Consistency and Soundness of the Balance of Power Theory* (University of Denver Press, Denver, Colo.).

Singer, J. D. (ed.) (1968) *Quantitive International Politics* (Free Press, New York).

Singer, J., Bremer, S. and Stuckey, J. (1972) 'Capability Distribution Uncertainty and Major Power War, 1820–1965', in B. Russett (ed.), *Peace, War and Numbers* (Sage, Beverly Hills).

Singer, J. D. and Small, M. (1966) 'National Alliance Commitments and War Involvement 1815–1945', *Peace Research Society (International) Papers*, Vol. 5, pp. 109–40.

Singer, J. D. and Small, M. (1968) 'Alliance Aggregation and the Onset of War 1815–1945', in J. D. Singer (ed.), *Quantitive International Politics* (Free Press, New York), pp. 247–86.

Siverson, R. M. and Sullivan, M. (1983) 'The Distribution of Power and the Onset of War', *Journal of Conflict Resolution,* Vol. 27, pp. 473–94.

Siverson, R. M. and Tennefoss, M. R. (1984) 'Power, Alliance and the Escalation of International Conflict 1815–1965', *American Political Science Review*, Vol. 78, pp. 1057–69.

Small, M. and Singer, J. D. (1970) 'Patterns in International Warfare 1816–1965', *Annals of the American Academy of Political and Social Sciences*, pp. 145–55.

Snyder, G. (1960) 'Balance of Power in the Missile Age', *Journal of International Affairs*, Vol. 14, No. 1, pp. 21–34.

Snyder, G. (1965) 'The Balance of Power and the Balance of Terror', in P Seabury (ed.), *Balance of Power* (Chandler, San Francisco), pp. 184–201.

Snyder, G. (1991) 'Alliances, Balance and Stability', *International Organisation*, Vol. 45, No. 1, pp. 121–42.

Sorel, A. (1969) *Europe and the French Revolution* (Collins, London).

Spanier, J. (1972) *Games Nations Play* (Nelson, London).

Spiegal, S. L. (1972) *Dominance and Diversity: The International Hierarchy* (Little Brown, Boston).

Spykman, N. (1942a) *America's Strategy in World Politics* (Harcourt Brace, New York).

Spykman, N. (1942b) 'U.S. Foreign Policy and the Balance of Power', *The Review of Politics* Vol. 1 (January), pp. 76–83.

Stall, R. J. (1984) 'Bloc Concentration and the Balance of Power: the European Major Powers 1824–1914', *Journal of Conflict Resolution*, Vol. 28, pp. 25–50.

Sterling, R. (1972) *Macropolitics* (New York).

Stoll, R. J. and Ward, M. D. (eds) (1989) *Power in World Politics* (Lynne Rienner, Boulder, Colo.).

Strausz-Hupé, R. (1957) 'The Balance of Tomorrow', *Orbis*, Vol. I, pp. 10–27.

Strausz-Hupé, R. and Possony, S. (1950) *International Relations in the Age of Conflict Between Democracy and Dictatorship* (New York).

Stubbs, W. (1986) *Seventeen Lectures on the Study of Medieval and Modern History* (Oxford).

Sullivan, J. D. (1974) 'International Alliances', in M. Haas (ed.), *International Systems* (Chandler, New York), pp. 99–122.

Sullivan, M. (1976) *International Relations: Theories and Evidence* (New Jersey).

Sullivan, R. (1973) 'Machiavelli's Balance of Power Theory', *Social Science Quarterly*, Vol. 54, pp. 258–70.

Sweet, P. (1941) *Friedrich von Gentz: Defender of the Old Order* (University of Wisconsin Press, Madison).

Swift, J. (1711) *The Conduct of the Allies* (London).

Swift, J. (ed.) (1757) *The Works of Sir William Temple* (London).

Syed, A. H. (1963) *Walter Lippmann's Philosophy of International Politics* (University of Pennsylvania Press, Philadelphia).

Tannenbaum, F. (1962) 'The Balance of Power Versus the Coordinate State', *Political Science Quarterly*, Vol. 67, No. 2, pp. 173–97.

Tardieu, A. (1908) *France and the Alliances: the Struggle for the Balance of Power* (New York).

Taylor, A. J. P. (1954) *The Struggle for Mastery in Europe 1848–1918* (Oxford University Press, Oxford).

Taylor, T. (1978a) 'Power Politics', in Trevor Taylor (ed.), *Approaches and Theory in International Relations* (Longman, London), pp. 122–40.

Taylor, T. (ed.) (1978b) *Approaches and Theory in International Relations* (Longman, London).

Thompson, K. (1958) 'The Limits of Principle in International Politics: Necessity and the New Balance of Power', *Journal of Politics*, Vol. 20, pp. 437–67.

Thompson, W. R. (1988) *On Global War: Historical–Structural Approaches to World Politics* (University of South Carolina Press, Columbia S.C.).

Thucydides (1954) *The Peloponnesian War*, trans Rex Warner (Penguin, Harmondsworth).

Towle, P. (1974) 'The European Balance of Power in 1914', *Army Quarterly*, Vol. 104, pp. 332–42.

Toynbee, A. J. (1934) *A Study of History*, Vol. III (Oxford).

Vagts, A. (1948) 'The Balance of Power: Growth of an Idea', *World Politics*, Vol. 1, pp. 82–101.

Vagts, A. and Vagts, D. (1979) 'The Balance of Power in International Law: A History of an Idea', *American Journal of International Law*, Vol. 73, pp. 555–79.

Van Dyke, V. (1966) *International Politics*, 2nd edn (New York).

Vattel, E. (1916) *The Law of Nations or the Principles of Natural Law Applied to the Conduct and to the Affairs of Nations and Sovereigns*, trans. of 1758 edn Charles Fenwick (Carnegie Institution, Washington, D.C.).

Wagner, R. H. (1986) 'The Theory of Games and the Balance of Power', *World Politics*, Vol. 38, No. 4, pp. 546–76.

Wallace, M. (1971) 'Power, Status and International War', *Journal of Peace Research*, Vol. 8, pp. 23–35.

Wallace, M. (1973) *War and Rank Among Nations* (Lexington Books, London).

Walt, S. M. (1985) 'Alliance Formation and the Balance of World Power', *International Security* (Spring), pp. 3–43.

Walt, S. M. (1987) *The Origins of Alliances* (Cornell University Press, Ithaca, N.Y.).

Waltz, K. (1959a) *Man, the State and War* (New York).

Waltz, K. (1959b) 'Realpolitik and Balance of Power Theory', in F. Greenstein and N. Polsby (eds), *International Politics* (Reading, Mass.), pp. 33–42.

Waltz, K. (1964) 'The Stability of the Bipolar World', *Daedalus*, Vol. 93, pp. 892–907.

Waltz, K. (1967) 'International Structure, National Force and the Balance of World Power', in J. C. Farrell and A. P. Smith (eds) *Theory and Reality in World Politics* (Columbia University Press, New York), pp. 31–47.

Waltz, K. (1979) *Theory of International Politics* (McGraw-Hill, New York and London).

Waltz, K. (1981) *The Spread of Nuclear Weapons: More May be Better*, Adelphi Paper No. 171 (London, IISS).

Waltz, K. (1988) 'The Origins of War in Neorealist Theory', *Journal of Interdisciplinary History*, Vol. 18, No. 4, pp. 615–28.

Ward, A. W. (1908) 'The Peace of Utrecht and the Supplementary Pacifications', in *The Cambridge Modern History,* Vol. V (Cambridge), pp. 437–59.

Ward, A. W. (ed.) (1907–8) *The Cambridge Modern History*, 14 vols (Cambridge).

Wasserman, B. (1959) 'The Scientific Pretensions of Professor Morgenthau's Theory of Power Politics', *Australian Outlook*, Vol. 13, No. 1, pp. 55–70.

Watson, A. (1992) *The Evolution of International Society* (Routledge, London).

Wayman, F. (1985) 'Bipolarity, Multipolarity, and the Threat of War', in A. N. Sabrowsky (ed.), *Polarity and War* (Westview, Boulder, Colo.), pp. 115–44.

Webster, C. K. (1934) *The Congress of Vienna* (London).

Weltman, J. (1973) *Systems Theory in International Relations: A Study in Metaphoric Hypertrophy* (Lexington Books, Lexington, Mass.).

Wessell, N. (1979) 'The Soviet Views of Multipolarity and the Emerging Balance of Power', *Orbis*, Vol. 22, pp. 785–813.

Wight, M. (1946) *Power Politics* (Royal Institute of International Affairs, London).

Wight, M. (1966) 'The Balance of Power', in H. Butterfield and M. Wight (eds) *Diplomatic Investigations* (London).

Wight, M. (1973) 'The Balance of Power and International Order', in A. James (ed.), *The Bases of International Order* (Oxford University Press, Oxford).

Wight, M. (1979) *Power Politics* (Pelican, Harmondsworth).

Wight, M. (1991) *International Theory: The Three Traditions* (Leicester University Press, London).

Wohlstetter, A. (1959) 'The Delicate Balance of Terror', *Foreign Affairs*, Vol. 37, pp. 211–34.

Wolf, J. B. (1951) *The Emergence of the Great Powers 1685–1715* (New York).

Wolf, J. B. (1970) *Towards a European Balance of Power 1620–1715* (Chicago).

Wolfers, A. (1959) 'The Balance of Power', *SAIS Review*, Vol. 3, No. 3, pp. 9–16.

Wolfers, A. (1962) *Discord and Collaboration* (Johns Hopkins University Press, Baltimore).

Wolfers, A. and Martin, L. W. (eds) (1956) *The Anglo-American Tradition in Foreign Affairs* (New Haven, Conn. and London).

Wright, M. (1975) *The Theory and Practice of the Balance of Power, 1486–1914* (Dent, London).

Wright, Q. (1942) *A Study of War* (University Chicago Press, Chicago).

Wright, Q. (1944) 'The Balance of Power', in H. Weigart and V. Steffanson (eds) *The Compass of the World*, (New York).

Zeller, G. (1956) 'Le principe d'équilibre dans la politique internationale avant 1789', *Revue historique*, Vol. 215, pp. 25–37.

Ziegler, D. (1977) *War, Peace and International Politics* (HarperCollins, Boston).

Zinnes, D. (1967) 'An Analytical Study of the Balance of Power Theories', *Journal of Peace Research*, Vol. 4, pp. 270–85.

Zinnes, D. (1970) 'Coalition Theories and the Balance of Power', in S Groennings, E. W. Kelley and M. Leiserson (eds) *The Study of Coalition Behaviour* (Holt, Reinhart & Winston, New York).

Index